Apache CloudStack 4.5 Administration Guide

A catalogue record for this book is available from the Hong Kong Public Libraries.

Published in Hong Kong by Samurai Media Limited.

Email: info@samuraimedia.org

ISBN 978-988-8381-83-8

This guide is aimed at Administrators of a CloudStack based Cloud, for Release Notes, Installation and General introduction to CloudStack see the following guides:

- Documentation Start
- Installation Guide
- Release Notes

Contents

## CHAPTER 1

User Interface

1.1 User Interface

1.1.1 Log In to the UI

CloudStack provides a web-based UI that can be used by both administrators and end users. The appropriate version of the UI is displayed depending on the credentials used to log in. The UI is available in popular browsers including IE7, IE8, IE9, Firefox 3.5+, Firefox 4, Safari 4, and Safari 5. The URL is: (substitute your own management server IP address)

```
http://<management-server-ip-address>:8080/client
```

On a fresh Management Server installation, a guided tour splash screen appears. On later visits, you'll see a login screen where you specify the following to proceed to your Dashboard:

Username -> The user ID of your account. The default username is admin.

Password -> The password associated with the user ID. The password for the default username is password.

Domain -> If you are a root user, leave this field blank.

If you are a user in the sub-domains, enter the full path to the domain, excluding the root domain.

For example, suppose multiple levels are created under the root domain, such as Comp1/hr. The users in the Comp1 domain should enter Comp1 in the Domain field, whereas the users in the Comp1/sales domain should enter Comp1/sales.

For more guidance about the choices that appear when you log in to this UI, see Logging In as the Root Administrator.

End User's UI Overview

The CloudStack UI helps users of cloud infrastructure to view and use their cloud resources, including virtual machines, templates and ISOs, data volumes and snapshots, guest networks, and IP addresses. If the user is a member or administrator of one or more CloudStack projects, the UI can provide a project-oriented view.

Root Administrator's UI Overview

The CloudStack UI helps the CloudStack administrator provision, view, and manage the cloud infrastructure, domains, user accounts, projects, and configuration settings. The first time you start the UI after a fresh Management Server installation, you can choose to follow a guided tour to provision your cloud infrastructure. On subsequent logins, the dashboard of the logged-in user appears. The various links in this screen and the navigation bar on the left provide access to a variety of administrative functions. The root administrator can also use the UI to perform all the same tasks that are present in the end-user's UI.

Logging In as the Root Administrator

After the Management Server software is installed and running, you can run the CloudStack user interface. This UI is there to help you provision, view, and manage your cloud infrastructure.

1. Open your favorite Web browser and go to this URL. Substitute the IP address of your own Management Server:

```
http://<management-server-ip-address>:8080/client
```

After logging into a fresh Management Server installation, a guided tour splash screen appears. On later visits, you'll be taken directly into the Dashboard.

2. If you see the first-time splash screen, choose one of the following.

   - **Continue with basic setup.** Choose this if you're just trying CloudStack, and you want a guided walk-through of the simplest possible configuration so that you can get started right away. We'll help you set up a cloud with the following features: a single machine that runs CloudStack software and uses NFS to provide storage; a single machine running VMs under the XenServer or KVM hypervisor; and a shared public network.

     The prompts in this guided tour should give you all the information you need, but if you want just a bit more detail, you can follow along in the Trial Installation Guide.

   - **I have used CloudStack before.** Choose this if you have already gone through a design phase and planned a more sophisticated deployment, or you are ready to start scaling up a trial cloud that you set up earlier with the basic setup screens. In the Administrator UI, you can start using the more powerful features of CloudStack, such as advanced VLAN networking, high availability, additional network elements such as load balancers and firewalls, and support for multiple hypervisors including Citrix XenServer, KVM, and VMware vSphere.

     The root administrator Dashboard appears.

3. You should set a new root administrator password. If you chose basic setup, you'll be prompted to create a new password right away. If you chose experienced user, use the steps in *Changing the Root Password*.

> **Warning:** You are logging in as the root administrator. This account manages the CloudStack deployment, including physical infrastructure. The root administrator can modify configuration settings to change basic functionality, create or delete user accounts, and take many actions that should be performed only by an authorized person. Please change the default password to a new, unique password.

Changing the Root Password

During installation and ongoing cloud administration, you will need to log in to the UI as the root administrator. The root administrator account manages the CloudStack deployment, including physical infrastructure. The root administrator can modify configuration settings to change basic functionality, create or delete user accounts, and take many actions that should be performed only by an authorized person. When first installing CloudStack, be sure to change the default password to a new, unique value.

1. Open your favorite Web browser and go to this URL. Substitute the IP address of your own Management Server:

```
http://<management-server-ip-address>:8080/client
```

2. Log in to the UI using the current root user ID and password. The default is admin, password.

3. Click Accounts.

4. Click the admin account name.

5. Click View Users.

6. Click the admin user name.

7. Click the Change Password button.

8. Type the new password, and click OK.

## CHAPTER 2

Managing Accounts, Users and Domains

2.1 Managing Accounts, Users and Domains

2.1.1 Accounts, Users, and Domains

Accounts

An account typically represents a customer of the service provider or a department in a large organization. Multiple users can exist in an account.

Domains

Accounts are grouped by domains. Domains usually contain multiple accounts that have some logical relationship to each other and a set of delegated administrators with some authority over the domain and its subdomains. For example, a service provider with several resellers could create a domain for each reseller.

For each account created, the Cloud installation creates three different types of user accounts: root administrator, domain administrator, and user.

Users

Users are like aliases in the account. Users in the same account are not isolated from each other, but they are isolated from users in other accounts. Most installations need not surface the notion of users; they just have one user per account. The same user cannot belong to multiple accounts.

Username is unique in a domain across accounts in that domain. The same username can exist in other domains, including sub-domains. Domain name can repeat only if the full pathname from root is unique. For example, you can create root/d1, as well as root/foo/d1, and root/sales/d1.

Administrators are accounts with special privileges in the system. There may be multiple administrators in the system. Administrators can create or delete other administrators, and change the password for any user in the system.

Domain Administrators

Domain administrators can perform administrative operations for users who belong to that domain. Domain administrators do not have visibility into physical servers or other domains.

Root Administrator

Root administrators have complete access to the system, including managing templates, service offerings, customer care administrators, and domains

Resource Ownership

Resources belong to the account, not individual users in that account. For example, billing, resource limits, and so on are maintained by the account, not the users. A user can operate on any resource in the account provided the user has privileges for that operation. The privileges are determined by the role. A root administrator can change the ownership of any virtual machine from one account to any other account by using the assignVirtualMachine API. A domain or sub-domain administrator can do the same for VMs within the domain from one account to any other account in the domain or any of its sub-domains.

2.1.2 Dedicating Resources to Accounts and Domains

The root administrator can dedicate resources to a specific domain or account that needs private infrastructure for additional security or performance guarantees. A zone, pod, cluster, or host can be reserved by the root administrator for a specific domain or account. Only users in that domain or its subdomain may use the infrastructure. For example, only users in a given domain can create guests in a zone dedicated to that domain.

There are several types of dedication available:

- Explicit dedication. A zone, pod, cluster, or host is dedicated to an account or domain by the root administrator during initial deployment and configuration.

- Strict implicit dedication. A host will not be shared across multiple accounts. For example, strict implicit dedication is useful for deployment of certain types of applications, such as desktops, where no host can be shared between different accounts without violating the desktop software's terms of license.

- Preferred implicit dedication. The VM will be deployed in dedicated infrastructure if possible. Otherwise, the VM can be deployed in shared infrastructure.

2.1.3 How to Dedicate a Zone, Cluster, Pod, or Host to an Account or Domain

For explicit dedication: When deploying a new zone, pod, cluster, or host, the root administrator can click the Dedicated checkbox, then choose a domain or account to own the resource.

To explicitly dedicate an existing zone, pod, cluster, or host: log in as the root admin, find the resource in the UI, and

click the Dedicate button.

For implicit dedication: The administrator creates a compute service offering and in the Deployment Planner field, chooses ImplicitDedicationPlanner. Then in Planner Mode, the administrator specifies either Strict or Preferred, depending on whether it is permissible to allow some use of shared resources when dedicated resources are not available. Whenever a user creates a VM based on this service offering, it is allocated on one of the dedicated hosts.

How to Use Dedicated Hosts

To use an explicitly dedicated host, use the explicit-dedicated type of affinity group (see "Affinity Groups"). For example, when creating a new VM, an end user can choose to place it on dedicated infrastructure. This operation will succeed only if some infrastructure has already been assigned as dedicated to the user's account or domain.

Behavior of Dedicated Hosts, Clusters, Pods, and Zones

The administrator can live migrate VMs away from dedicated hosts if desired, whether the destination is a host reserved for a different account/domain or a host that is shared (not dedicated to any particular account or domain). CloudStack will generate an alert, but the operation is allowed.

Dedicated hosts can be used in conjunction with host tags. If both a host tag and dedication are requested, the VM will be placed only on a host that meets both requirements. If there is no dedicated resource available to that user that also has the host tag requested by the user, then the VM will not deploy.

If you delete an account or domain, any hosts, clusters, pods, and zones that were dedicated to it are freed up. They will now be available to be shared by any account or domain, or the administrator may choose to re-dedicate them to a different account or domain.

System VMs and virtual routers affect the behavior of host dedication. System VMs and virtual routers are owned by the CloudStack system account, and they can be deployed on any host. They do not adhere to explicit dedication. The presence of system vms and virtual routers on a host makes it unsuitable for strict implicit dedication. The host can not be used for strict implicit dedication, because the host already has VMs of a specific account (the default system account). However, a host with system VMs or virtual routers can be used for preferred implicit dedication.

2.1.4 Using an LDAP Server for User Authentication

You can use an external LDAP server such as Microsoft Active Directory or ApacheDS to authenticate CloudStack end-users. CloudStack will search the external LDAP directory tree starting at a specified base directory and gets user info such as first name, last name, email and username.

To authenticate, username and password entered by the user are used. Cloudstack does a search for a user with the given username. If it exists, it does a bind request with DN and password.

To set up LDAP authentication in CloudStack, call the CloudStack API command `addLdapConfiguration` and provide Hostname or IP address and listening port of the LDAP server. You could configure multiple servers as well. These are expected to be replicas. If one fails, the next one is used.

The following global configurations should also be configured (the default values are for openldap)

- `ldap.basedn`: Sets the basedn for LDAP. Ex: **OU=APAC,DC=company,DC=com**
- `ldap.bind.principal`, `ldap.bind.password`: DN and password for a user who can list all the users in the above basedn. Ex: **CN=Administrator, OU=APAC, DC=company, DC=com**
- `ldap.user.object`: object type of users within LDAP. Defaults value is **user** for AD and **interorgperson** for openldap.
- `ldap.email.attribute`: email attribute within ldap for a user. Default value for AD and openldap is **mail**.
- `ldap.firstname.attribute`: firstname attribute within ldap for a user. Default value for AD and openldap is **givenname**.
- `ldap.lastname.attribute`: lastname attribute within ldap for a user. Default value for AD and openldap is **sn**.
- `ldap.username.attribute`: username attribute for a user within LDAP. Default value is **SAMAccountName** for AD and **uid** for openldap.

Restricting LDAP users to a group:

- `ldap.search.group.principle`: this is optional and if set only users from this group are listed.

LDAP SSL:

If the LDAP server requires SSL, you need to enable the below configurations. Before enabling SSL for LDAP, you need to get the certificate which the LDAP server is using and add it to a trusted keystore. You will need to know the path to the keystore and the password.

- `ldap.truststore` : truststore path

- `ldap.truststore.password` : truststore password

LDAP groups:

- `ldap.group.object`: object type of groups within LDAP. Default value is group for AD and **groupOfU-niqueNames** for openldap.

- `ldap.group.user.uniquemember`: attribute for uniquemembers within a group. Default value is **member** for AD and **uniquemember** for openldap.

Once configured, on Add Account page, you will see an "Add LDAP Account" button which opens a dialog and the selected users can be imported.

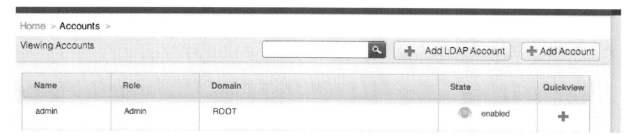

You could also use api commands: `listLdapUsers`, `ldapCreateAccount` and `importLdapUsers`.

Once LDAP is enabled, the users will not be allowed to changed password directly in cloudstack.

2.1.5 Using a SAML 2.0 Identity Provider for User Authentication

You can use a SAML 2.0 Identity Provider with CloudStack for user authentication. This will require enabling the SAML 2.0 service provider plugin in CloudStack. To do that first, enable the SAML plugin by setting `saml2.enabled` to `true` and restart management server.

Starting 4.5.2, the SAML plugin uses an authorization workflow where users should be authorized by an admin using `authorizeSamlSso` API before those users can use Single Sign On against a specific IDP. This can be done by ticking the enable SAML Single Sign On checkbox and selecting a IDP when adding or importing users. For existing users, admin can go to the user's page and click on configure SAML SSO option to enable/disable SSO for a user and select a Identity Provider. A user can be authorized to authenticate against only one IDP.

The CloudStack service provider metadata is accessible using the `getSPMetadata` API command, or from the URL http://acs-server:8080/client/api?command=getSPMetadata where acs-server is the domain name or IP address of the management server. The IDP administrator can get the SP metadata from CloudStack and add it to their IDP server.

To start a SAML 2.0 Single Sign-On authentication, on the login page users need to select the Identity Provider or Institution/Department they can authenticate with and click on Login button. This action call the `samlsso` API command which will redirect the user to the Identity Provider's login page. Upon successful authentication, the IdP will redirect the user to CloudStack. In case a user has multiple user accounts with the same username (across domains) for the same authorized IDP, that user would need to specify domainpath after selecting their IDP server from the dropdown list. By default, users don't need to specify any domain path. After a user is successfully authenticated by an IDP server, the SAML authentication plugin finds user accounts whose username match the username attribute value returned by the SAML authentication response; it fails only when it finds that there are multiple user accounts with the same user name for the specific IDP otherwise the unique useraccount is allowed to proceed and the user is logged into their account.

Limitations:

- The plugin uses a user attribute returned by the IDP server in the SAML response to find and map the authorized user in CloudStack. The default attribute is *uid*.

- The SAML authentication plugin supports HTTP-Redirect and HTTP-Post bindings.

- Tested with Shibboleth 2.4, SSOCircle, Microsoft ADFS, OneLogin, Feide OpenIDP, PingIdentity.

The following global configuration should be configured:

- `saml2.enabled`: Indicates whether SAML SSO plugin is enabled or not true. Default is **false**

- `saml2.sp.id`: SAML2 Service Provider Identifier string

- `saml2.idp.metadata.url`: SAML2 Identity Provider Metadata XML Url or Filename. If a URL is not provided, it will look for a file in the config directory /etc/cloudstack/management

- `saml2.default.idpid`: The default IdP entity ID to use only in case of multiple IdPs

- `saml2.sigalg`: The algorithm to use to when signing a SAML request. Default is SHA1, allowed algorithms: SHA1, SHA256, SHA384, SHA512.

- `saml2.redirect.url`: The CloudStack UI url the SSO should redirected to when successful. Default is **http://localhost:8080/client**

- `saml2.sp.org.name`: SAML2 Service Provider Organization Name

- `saml2.sp.org.url`: SAML2 Service Provider Organization URL

- `saml2.sp.contact.email`: SAML2 Service Provider Contact Email Address

- `saml2.sp.contact.person`: SAML2 Service Provider Contact Person Name

- `saml2.sp.slo.url`: SAML2 CloudStack Service Provider Single Log Out URL

- `saml2.sp.sso.url`: SAML2 CloudStack Service Provider Single Sign On URL

- `saml2.user.attribute`: Attribute name to be looked for in SAML response that will contain the username. Default is **uid**

- `saml2.timeout`: SAML2 IDP Metadata refresh interval in seconds, minimum value is set to 300. Default is 1800

## CHAPTER 3

Using Projects to Organize User Resources

3.1 Using Projects to Organize Users and Resources

3.1.1 Overview of Projects

Projects are used to organize people and resources. CloudStack users within a single domain can group themselves into project teams so they can collaborate and share virtual resources such as VMs, snapshots, templates, data disks, and IP addresses. CloudStack tracks resource usage per project as well as per user, so the usage can be billed to either a user account or a project. For example, a private cloud within a software company might have all members of the QA department assigned to one project, so the company can track the resources used in testing while the project members can more easily isolate their efforts from other users of the same cloud

You can configure CloudStack to allow any user to create a new project, or you can restrict that ability to just Cloud-Stack administrators. Once you have created a project, you become that project's administrator, and you can add others within your domain to the project. CloudStack can be set up either so that you can add people directly to a project, or so that you have to send an invitation which the recipient must accept. Project members can view and manage all virtual resources created by anyone in the project (for example, share VMs). A user can be a member of any number of projects and can switch views in the CloudStack UI to show only project-related information, such as project VMs, fellow project members, project-related alerts, and so on.

The project administrator can pass on the role to another project member. The project administrator can also add more members, remove members from the project, set new resource limits (as long as they are below the global defaults set by the CloudStack administrator), and delete the project. When the administrator removes a member from the project, resources created by that user, such as VM instances, remain with the project. This brings us to the subject of resource ownership and which resources can be used by a project.

Resources created within a project are owned by the project, not by any particular CloudStack account, and they can be used only within the project. A user who belongs to one or more projects can still create resources outside of those projects, and those resources belong to the user's account; they will not be counted against the project's usage or resource limits. You can create project-level networks to isolate traffic within the project and provide network services such as port forwarding, load balancing, VPN, and static NAT. A project can also make use of certain types of resources from outside the project, if those resources are shared. For example, a shared network or public template is available to any project in the domain. A project can get access to a private template if the template's owner will grant permission. A project can use any service offering or disk offering available in its domain; however, you can not create private service and disk offerings at the project level..

3.1.2 Configuring Projects

Before CloudStack users start using projects, the CloudStack administrator must set up various systems to support them, including membership invitations, limits on project resources, and controls on who can create projects.

Setting Up Invitations

CloudStack can be set up either so that project administrators can add people directly to a project, or so that it is necessary to send an invitation which the recipient must accept. The invitation can be sent by email or through the user's CloudStack account. If you want administrators to use invitations to add members to projects, turn on and set up the invitations feature in CloudStack.

1. Log in as administrator to the CloudStack UI.

2. In the left navigation, click Global Settings.

3. In the search box, type project and click the search button.

4. In the search results, you can see a few other parameters you need to set to control how invitations behave. The table below shows global configuration parameters related to project invitations. Click the edit button to set each parameter.

Configuration Parameters	Description
project.invite.required	Set to true to turn on the invitations feature.
project.email.sender	The email address to show in the From field of invitation emails.
project.invite.timeout	Amount of time to allow for a new member to respond to the invitation.
project.smtp.host	Name of the host that acts as an email server to handle invitations.
project.smtp.password	(Optional) Password required by the SMTP server. You must also set project.smtp.username and set project.smtp.useAuth to true.
project.smtp.port	SMTP server's listening port.
project.smtp.useAuth	Set to true if the SMTP server requires a username and password.
project.smtp.username	(Optional) User name required by the SMTP server for authentication. You must also set project.smtp.password and set project.smtp.useAuth to true..

5. Restart the Management Server:

```
service cloudstack-management restart
```

Setting Resource Limits for Projects

The CloudStack administrator can set global default limits to control the amount of resources that can be owned by each project in the cloud. This serves to prevent uncontrolled usage of resources such as snapshots, IP addresses, and virtual machine instances. Domain administrators can override these resource limits for individual projects with their domains, as long as the new limits are below the global defaults set by the CloudStack root administrator. The root administrator can also set lower resource limits for any project in the cloud

Setting Per-Project Resource Limits

The CloudStack root administrator or the domain administrator of the domain where the project resides can set new resource limits for an individual project. The project owner can set resource limits only if the owner is also a domain or root administrator.

The new limits must be below the global default limits set by the CloudStack administrator (as described in *"Setting Resource Limits for Projects"*). If the project already owns more of a given type of resource than the new maximum, the resources are not affected; however, the project can not add any new resources of that type until the total drops below the new limit.

1. Log in as administrator to the CloudStack UI.

2. In the left navigation, click Projects.

3. In Select View, choose Projects.

4. Click the name of the project you want to work with.

5. Click the Resources tab. This tab lists the current maximum amount that the project is allowed to own for each type of resource.

6. Type new values for one or more resources.

7. Click Apply.

Setting the Global Project Resource Limits

1. Log in as administrator to the CloudStack UI.

2. In the left navigation, click Global Settings.

3. In the search box, type max.projects and click the search button.

4. In the search results, you will see the parameters you can use to set per-project maximum resource amounts that apply to all projects in the cloud. No project can have more resources, but an individual project can have lower

   limits. Click the edit button to set each parameter.

max.project.public.ip	Maximum number of public IP addresses that can be owned by any project in the cloud. See About Public IP Addresses.
max.project.snapshot	Maximum number of snapshots that can be owned by any project in the cloud. See Working with Snapshots.
max.project.template	Maximum number of templates that can be owned by any project in the cloud. See Working with Templates.
max.project.uservm	Maximum number of guest virtual machines that can be owned by any project in the cloud. See Working With Virtual Machines.
max.project.volume	Maximum number of data volumes that can be owned by any project in the cloud. See Working with Volumes.

5. Restart the Management Server.

```
# service cloudstack-management restart
```

Setting Project Creator Permissions

You can configure CloudStack to allow any user to create a new project, or you can restrict that ability to just Cloud-Stack administrators.

1. Log in as administrator to the CloudStack UI.

2. In the left navigation, click Global Settings.

3. In the search box, type allow.user.create.projects.

4. Click the edit button to set the parameter.

   ```
   allow.user.create.projects
   ```

   Set to true to allow end users to create projects. Set to false if you want only the CloudStack root administrator and domain administrators to create projects.

5. Restart the Management Server.

```
# service cloudstack-management restart
```

3.1.3 Creating a New Project

CloudStack administrators and domain administrators can create projects. If the global configuration parameter allow.user.create.projects is set to true, end users can also create projects.

1. Log in as administrator to the CloudStack UI.
2. In the left navigation, click Projects.
3. In Select view, click Projects.
4. Click New Project.
5. Give the project a name and description for display to users, then click Create Project.
6. A screen appears where you can immediately add more members to the project. This is optional. Click Next when you are ready to move on.
7. Click Save.

3.1.4 Adding Members to a Project

New members can be added to a project by the project's administrator, the domain administrator of the domain where the project resides or any parent domain, or the CloudStack root administrator. There are two ways to add members in CloudStack, but only one way is enabled at a time:

- If invitations have been enabled, you can send invitations to new members.
- If invitations are not enabled, you can add members directly through the UI.

Sending Project Membership Invitations

Use these steps to add a new member to a project if the invitations feature is enabled in the cloud as described in *"Setting Up Invitations"*. If the invitations feature is not turned on, use the procedure in Adding Project Members From the UI.

1. Log in to the CloudStack UI.
2. In the left navigation, click Projects.
3. In Select View, choose Projects.
4. Click the name of the project you want to work with.
5. Click the Invitations tab.
6. In Add by, select one of the following:

    (a) Account – The invitation will appear in the user's Invitations tab in the Project View. See Using the Project View.

    (b) Email – The invitation will be sent to the user's email address. Each emailed invitation includes a unique code called a token which the recipient will provide back to CloudStack when accepting the invitation. Email invitations will work only if the global parameters related to the SMTP server have been set. See *"Setting Up Invitations"*.

7. Type the user name or email address of the new member you want to add, and click Invite. Type the CloudStack user name if you chose Account in the previous step. If you chose Email, type the email address. You can invite only people who have an account in this cloud within the same domain as the project. However, you can send the invitation to any email address.

8. To view and manage the invitations you have sent, return to this tab. When an invitation is accepted, the new member will appear in the project's Accounts tab.

Adding Project Members From the UI

The steps below tell how to add a new member to a project if the invitations feature is not enabled in the cloud. If the invitations feature is enabled cloud,as described in *"Setting Up Invitations"*, use the procedure in *"Sending Project Membership Invitations"*.

1. Log in to the CloudStack UI.

2. In the left navigation, click Projects.

3. In Select View, choose Projects.

4. Click the name of the project you want to work with.

5. Click the Accounts tab. The current members of the project are listed.

6. Type the account name of the new member you want to add, and click Add Account. You can add only people who have an account in this cloud and within the same domain as the project.

3.1.5 Accepting a Membership Invitation

If you have received an invitation to join a CloudStack project, and you want to accept the invitation, follow these steps:

1. Log in to the CloudStack UI.

2. In the left navigation, click Projects.

3. In Select View, choose Invitations.

4. If you see the invitation listed onscreen, click the Accept button.

   Invitations listed on screen were sent to you using your CloudStack account name.

5. If you received an email invitation, click the Enter Token button, and provide the project ID and unique ID code (token) from the email.

3.1.6 Suspending or Deleting a Project

When a project is suspended, it retains the resources it owns, but they can no longer be used. No new resources or members can be added to a suspended project.

When a project is deleted, its resources are destroyed, and member accounts are removed from the project. The project's status is shown as Disabled pending final deletion.

A project can be suspended or deleted by the project administrator, the domain administrator of the domain the project belongs to or of its parent domain, or the CloudStack root administrator.

1. Log in to the CloudStack UI.

2. In the left navigation, click Projects.

3. In Select View, choose Projects.

4. Click the name of the project.

5. Click one of the buttons:

    To delete, use

    To suspend, use

3.1.7 Using the Project View

If you are a member of a project, you can use CloudStack's project view to see project members, resources consumed, and more. The project view shows only information related to one project. It is a useful way to filter out other information so you can concentrate on a project status and resources.

1. Log in to the CloudStack UI.

2. Click Project View.

3. The project dashboard appears, showing the project's VMs, volumes, users, events, network settings, and more. From the dashboard, you can:

    - Click the Accounts tab to view and manage project members. If you are the project administrator, you can add new members, remove members, or change the role of a member from user to admin. Only one member at a time can have the admin role, so if you set another user's role to admin, your role will change to regular user.

    - (If invitations are enabled) Click the Invitations tab to view and manage invitations that have been sent to new project members but not yet accepted. Pending invitations will remain in this list until the new member accepts, the invitation timeout is reached, or you cancel the invitation.

## CHAPTER 4

Service Offerings

4.1 Service Offerings

In addition to the physical and logical infrastructure of your cloud and the CloudStack software and servers, you also need a layer of user services so that people can actually make use of the cloud. This means not just a user UI, but a set of options and resources that users can choose from, such as templates for creating virtual machines, disk storage, and more. If you are running a commercial service, you will be keeping track of what services and resources users are consuming and charging them for that usage. Even if you do not charge anything for people to use your cloud – say, if the users are strictly internal to your organization, or just friends who are sharing your cloud – you can still keep track of what services they use and how much of them.

4.1.1 Service Offerings, Disk Offerings, Network Offerings, and Templates

A user creating a new instance can make a variety of choices about its characteristics and capabilities. CloudStack provides several ways to present users with choices when creating a new instance:

- Service Offerings, defined by the CloudStack administrator, provide a choice of CPU speed, number of CPUs, RAM size, tags on the root disk, and other choices. See Creating a New Compute Offering.

- Disk Offerings, defined by the CloudStack administrator, provide a choice of disk size and IOPS (Quality of Service) for primary data storage. See Creating a New Disk Offering.

- Network Offerings, defined by the CloudStack administrator, describe the feature set that is available to end users from the virtual router or external networking devices on a given guest network. See Network Offerings.

- Templates, defined by the CloudStack administrator or by any CloudStack user, are the base OS images that the user can choose from when creating a new instance. For example, CloudStack includes CentOS as a template. See Working with Templates.

In addition to these choices that are provided for users, there is another type of service offering which is available only to the CloudStack root administrator, and is used for configuring virtual infrastructure resources. For more information, see Upgrading a Virtual Router with System Service Offerings.

4.1.2 Compute and Disk Service Offerings

A service offering is a set of virtual hardware features such as CPU core count and speed, memory, and disk size. The CloudStack administrator can set up various offerings, and then end users choose from the available offerings when they create a new VM. Based on the user's selected offering, CloudStack emits usage records that can be integrated with billing systems.

Some characteristics of service offerings must be defined by the CloudStack administrator, and others can be left undefined so that the end-user can enter their own desired values. This is useful to reduce the number of offerings the CloudStack administrator has to define. Instead of defining a compute offering for every imaginable combination of values that a user might want, the administrator can define offerings that provide some flexibility to the users and can serve as the basis for several different VM configurations.

A service offering includes the following elements:

- CPU, memory, and network resource guarantees
- How resources are metered
- How the resource usage is charged
- How often the charges are generated

For example, one service offering might allow users to create a virtual machine instance that is equivalent to a 1 GHz Intel® Core™ 2 CPU, with 1 GB memory at $0.20/hour, with network traffic metered at $0.10/GB.

CloudStack separates service offerings into compute offerings and disk offerings. The compute service offering specifies:

- Guest CPU (optional). If not defined by the CloudStack administrator, users can pick the CPU attributes.
- Guest RAM (optional). If not defined by the CloudStack administrator, users can pick the RAM.
- Guest Networking type (virtual or direct)
- Tags on the root disk

The disk offering specifies:

- Disk size (optional). If not defined by the CloudStack administrator, users can pick the disk size.
- Tags on the data disk

Custom Compute Offering

CloudStack provides you the flexibility to specify the desired values for the number of CPU, CPU speed, and memory while deploying a VM. As an admin, you create a Compute Offering by marking it as custom, and the users will be able to customize this dynamic Compute Offering by specifying the memory, and CPU at the time of VM creation or upgrade. Custom Compute Offering is same as the normal Compute Offering except that the values of the dynamic parameters will be set to zeros in the given set of templates. Use this offering to deploy VM by specifying custom values for the dynamic parameters. Memory, CPU and number of CPUs are considered as dynamic parameters.

Dynamic Compute Offerings can be used in following cases: deploying a VM, changing the compute offering of a stopped VM and running VMs, which is nothing but scaling up. To support this feature a new field, Custom, has been added to the Create Compute Offering page. If the Custom field is checked, the user will be able to create a custom Compute Offering by filling in the desired values for number of CPU, CPU speed, and memory. See ? for more information on this.

Recording Usage Events for Dynamically Assigned Resources.

To support this feature, usage events has been enhanced to register events for dynamically assigned resources. Usage events are registered when a VM is created from a custom compute offering, and upon changing the compute offering of a stopped or running VM. The values of the parameters, such as CPU, speed, RAM are recorded.

Creating a New Compute Offering

To create a new compute offering:

1. Log in with admin privileges to the CloudStack UI.

2. In the left navigation bar, click Service Offerings.

3. In Select Offering, choose Compute Offering.

4. Click Add Compute Offering.

5. In the dialog, make the following choices:

  - **Name**: Any desired name for the service offering.

  - **Description**: A short description of the offering that can be displayed to users

  - **Storage type**: The type of disk that should be allocated. Local allocates from storage attached directly to the host where the system VM is running. Shared allocates from storage accessible via NFS.

  - **Custom**: Custom compute offerings can be used in following cases: deploying a VM, changing the compute offering of a stopped VM and running VMs, which is nothing but scaling up.

    If the Custom field is checked, the end-user must fill in the desired values for number of CPU, CPU speed, and RAM Memory when using a custom compute offering. When you check this box, those three input fields are hidden in the dialog box.

  - **# of CPU cores**: The number of cores which should be allocated to a system VM with this offering. If Custom is checked, this field does not appear.

  - **CPU (in MHz)**: The CPU speed of the cores that the system VM is allocated. For example, "2000" would provide for a 2 GHz clock. If Custom is checked, this field does not appear.

  - **Memory (in MB)**: The amount of memory in megabytes that the system VM should be allocated. For example, "2048" would provide for a 2 GB RAM allocation. If Custom is checked, this field does not appear.

  - **Network Rate**: Allowed data transfer rate in MB per second.

  - **Disk Read Rate**: Allowed disk read rate in bits per second.

  - **Disk Write Rate**: Allowed disk write rate in bits per second.

  - **Disk Read Rate**: Allowed disk read rate in IOPS (input/output operations per second).

  - **Disk Write Rate**: Allowed disk write rate in IOPS (input/output operations per second).

  - **Offer HA**: If yes, the administrator can choose to have the system VM be monitored and as highly available as possible.

  - **QoS Type**: Three options: Empty (no Quality of Service), hypervisor (rate limiting enforced on the hypervisor side), and storage (guaranteed minimum and maximum IOPS enforced on the storage side). If leveraging QoS, make sure that the hypervisor or storage system supports this feature.

  - **Custom IOPS**: If checked, the user can set their own IOPS. If not checked, the root administrator can define values. If the root admin does not set values when using storage QoS, default values are used (the defaults can be overridden if the proper parameters are passed into CloudStack when creating the primary storage in question).

  - **Min IOPS**: Appears only if storage QoS is to be used. Set a guaranteed minimum number of IOPS to be enforced on the storage side.

  - **Max IOPS**: Appears only if storage QoS is to be used. Set a maximum number of IOPS to be enforced on the storage side (the system may go above this limit in certain circumstances for short intervals).

  - **Hypervisor Snapshot Reserve**: For managed storage only. This is a value that is a percentage of the size of the root disk. For example: if the root disk is 20 GB and Hypervisor Snapshot Reserve is 200%, the storage volume that backs the storage repository (XenServer) or datastore (VMware) in question is sized at 60 GB (20 GB + (20 GB * 2)). This enables space for hypervisor snapshots in addition to the virtual disk that represents the root disk. This does not apply for KVM.

- **Storage Tags**: The tags that should be associated with the primary storage used by the system VM.

- **Host Tags**: (Optional) Any tags that you use to organize your hosts

- **CPU cap**: Whether to limit the level of CPU usage even if spare capacity is available.

- **Public**: Indicate whether the service offering should be available all domains or only some domains. Choose Yes to make it available to all domains. Choose No to limit the scope to a subdomain; CloudStack will then prompt for the subdomain's name.

- **isVolatile**: If checked, VMs created from this service offering will have their root disks reset upon reboot. This is useful for secure environments that need a fresh start on every boot and for desktops that should not retain state.

- **Deployment Planner**: Choose the technique that you would like CloudStack to use when deploying VMs based on this service offering.

  First Fit places new VMs on the first host that is found having sufficient capacity to support the VM's requirements.

  User Dispersing makes the best effort to evenly distribute VMs belonging to the same account on different clusters or pods.

  User Concentrated prefers to deploy VMs belonging to the same account within a single pod.

  Implicit Dedication will deploy VMs on private infrastructure that is dedicated to a specific domain or account. If you choose this planner, then you must also pick a value for Planner Mode. See "Dedicating Resources to Accounts and Domains".

  Bare Metal is used with bare metal hosts. See Bare Metal Installation in the Installation Guide.

- **Planner Mode**: Used when ImplicitDedicationPlanner is selected in the previous field. The planner mode determines how VMs will be deployed on private infrastructure that is dedicated to a single domain or account.

  Strict: A host will not be shared across multiple accounts. For example, strict implicit dedication is useful for deployment of certain types of applications, such as desktops, where no host can be shared between different accounts without violating the desktop software's terms of license.

  Preferred: The VM will be deployed in dedicated infrastructure if possible. Otherwise, the VM can be deployed in shared infrastructure.

- **GPU: Assign a physical GPU(GPU-passthrough) or a portion of a physicalGPU** GPU card(vGPU) to the guest VM. It allows graphical applications to run on the VM. Select the card from the supported list of cards.

  The options given are NVIDIA GRID K1 and NVIDIA GRID K2. These are vGPU capable cards that allow multiple vGPUs on a single physical GPU. If you want to use a card other than these, follow the instructions in the **"GPU and vGPU support for CloudStack Guest VMs"** page in the Cloudstack Version 4.4 Design Docs found in the Cloudstack Wiki.

- **vGPU Type**: Represents the type of virtual GPU to be assigned to a guest VM. In this case, only a portion of a physical GPU card (vGPU) is assigned to the guest VM.

  Additionally, the **passthrough vGPU** type is defined to represent a physical GPU device. A **passthrough vGPU** can directly be assigned to a single guest VM. In this case, a physical GPU device is exclusively allotted to a single guest VM.

6. Click Add.

Creating a New Disk Offering

To create a new disk offering:

1. Log in with admin privileges to the CloudStack UI.

2. In the left navigation bar, click Service Offerings.

3. In Select Offering, choose Disk Offering.

4. Click Add Disk Offering.

5. In the dialog, make the following choices:

   - **Name**: Any desired name for the disk offering.

   - **Description**: A short description of the offering that can be displayed to users

   - **Custom Disk Size**: If checked, the user can set their own disk size. If not checked, the root administrator must define a value in Disk Size.

   - **Disk Size**: Appears only if Custom Disk Size is not selected. Define the volume size in GB (2^30 1GB = 1,073,741,824 Bytes).

   - **QoS Type**: Three options: Empty (no Quality of Service), hypervisor (rate limiting enforced on the hypervisor side), and storage (guaranteed minimum and maximum IOPS enforced on the storage side). If leveraging QoS, make sure that the hypervisor or storage system supports this feature.

   - **Custom IOPS**: If checked, the user can set their own IOPS. If not checked, the root administrator can define values. If the root admin does not set values when using storage QoS, default values are used (the defauls can be overridden if the proper parameters are passed into CloudStack when creating the primary storage in question).

   - **Min IOPS**: Appears only if storage QoS is to be used. Set a guaranteed minimum number of IOPS to be enforced on the storage side.

   - **Max IOPS**: Appears only if storage QoS is to be used. Set a maximum number of IOPS to be enforced on the storage side (the system may go above this limit in certain circumstances for short intervals).

   - **Hypervisor Snapshot Reserve**: For managed storage only. This is a value that is a percentage of the size of the data disk. For example: if the data disk is 20 GB and Hypervisor Snapshot Reserve is 200%, the storage volume that backs the storage repository (XenServer) or datastore (VMware) in question is sized at 60 GB (20 GB + (20 GB * 2)). This enables space for hypervisor snapshots in addition to the virtual disk that represents the data disk. This does not apply for KVM.

   - **(Optional)Storage Tags**: The tags that should be associated with the primary storage for this disk. Tags are a comma separated list of attributes of the storage. For example "ssd,blue". Tags are also added on Primary Storage. CloudStack matches tags on a disk offering to tags on the storage. If a tag is present on a disk offering that tag (or tags) must also be present on Primary Storage for the volume to be provisioned. If no such primary storage exists, allocation from the disk offering will fail..

   - **Public**: Indicate whether the service offering should be available all domains or only some domains. Choose Yes to make it available to all domains. Choose No to limit the scope to a subdomain; CloudStack will then prompt for the subdomain's name.

6. Click Add.

Modifying or Deleting a Service Offering

Service offerings cannot be changed once created. This applies to both compute offerings and disk offerings.

A service offering can be deleted. If it is no longer in use, it is deleted immediately and permanently. If the service offering is still in use, it will remain in the database until all the virtual machines referencing it have been deleted. After deletion by the administrator, a service offering will not be available to end users that are creating new instances.

4.1.3 System Service Offerings

System service offerings provide a choice of CPU speed, number of CPUs, tags, and RAM size, just as other service offerings do. But rather than being used for virtual machine instances and exposed to users, system service offerings are used to change the default properties of virtual routers, console proxies, and other system VMs. System service offerings are visible only to the CloudStack root administrator. CloudStack provides default system service offerings. The CloudStack root administrator can create additional custom system service offerings.

When CloudStack creates a virtual router for a guest network, it uses default settings which are defined in the system service offering associated with the network offering. You can upgrade the capabilities of the virtual router by applying a new network offering that contains a different system service offering. All virtual routers in that network will begin using the settings from the new service offering.

Creating a New System Service Offering

To create a system service offering:

1. Log in with admin privileges to the CloudStack UI.

2. In the left navigation bar, click Service Offerings.

3. In Select Offering, choose System Offering.

4. Click Add System Service Offering.

5. In the dialog, make the following choices:

   - Name. Any desired name for the system offering.

   - Description. A short description of the offering that can be displayed to users

   - System VM Type. Select the type of system virtual machine that this offering is intended to support.

   - Storage type. The type of disk that should be allocated. Local allocates from storage attached directly to the host where the system VM is running. Shared allocates from storage accessible via NFS.

   - # of CPU cores. The number of cores which should be allocated to a system VM with this offering

   - CPU (in MHz). The CPU speed of the cores that the system VM is allocated. For example, "2000" would provide for a 2 GHz clock.

   - Memory (in MB). The amount of memory in megabytes that the system VM should be allocated. For example, "2048" would provide for a 2 GB RAM allocation.

   - Network Rate. Allowed data transfer rate in MB per second.

   - Offer HA. If yes, the administrator can choose to have the system VM be monitored and as highly available as possible.

   - Storage Tags. The tags that should be associated with the primary storage used by the system VM.

   - Host Tags. (Optional) Any tags that you use to organize your hosts

   - CPU cap. Whether to limit the level of CPU usage even if spare capacity is available.

   - Public. Indicate whether the service offering should be available all domains or only some domains. Choose Yes to make it available to all domains. Choose No to limit the scope to a subdomain; CloudStack will then prompt for the subdomain's name.

6. Click Add.

4.1.4 Network Throttling

Network throttling is the process of controlling the network access and bandwidth usage based on certain rules. Cloud-Stack controls this behaviour of the guest networks in the cloud by using the network rate parameter. This parameter is defined as the default data transfer rate in Mbps (Megabits Per Second) allowed in a guest network. It defines the upper limits for network utilization. If the current utilization is below the allowed upper limits, access is granted, else revoked.

You can throttle the network bandwidth either to control the usage above a certain limit for some accounts, or to control network congestion in a large cloud environment. The network rate for your cloud can be configured on the following:

- Network Offering
- Service Offering
- Global parameter

If network rate is set to NULL in service offering, the value provided in the vm.network.throttling.rate global parameter is applied. If the value is set to NULL for network offering, the value provided in the network.throttling.rate global parameter is considered.

For the default public, storage, and management networks, network rate is set to 0. This implies that the public, storage, and management networks will have unlimited bandwidth by default. For default guest networks, network rate is set to NULL. In this case, network rate is defaulted to the global parameter value.

The following table gives you an overview of how network rate is applied on different types of networks in CloudStack.

Networks	Network Rate Is Taken from
Guest network of Virtual Router	Guest Network Offering
Public network of Virtual Router	Guest Network Offering
Storage network of Secondary Storage VM	System Network Offering
Management network of Secondary Storage VM	System Network Offering
Storage network of Console Proxy VM	System Network Offering
Management network of Console Proxy VM	System Network Offering
Storage network of Virtual Router	System Network Offering
Management network of Virtual Router	System Network Offering
Public network of Secondary Storage VM	System Network Offering
Public network of Console Proxy VM	System Network Offering
Default network of a guest VM	Compute Offering
Additional networks of a guest VM	Corresponding Network Offerings

A guest VM must have a default network, and can also have many additional networks. Depending on various parameters, such as the host and virtual switch used, you can observe a difference in the network rate in your cloud. For example, on a VMware host the actual network rate varies based on where they are configured (compute offering, network offering, or both); the network type (shared or isolated); and traffic direction (ingress or egress).

The network rate set for a network offering used by a particular network in CloudStack is used for the traffic shaping policy of a port group, for example: port group A, for that network: a particular subnet or VLAN on the actual network. The virtual routers for that network connects to the port group A, and by default instances in that network connects to this port group. However, if an instance is deployed with a compute offering with the network rate set, and if this rate is used for the traffic shaping policy of another port group for the network, for example port group B, then instances using this compute offering are connected to the port group B, instead of connecting to port group A.

The traffic shaping policy on standard port groups in VMware only applies to the egress traffic, and the net effect depends on the type of network used in CloudStack. In shared networks, ingress traffic is unlimited for CloudStack, and egress traffic is limited to the rate that applies to the port group used by the instance if any. If the compute offering has a network rate configured, this rate applies to the egress traffic, otherwise the network rate set for the network offering applies. For isolated networks, the network rate set for the network offering, if any, effectively applies to the ingress traffic. This is mainly because the network rate set for the network offering applies to the egress traffic from the virtual router to the instance. The egress traffic is limited by the rate that applies to the port group used by the instance if any, similar to shared networks.

For example:

Network rate of network offering = 10 Mbps

Network rate of compute offering = 200 Mbps

In shared networks, ingress traffic will not be limited for CloudStack, while egress traffic will be limited to 200 Mbps. In an isolated network, ingress traffic will be limited to 10 Mbps and egress to 200 Mbps.

4.1.5 Changing the Default System Offering for System VMs

You can manually change the system offering for a particular System VM. Additionally, as a CloudStack administrator, you can also change the default system offering used for System VMs.

1. Create a new system offering.

   For more information, see Creating a New System Service Offering.

2. Back up the database:

```
mysqldump -u root -p cloud | bzip2 > cloud_backup.sql.bz2
```

3. Open an MySQL prompt:

```
mysql -u cloud -p cloud
```

4. Run the following queries on the cloud database.

   (a) In the disk_offering table, identify the original default offering and the new offering you want to use by default.

   Take a note of the ID of the new offering.

```
select id,name,unique_name,type from disk_offering;
```

   (b) For the original default offering, set the value of unique_name to NULL.

```
# update disk_offering set unique_name = NULL where id = 10;
```

   Ensure that you use the correct value for the ID.

   (c) For the new offering that you want to use by default, set the value of unique_name as follows:

   For the default Console Proxy VM (CPVM) offering,set unique_name to 'Cloud.com-ConsoleProxy'. For the default Secondary Storage VM (SSVM) offering, set unique_name to 'Cloud.com-SecondaryStorage'. For example:

```
update disk_offering set unique_name = 'Cloud.com-ConsoleProxy' where id = 16;
```

5. Restart CloudStack Management Server. Restarting is required because the default offerings are loaded into the memory at startup.

```
service cloudstack-management restart
```

6. Destroy the existing CPVM or SSVM offerings and wait for them to be recreated. The new CPVM or SSVM are configured with the new offering.

## CHAPTER 5

Setting up Networking for Users

5.1 Setting Up Networking for Users

5.1.1 Overview of Setting Up Networking for Users

People using cloud infrastructure have a variety of needs and preferences when it comes to the networking services provided by the cloud. As a CloudStack administrator, you can do the following things to set up networking for your users:

- Set up physical networks in zones

- Set up several different providers for the same service on a single physical network (for example, both Cisco and Juniper firewalls)

- Bundle different types of network services into network offerings, so users can choose the desired network services for any given virtual machine

- Add new network offerings as time goes on so end users can upgrade to a better class of service on their network

- Provide more ways for a network to be accessed by a user, such as through a project of which the user is a member

5.1.2 About Virtual Networks

A virtual network is a logical construct that enables multi-tenancy on a single physical network. In CloudStack a virtual network can be shared or isolated.

Isolated Networks

An isolated network can be accessed only by virtual machines of a single account. Isolated networks have the following properties.

- Resources such as VLAN are allocated and garbage collected dynamically

- There is one network offering for the entire network

- The network offering can be upgraded or downgraded but it is for the entire network

For more information, see "Configure Guest Traffic in an Advanced Zone".

Shared Networks

A shared network can be accessed by virtual machines that belong to many different accounts. Network Isolation on shared networks is accomplished by using techniques such as security groups, which is supported only in Basic zones in CloudStack 3.0.3 and later versions.

- Shared Networks are created by the administrator

- Shared Networks can be designated to a certain domain

- Shared Network resources such as VLAN and physical network that it maps to are designated by the administrator

- Shared Networks can be isolated by security groups

- Public Network is a shared network that is not shown to the end users

- Source NAT per zone is not supported in Shared Network when the service provider is virtual router. However, Source NAT per account is supported. For information, see "Configuring a Shared Guest Network".

Runtime Allocation of Virtual Network Resources

When you define a new virtual network, all your settings for that network are stored in CloudStack. The actual network resources are activated only when the first virtual machine starts in the network. When all virtual machines have left the virtual network, the network resources are garbage collected so they can be allocated again. This helps to conserve network resources.

5.1.3 Network Service Providers

Note: For the most up-to-date list of supported network service providers, see the CloudStack UI or call *listNetwork-ServiceProviders*.

A service provider (also called a network element) is hardware or virtual appliance that makes a network service possible; for example, a firewall appliance can be installed in the cloud to provide firewall service. On a single network, multiple providers can provide the same network service. For example, a firewall service may be provided by Cisco or Juniper devices in the same physical network.

You can have multiple instances of the same service provider in a network (say, more than one Juniper SRX device).

If different providers are set up to provide the same service on the network, the administrator can create network offerings so users can specify which network service provider they prefer (along with the other choices offered in network offerings). Otherwise, CloudStack will choose which provider to use whenever the service is called for.

Supported Network Service Providers

CloudStack ships with an internal list of the supported service providers, and you can choose from this list when creating a network offering.

	Virtual Router	Citrix NetScaler	Juniper SRX	F5 BigIP	Host based (KVM/Xen)
Remote Access VPN	Yes	No	No	No	No
DNS/DHCP/User Data	Yes	No	No	No	No
Firewall	Yes	No	Yes	No	No
Load Balancing	Yes	Yes	No	Yes	No
Elastic IP	No	Yes	No	No	No
Elastic LB	No	Yes	No	No	No
Source NAT	Yes	No	Yes	No	No
Static NAT	Yes	Yes	Yes	No	No
Port Forwarding	Yes	No	Yes	No	No

5.1.4 Network Offerings

Note: For the most up-to-date list of supported network services, see the CloudStack UI or call listNetworkServices.

A network offering is a named set of network services, such as:

- DHCP
- DNS
- Source NAT
- Static NAT
- Port Forwarding
- Load Balancing
- Firewall
- VPN
- (Optional) Name one of several available providers to use for a given service, such as Juniper for the firewall
- (Optional) Network tag to specify which physical network to use

When creating a new VM, the user chooses one of the available network offerings, and that determines which network services the VM can use.

The CloudStack administrator can create any number of custom network offerings, in addition to the default network offerings provided by CloudStack. By creating multiple custom network offerings, you can set up your cloud to offer different classes of service on a single multi-tenant physical network. For example, while the underlying physical wiring may be the same for two tenants, tenant A may only need simple firewall protection for their website, while tenant B may be running a web server farm and require a scalable firewall solution, load balancing solution, and alternate networks for accessing the database backend.

Note: If you create load balancing rules while using a network service offering that includes an external load balancer device such as NetScaler, and later change the network service offering to one that uses the CloudStack virtual router, you must create a firewall rule on the virtual router for each of your existing load balancing rules so that they continue to function.

When creating a new virtual network, the CloudStack administrator chooses which network offering to enable for that network. Each virtual network is associated with one network offering. A virtual network can be upgraded or downgraded by changing its associated network offering. If you do this, be sure to reprogram the physical network to match.

CloudStack also has internal network offerings for use by CloudStack system VMs. These network offerings are not visible to users but can be modified by administrators.

Creating a New Network Offering

To create a network offering:

1. Log in with admin privileges to the CloudStack UI.

2. In the left navigation bar, click Service Offerings.

3. In Select Offering, choose Network Offering.

4. Click Add Network Offering.

5. In the dialog, make the following choices:

   - **Name**. Any desired name for the network offering.

   - **Description**. A short description of the offering that can be displayed to users.

   - **Network Rate**. Allowed data transfer rate in MB per second.

   - **Guest Type**. Choose whether the guest network is isolated or shared.

     For a description of this term, see *"About Virtual Networks"*.

   - **Persistent**. Indicate whether the guest network is persistent or not. The network that you can provision without having to deploy a VM on it is termed persistent network. For more information, see "Persistent Networks".

   - **Specify VLAN**. (Isolated guest networks only) Indicate whether a VLAN could be specified when this offering is used. If you select this option and later use this network offering while creating a VPC tier or an isolated network, you will be able to specify a VLAN ID for the network you create.

   - **VPC**. This option indicate whether the guest network is Virtual Private Cloud-enabled. A Virtual Private Cloud (VPC) is a private, isolated part of CloudStack. A VPC can have its own virtual network topology that resembles a traditional physical network. For more information on VPCs, see "About Virtual Private Clouds".

   - **Supported Services**. Select one or more of the possible network services. For some services, you must also choose the service provider; for example, if you select Load Balancer, you can choose the CloudStack virtual router or any other load balancers that have been configured in the cloud. Depending on which services you choose, additional fields may appear in the rest of the dialog box.

     Based on the guest network type selected, you can see the following supported services:

Sup-ported Services	Description	Iso-lated	Shared
DHCP	For more information, see "DNS and DHCP".	Supported	Supported
DNS	For more information, see "DNS and DHCP".	Supported	Supported
Load Balancer	If you select Load Balancer, you can choose the CloudStack virtual router or any other load balancers that have been configured in the cloud.	Supported	Supported
Firewall	For more information, see the Administration Guide.	Supported	Supported
Source NAT	If you select Source NAT, you can choose the CloudStack virtual router or any other Source NAT providers that have been configured in the cloud.	Supported	Supported
Static NAT	If you select Static NAT, you can choose the CloudStack virtual router or any other Static NAT providers that have been configured in the cloud.	Supported	Supported
Port For-warding	If you select Port Forwarding, you can choose the CloudStack virtual router or any other Port Forwarding providers that have been configured in the cloud.	Supported	Not Supported
VPN	For more information, see "Remote Access VPN".	Supported	Not Supported
User Data	For more information, see "User Data and Meta Data".	Not Supported	Supported
Network ACL	For more information, see "Configuring Network Access Control List".	Supported	Not Supported
Security Groups	For more information, see "Adding a Security Group".	Not Supported	Supported

- **System Offering**. If the service provider for any of the services selected in Supported Services is a virtual router, the System Offering field appears. Choose the system service offering that you want virtual routers to use in this network. For example, if you selected Load Balancer in Supported Services and selected a virtual router to provide load balancing, the System Offering field appears so you can choose between the CloudStack default system service offering and any custom system service offerings that have been defined by the CloudStack root administrator.

For more information, see "System Service Offerings".

- **LB Isolation**: Specify what type of load balancer isolation you want for the network: Shared or Dedicated.

Dedicated: If you select dedicated LB isolation, a dedicated load balancer device is assigned for the network from the pool of dedicated load balancer devices provisioned in the zone. If no sufficient dedicated load balancer devices are available in the zone, network creation fails. Dedicated device is a good choice for the high-traffic networks that make full use of the device's resources.

Shared: If you select shared LB isolation, a shared load balancer device is assigned for the network from the pool of shared load balancer devices provisioned in the zone. While provisioning CloudStack picks the shared load balancer device that is used by the least number of accounts. Once the device reaches its maximum capacity, the device will not be allocated to a new account.

- **Mode**: You can select either Inline mode or Side by Side mode:

Inline mode: Supported only for Juniper SRX firewall and BigF5 load balancer devices. In inline mode, a firewall device is placed in front of a load balancing device. The firewall acts as the gateway for all the incoming traffic, then redirect the load balancing traffic to the load balancer behind it. The load balancer in this case will not have the direct access to the public network.

Side by Side: In side by side mode, a firewall device is deployed in parallel with the load balancer device. So the traffic to the load balancer public IP is not routed through the firewall, and therefore, is exposed to the public network.

- **Associate Public IP**: Select this option if you want to assign a public IP address to the VMs deployed in the guest network. This option is available only if

    - Guest network is shared.

    - StaticNAT is enabled.

    - Elastic IP is enabled.

    For information on Elastic IP, see "About Elastic IP".

- **Redundant router capability**: Available only when Virtual Router is selected as the Source NAT provider. Select this option if you want to use two virtual routers in the network for uninterrupted connection: one operating as the master virtual router and the other as the backup. The master virtual router receives requests from and sends responses to the user's VM. The backup virtual router is activated only when the master is down. After the failover, the backup becomes the master virtual router. CloudStack deploys the routers on different hosts to ensure reliability if one host is down.

- **Conserve mode**: Indicate whether to use conserve mode. In this mode, network resources are allocated only when the first virtual machine starts in the network. When conservative mode is off, the public IP can only be used for a single service. For example, a public IP used for a port forwarding rule cannot be used for defining other services, such as StaticNAT or load balancing. When the conserve mode is on, you can define more than one service on the same public IP.

Note: If StaticNAT is enabled, irrespective of the status of the conserve mode, no port forwarding or load balancing rule can be created for the IP. However, you can add the firewall rules by using the createFirewallRule command.

- **Tags**: Network tag to specify which physical network to use.

- **Default egress policy**: Configure the default policy for firewall egress rules. Options are Allow and Deny. Default is Allow if no egress policy is specified, which indicates that all the egress traffic is accepted when a guest network is created from this offering.

    To block the egress traffic for a guest network, select Deny. In this case, when you configure an egress rules for an isolated guest network, rules are added to allow the specified traffic.

6. Click Add.

## CHAPTER 6

Working with Virtual Machines

6.1 Working with Virtual Machines

6.1.1 About Working with Virtual Machines

CloudStack provides administrators with complete control over the lifecycle of all guest VMs executing in the cloud. CloudStack provides several guest management operations for end users and administrators. VMs may be stopped, started, rebooted, and destroyed.

Guest VMs have a name and group. VM names and groups are opaque to CloudStack and are available for end users to organize their VMs. Each VM can have three names for use in different contexts. Only two of these names can be controlled by the user:

- Instance name – a unique, immutable ID that is generated by CloudStack and can not be modified by the user. This name conforms to the requirements in IETF RFC 1123.

- Display name – the name displayed in the CloudStack web UI. Can be set by the user. Defaults to instance name.

- Name – host name that the DHCP server assigns to the VM. Can be set by the user. Defaults to instance name

---

Note: You can append the display name of a guest VM to its internal name. For more information, see *"Appending a Display Name to the Guest VM's Internal Name"*.

Guest VMs can be configured to be Highly Available (HA). An HA-enabled VM is monitored by the system. If the system detects that the VM is down, it will attempt to restart the VM, possibly on a different host. For more information, see HA-Enabled Virtual Machines on

Each new VM is allocated one public IP address. When the VM is started, CloudStack automatically creates a static NAT between this public IP address and the private IP address of the VM.

If elastic IP is in use (with the NetScaler load balancer), the IP address initially allocated to the new VM is not marked as elastic. The user must replace the automatically configured IP with a specifically acquired elastic IP, and set up the static NAT mapping between this new IP and the guest VM's private IP. The VM's original IP address is then released and returned to the pool of available public IPs. Optionally, you can also decide not to allocate a public IP to a VM in an EIP-enabled Basic zone. For more information on Elastic IP, see "About Elastic IP".

CloudStack cannot distinguish a guest VM that was shut down by the user (such as with the "shutdown" command in Linux) from a VM that shut down unexpectedly. If an HA-enabled VM is shut down from inside the VM, CloudStack will restart it. To shut down an HA-enabled VM, you must go through the CloudStack UI or API.

6.1.2 Best Practices for Virtual Machines

For VMs to work as expected and provide excellent service, follow these guidelines.

Monitor VMs for Max Capacity

The CloudStack administrator should monitor the total number of VM instances in each cluster, and disable allocation to the cluster if the total is approaching the maximum that the hypervisor can handle. Be sure to leave a safety margin to allow for the possibility of one or more hosts failing, which would increase the VM load on the other hosts as the VMs are automatically redeployed. Consult the documentation for your chosen hypervisor to find the maximum permitted number of VMs per host, then use CloudStack global configuration settings to set this as the default limit. Monitor the VM activity in each cluster at all times. Keep the total number of VMs below a safe level that allows for the occasional host failure. For example, if there are N hosts in the cluster, and you want to allow for one host in the cluster to be down at any given time, the total number of VM instances you can permit in the cluster is at most (N-1) * (per-host-limit). Once a cluster reaches this number of VMs, use the CloudStack UI to disable allocation of more VMs to the cluster.

Install Required Tools and Drivers

Be sure the following are installed on each VM:

- For XenServer, install PV drivers and Xen tools on each VM. This will enable live migration and clean guest shutdown. Xen tools are required in order for dynamic CPU and RAM scaling to work.

- For vSphere, install VMware Tools on each VM. This will enable console view to work properly. VMware Tools are required in order for dynamic CPU and RAM scaling to work.

To be sure that Xen tools or VMware Tools is installed, use one of the following techniques:

- Create each VM from a template that already has the tools installed; or,

- When registering a new template, the administrator or user can indicate whether tools are installed on the template. This can be done through the UI or using the updateTemplate API; or,

- If a user deploys a virtual machine with a template that does not have Xen tools or VMware Tools, and later installs the tools on the VM, then the user can inform CloudStack using the updateVirtualMachine API. After installing the tools and updating the virtual machine, stop and start the VM.

6.1.3 VM Lifecycle

Virtual machines can be in the following states:

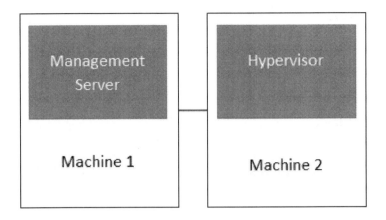

Simplified view of a basic deployment

Once a virtual machine is destroyed, it cannot be recovered. All the resources used by the virtual machine will be reclaimed by the system. This includes the virtual machine's IP address.

A stop will attempt to gracefully shut down the operating system, which typically involves terminating all the running applications. If the operation system cannot be stopped, it will be forcefully terminated. This has the same effect as pulling the power cord to a physical machine.

A reboot is a stop followed by a start.

CloudStack preserves the state of the virtual machine hard disk until the machine is destroyed.

A running virtual machine may fail because of hardware or network issues. A failed virtual machine is in the down state.

The system places the virtual machine into the down state if it does not receive the heartbeat from the hypervisor for three minutes.

The user can manually restart the virtual machine from the down state.

The system will start the virtual machine from the down state automatically if the virtual machine is marked as HA-enabled.

6.1.4 Creating VMs

Virtual machines are usually created from a template. Users can also create blank virtual machines. A blank virtual machine is a virtual machine without an OS template. Users can attach an ISO file and install the OS from the CD/DVD-ROM.

Note: You can create a VM without starting it. You can determine whether the VM needs to be started as part of the VM deployment. A request parameter, startVM, in the deployVm API provides this feature. For more information, see the Developer's Guide.

To create a VM from a template:

1. Log in to the CloudStack UI as an administrator or user.

2. In the left navigation bar, click Instances.

3. Click Add Instance.

4. Select a zone.

5. Select a template, then follow the steps in the wizard. For more information about how the templates came to be in this list, see *Working with Templates*.

6. Be sure that the hardware you have allows starting the selected service offering.

7. Click Submit and your VM will be created and started.

> **Note:** For security reason, the internal name of the VM is visible only to the root admin.

To create a VM from an ISO:

> **Note:** (XenServer) Windows VMs running on XenServer require PV drivers, which may be provided in the template or added after the VM is created. The PV drivers are necessary for essential management functions such as mounting additional volumes and ISO images, live migration, and graceful shutdown.

1. Log in to the CloudStack UI as an administrator or user.

2. In the left navigation bar, click Instances.

3. Click Add Instance.

4. Select a zone.

5. Select ISO Boot, and follow the steps in the wizard.

6. Click Submit and your VM will be created and started.

6.1.5 Accessing VMs

Any user can access their own virtual machines. The administrator can access all VMs running in the cloud.

To access a VM through the CloudStack UI:

1. Log in to the CloudStack UI as a user or admin.

2. Click Instances, then click the name of a running VM.

3. Click the View Console button .

To access a VM directly over the network:

1. The VM must have some port open to incoming traffic. For example, in a basic zone, a new VM might be assigned to a security group which allows incoming traffic. This depends on what security group you picked when creating the VM. In other cases, you can open a port by setting up a port forwarding policy. See "IP Forwarding and Firewalling".

2. If a port is open but you can not access the VM using ssh, it's possible that ssh is not already enabled on the VM. This will depend on whether ssh is enabled in the template you picked when creating the VM. Access the VM through the CloudStack UI and enable ssh on the machine using the commands for the VM's operating system.

3. If the network has an external firewall device, you will need to create a firewall rule to allow access. See "IP Forwarding and Firewalling".

6.1.6 Stopping and Starting VMs

Once a VM instance is created, you can stop, restart, or delete it as needed. In the CloudStack UI, click Instances, select the VM, and use the Stop, Start, Reboot, and Destroy buttons.

6.1.7 Assigning VMs to Hosts

At any point in time, each virtual machine instance is running on a single host. How does CloudStack determine which host to place a VM on? There are several ways:

- Automatic default host allocation. CloudStack can automatically pick the most appropriate host to run each virtual machine.

- Instance type preferences. CloudStack administrators can specify that certain hosts should have a preference for particular types of guest instances. For example, an administrator could state that a host should have a preference to run Windows guests. The default host allocator will attempt to place guests of that OS type on such hosts first. If no such host is available, the allocator will place the instance wherever there is sufficient physical capacity.

- Vertical and horizontal allocation. Vertical allocation consumes all the resources of a given host before allocating any guests on a second host. This reduces power consumption in the cloud. Horizontal allocation places a guest on each host in a round-robin fashion. This may yield better performance to the guests in some cases.

- End user preferences. Users can not control exactly which host will run a given VM instance, but they can specify a zone for the VM. CloudStack is then restricted to allocating the VM only to one of the hosts in that zone.

- Host tags. The administrator can assign tags to hosts. These tags can be used to specify which host a VM should use. The CloudStack administrator decides whether to define host tags, then create a service offering using those tags and offer it to the user.

- Affinity groups. By defining affinity groups and assigning VMs to them, the user or administrator can influence (but not dictate) which VMs should run on separate hosts. This feature is to let users specify that certain VMs won't be on the same host.

- CloudStack also provides a pluggable interface for adding new allocators. These custom allocators can provide any policy the administrator desires.

Affinity Groups

By defining affinity groups and assigning VMs to them, the user or administrator can influence (but not dictate) which VMs should run on separate hosts. This feature is to let users specify that VMs with the same "host anti-affinity" type won't be on the same host. This serves to increase fault tolerance. If a host fails, another VM offering the same service (for example, hosting the user's website) is still up and running on another host.

The scope of an affinity group is per user account.

Creating a New Affinity Group

To add an affinity group:

1. Log in to the CloudStack UI as an administrator or user.

2. In the left navigation bar, click Affinity Groups.

3. Click Add affinity group. In the dialog box, fill in the following fields:

   - Name. Give the group a name.

   - Description. Any desired text to tell more about the purpose of the group.

   - Type. The only supported type shipped with CloudStack is Host Anti-Affinity. This indicates that the VMs in this group should avoid being placed on the same host with each other. If you see other types in this list, it means that your installation of CloudStack has been extended with customized affinity group plugins.

Assign a New VM to an Affinity Group

To assign a new VM to an affinity group:

- Create the VM as usual, as described in "Creating VMs". In the Add Instance wizard, there is a new Affinity tab where you can select the affinity group.

Change Affinity Group for an Existing VM

To assign an existing VM to an affinity group:

1. Log in to the CloudStack UI as an administrator or user.

2. In the left navigation bar, click Instances.

3. Click the name of the VM you want to work with.

4. Stop the VM by clicking the Stop button.

5. Click the Change Affinity button.

View Members of an Affinity Group

To see which VMs are currently assigned to a particular affinity group:

1. In the left navigation bar, click Affinity Groups.

2. Click the name of the group you are interested in.

3. Click View Instances. The members of the group are listed.

   From here, you can click the name of any VM in the list to access all its details and controls.

Delete an Affinity Group

To delete an affinity group:

1. In the left navigation bar, click Affinity Groups.

2. Click the name of the group you are interested in.

3. Click Delete.

   Any VM that is a member of the affinity group will be disassociated from the group. The former group members will continue to run normally on the current hosts, but if the VM is restarted, it will no longer follow the host allocation rules from its former affinity group.

6.1.8 Virtual Machine Snapshots

(Supported on VMware and XenServer)

In addition to the existing CloudStack ability to snapshot individual VM volumes, you can take a VM snapshot to preserve all the VM's data volumes as well as (optionally) its CPU/memory state. This is useful for quick restore of a VM. For example, you can snapshot a VM, then make changes such as software upgrades. If anything goes wrong, simply restore the VM to its previous state using the previously saved VM snapshot.

The snapshot is created using the hypervisor's native snapshot facility. The VM snapshot includes not only the data volumes, but optionally also whether the VM is running or turned off (CPU state) and the memory contents. The snapshot is stored in CloudStack's primary storage.

VM snapshots can have a parent/child relationship. Each successive snapshot of the same VM is the child of the snapshot that came before it. Each time you take an additional snapshot of the same VM, it saves only the differences between the current state of the VM and the state stored in the most recent previous snapshot. The previous snapshot becomes a parent, and the new snapshot is its child. It is possible to create a long chain of these parent/child snapshots, which amount to a "redo" record leading from the current state of the VM back to the original.

If you need more information about VM snapshots on VMware, check out the VMware documentation and the VMware Knowledge Base, especially Understanding virtual machine snapshots.

Limitations on VM Snapshots

- If a VM has some stored snapshots, you can't attach new volume to the VM or delete any existing volumes. If you change the volumes on the VM, it would become impossible to restore the VM snapshot which was created with the previous volume structure. If you want to attach a volume to such a VM, first delete its snapshots.

- VM snapshots which include both data volumes and memory can't be kept if you change the VM's service offering. Any existing VM snapshots of this type will be discarded.

- You can't make a VM snapshot at the same time as you are taking a volume snapshot.

- You should use only CloudStack to create VM snapshots on hosts managed by CloudStack. Any snapshots that you make directly on the hypervisor will not be tracked in CloudStack.

Configuring VM Snapshots

The cloud administrator can use global configuration variables to control the behavior of VM snapshots. To set these variables, go through the Global Settings area of the CloudStack UI.

Configuration Setting Name

Description

vmsnapshots.max

The maximum number of VM snapshots that can be saved for any given virtual machine in the cloud. The total possible number of VM snapshots in the cloud is (number of VMs) * vmsnapshots.max. If the number of snapshots for any VM ever hits the maximum, the older ones are removed by the snapshot expunge job.

vmsnapshot.create.wait

Number of seconds to wait for a snapshot job to succeed before declaring failure and issuing an error.

Using VM Snapshots

To create a VM snapshot using the CloudStack UI:

1. Log in to the CloudStack UI as a user or administrator.

2. Click Instances.

3. Click the name of the VM you want to snapshot.

4. Click the Take VM Snapshot button.

> **Note:** If a snapshot is already in progress, then clicking this button will have no effect.

5. Provide a name and description. These will be displayed in the VM Snapshots list.

6. (For running VMs only) If you want to include the VM's memory in the snapshot, click the Memory checkbox. This saves the CPU and memory state of the virtual machine. If you don't check this box, then only the current state of the VM disk is saved. Checking this box makes the snapshot take longer.

7. Quiesce VM: check this box if you want to quiesce the file system on the VM before taking the snapshot. Not supported on XenServer when used with CloudStack-provided primary storage.

   When this option is used with CloudStack-provided primary storage, the quiesce operation is performed by the underlying hypervisor (VMware is supported). When used with another primary storage vendor's plugin, the quiesce operation is provided according to the vendor's implementation.

8. Click OK.

To delete a snapshot or restore a VM to the state saved in a particular snapshot:

1. Navigate to the VM as described in the earlier steps.

2. Click View VM Snapshots.

3. In the list of snapshots, click the name of the snapshot you want to work with.

4. Depending on what you want to do:

   To delete the snapshot, click the Delete button.

   To revert to the snapshot, click the Revert button.

> **Note:** VM snapshots are deleted automatically when a VM is destroyed. You don't have to manually delete the snapshots in this case.

6.1.9 Changing the VM Name, OS, or Group

After a VM is created, you can modify the display name, operating system, and the group it belongs to.

To access a VM through the CloudStack UI:

1. Log in to the CloudStack UI as a user or admin.

2. In the left navigation, click Instances.

3. Select the VM that you want to modify.

4. Click the Stop button to stop the VM.

5. Click Edit.

6. Make the desired changes to the following:

7. **Display name**: Enter a new display name if you want to change the name of the VM.

8. **OS Type**: Select the desired operating system.

9. **Group**: Enter the group name for the VM.

10. Click Apply.

6.1.10 Appending a Display Name to the Guest VM's Internal Name

Every guest VM has an internal name. The host uses the internal name to identify the guest VMs. CloudStack gives you an option to provide a guest VM with a display name. You can set this display name as the internal name so that the vCenter can use it to identify the guest VM. A new global parameter, vm.instancename.flag, has now been added to achieve this functionality.

The default format of the internal name is i-<user_id>-<vm_id>-<instance.name>, where instance.name is a global parameter. However, If vm.instancename.flag is set to true, and if a display name is provided during the creation of a guest VM, the display name is appended to the internal name of the guest VM on the host. This makes the internal name format as i-<user_id>-<vm_id>-<displayName>. The default value of vm.instancename.flag is set to false. This feature is intended to make the correlation between instance names and internal names easier in large data center deployments.

The following table explains how a VM name is displayed in different scenarios.

User-Provided Display Name	vm.instancename.flag	Name displayed on the VM	Name on vCenter	Internal Name
Yes	True	Display name	i-<user_id>-<vm_id>-displayName	i-<user_id>-<vm_id>-displayName
No	True	UUID	i-<user_id>-<vm_id>-<instance.name>	i-<user_id>-<vm_id>-<instance.name>
Yes	False	Display name	i-<user_id>-<vm_id>-<instance.name>	i-<user_id>-<vm_id>-<instance.name>
No	False	UUID	i-<user_id>-<vm_id>-<instance.name>	i-<user_id>-<vm_id>-<instance.name>

6.1.11 Changing the Service Offering for a VM

To upgrade or downgrade the level of compute resources available to a virtual machine, you can change the VM's compute offering.

1. Log in to the CloudStack UI as a user or admin.

2. In the left navigation, click Instances.

3. Choose the VM that you want to work with.

4. (Skip this step if you have enabled dynamic VM scaling; see *CPU and Memory Scaling for Running VMs*.)

   Click the Stop button to stop the VM.

5. Click the Change Service button.

   The Change service dialog box is displayed.

6. Select the offering you want to apply to the selected VM.

7. Click OK.

CPU and Memory Scaling for Running VMs

(Supported on VMware and XenServer)

It is not always possible to accurately predict the CPU and RAM requirements when you first deploy a VM. You might need to increase these resources at any time during the life of a VM. You can dynamically modify CPU and RAM levels to scale up these resources for a running VM without incurring any downtime.

Dynamic CPU and RAM scaling can be used in the following cases:

- User VMs on hosts running VMware and XenServer.

- System VMs on VMware.

- VMware Tools or XenServer Tools must be installed on the virtual machine.

- The new requested CPU and RAM values must be within the constraints allowed by the hypervisor and the VM operating system.

- New VMs that are created after the installation of CloudStack 4.2 can use the dynamic scaling feature. If you are upgrading from a previous version of CloudStack, your existing VMs created with previous versions will not have the dynamic scaling capability unless you update them using the following procedure.

Updating Existing VMs

If you are upgrading from a previous version of CloudStack, and you want your existing VMs created with previous versions to have the dynamic scaling capability, update the VMs using the following steps:

1. Make sure the zone-level setting enable.dynamic.scale.vm is set to true. In the left navigation bar of the Cloud-Stack UI, click Infrastructure, then click Zones, click the zone you want, and click the Settings tab.

2. Install Xen tools (for XenServer hosts) or VMware Tools (for VMware hosts) on each VM if they are not already installed.

3. Stop the VM.

4. Click the Edit button.

5. Click the Dynamically Scalable checkbox.

6. Click Apply.

7. Restart the VM.

Configuring Dynamic CPU and RAM Scaling

To configure this feature, use the following new global configuration variables:

- enable.dynamic.scale.vm: Set to True to enable the feature. By default, the feature is turned off.

- scale.retry: How many times to attempt the scaling operation. Default = 2.

How to Dynamically Scale CPU and RAM

To modify the CPU and/or RAM capacity of a virtual machine, you need to change the compute offering of the VM to a new compute offering that has the desired CPU and RAM values. You can use the same steps described above in *"Changing the Service Offering for a VM"*, but skip the step where you stop the virtual machine. Of course, you might have to create a new compute offering first.

When you submit a dynamic scaling request, the resources will be scaled up on the current host if possible. If the host does not have enough resources, the VM will be live migrated to another host in the same cluster. If there is no host in the cluster that can fulfill the requested level of CPU and RAM, the scaling operation will fail. The VM will continue to run as it was before.

Limitations

- You can not do dynamic scaling for system VMs on XenServer.

- CloudStack will not check to be sure that the new CPU and RAM levels are compatible with the OS running on the VM.

- When scaling memory or CPU for a Linux VM on VMware, you might need to run scripts in addition to the other steps mentioned above. For more information, see Hot adding memory in Linux (1012764) in the VMware Knowledge Base.

- (VMware) If resources are not available on the current host, scaling up will fail on VMware because of a known issue where CloudStack and vCenter calculate the available capacity differently. For more information, see https://issues.apache.org/jira/browse/CLOUDSTACK-1809.

- On VMs running Linux 64-bit and Windows 7 32-bit operating systems, if the VM is initially assigned a RAM of less than 3 GB, it can be dynamically scaled up to 3 GB, but not more. This is due to a known issue with these operating systems, which will freeze if an attempt is made to dynamically scale from less than 3 GB to more than 3 GB.

6.1.12 Resetting the Virtual Machine Root Volume on Reboot

For secure environments, and to ensure that VM state is not persisted across reboots, you can reset the root disk. For more information, see "Reset VM to New Root Disk on Reboot".

6.1.13 Moving VMs Between Hosts (Manual Live Migration)

The CloudStack administrator can move a running VM from one host to another without interrupting service to users or going into maintenance mode. This is called manual live migration, and can be done under the following conditions:

- The root administrator is logged in. Domain admins and users can not perform manual live migration of VMs.

- The VM is running. Stopped VMs can not be live migrated.

- The destination host must have enough available capacity. If not, the VM will remain in the "migrating" state until memory becomes available.

- (KVM) The VM must not be using local disk storage. (On XenServer and VMware, VM live migration with local disk is enabled by CloudStack support for XenMotion and vMotion.)

- (KVM) The destination host must be in the same cluster as the original host. (On XenServer and VMware, VM live migration from one cluster to another is enabled by CloudStack support for XenMotion and vMotion.)

To manually live migrate a virtual machine

1. Log in to the CloudStack UI as a user or admin.

2. In the left navigation, click Instances.

3. Choose the VM that you want to migrate.

4. Click the Migrate Instance button.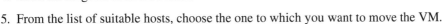

5. From the list of suitable hosts, choose the one to which you want to move the VM.

Note: If the VM's storage has to be migrated along with the VM, this will be noted in the host list. CloudStack will take care of the storage migration for you.

---

6. Click OK.

6.1.14 Deleting VMs

Users can delete their own virtual machines. A running virtual machine will be abruptly stopped before it is deleted. Administrators can delete any virtual machines.

To delete a virtual machine:

1. Log in to the CloudStack UI as a user or admin.

2. In the left navigation, click Instances.

3. Choose the VM that you want to delete.

4. Click the Destroy Instance button.

6.1.15 Working with ISOs

CloudStack supports ISOs and their attachment to guest VMs. An ISO is a read-only file that has an ISO/CD-ROM style file system. Users can upload their own ISOs and mount them on their guest VMs.

ISOs are uploaded based on a URL. HTTP is the supported protocol. Once the ISO is available via HTTP specify an upload URL such as http://my.web.server/filename.iso.

ISOs may be public or private, like templates.ISOs are not hypervisor-specific. That is, a guest on vSphere can mount the exact same image that a guest on KVM can mount.

ISO images may be stored in the system and made available with a privacy level similar to templates. ISO images are classified as either bootable or not bootable. A bootable ISO image is one that contains an OS image. CloudStack allows a user to boot a guest VM off of an ISO image. Users can also attach ISO images to guest VMs. For example, this enables installing PV drivers into Windows. ISO images are not hypervisor-specific.

Adding an ISO

To make additional operating system or other software available for use with guest VMs, you can add an ISO. The ISO is typically thought of as an operating system image, but you can also add ISOs for other types of software, such as desktop applications that you want to be installed as part of a template.

1. Log in to the CloudStack UI as an administrator or end user.

2. In the left navigation bar, click Templates.

3. In Select View, choose ISOs.

4. Click Add ISO.

5. In the Add ISO screen, provide the following:

   - **Name**: Short name for the ISO image. For example, CentOS 6.2 64-bit.

   - **Description**: Display test for the ISO image. For example, CentOS 6.2 64-bit.

   - **URL**: The URL that hosts the ISO image. The Management Server must be able to access this location via HTTP. If needed you can place the ISO image directly on the Management Server

   - **Zone**: Choose the zone where you want the ISO to be available, or All Zones to make it available throughout CloudStack.

   - **Bootable**: Whether or not a guest could boot off this ISO image. For example, a CentOS ISO is bootable, a Microsoft Office ISO is not bootable.

- **OS Type**: This helps CloudStack and the hypervisor perform certain operations and make assumptions that improve the performance of the guest. Select one of the following.

  - If the operating system of your desired ISO image is listed, choose it.

  - If the OS Type of the ISO is not listed or if the ISO is not bootable, choose Other.

  - (XenServer only) If you want to boot from this ISO in PV mode, choose Other PV (32-bit) or Other PV (64-bit)

  - (KVM only) If you choose an OS that is PV-enabled, the VMs created from this ISO will have a SCSI (virtio) root disk. If the OS is not PV-enabled, the VMs will have an IDE root disk. The PV-enabled types are:

    * Fedora 13

    * Fedora 12

    * Fedora 11

    * Fedora 10

    * Fedora 9

    * Other PV

    * Debian GNU/Linux

    * CentOS 5.3

    * CentOS 5.4

    * CentOS 5.5

    * Red Hat Enterprise Linux 5.3

    * Red Hat Enterprise Linux 5.4

    * Red Hat Enterprise Linux 5.5

    * Red Hat Enterprise Linux 6

Note: It is not recommended to choose an older version of the OS than the version in the image. For example, choosing CentOS 5.4 to support a CentOS 6.2 image will usually not work. In these cases, choose Other.

- **Extractable**: Choose Yes if the ISO should be available for extraction.

- **Public**: Choose Yes if this ISO should be available to other users.

- **Featured**: Choose Yes if you would like this ISO to be more prominent for users to select. The ISO will appear in the Featured ISOs list. Only an administrator can make an ISO Featured.

6. Click OK.

   The Management Server will download the ISO. Depending on the size of the ISO, this may take a long time. The ISO status column will display Ready once it has been successfully downloaded into secondary storage. Clicking Refresh updates the download percentage.

7. **Important**: Wait for the ISO to finish downloading. If you move on to the next task and try to use the ISO right away, it will appear to fail. The entire ISO must be available before CloudStack can work with it.

Attaching an ISO to a VM

1. In the left navigation, click Instances.

2. Choose the virtual machine you want to work with.

3. Click the Attach ISO button.

4. In the Attach ISO dialog box, select the desired ISO.

5. Click OK.

Changing a VM's Base Image

Every VM is created from a base image, which is a template or ISO which has been created and stored in CloudStack. Both cloud administrators and end users can create and modify templates, ISOs, and VMs.

In CloudStack, you can change an existing VM's base image from one template to another, or from one ISO to another. (You can not change from an ISO to a template, or from a template to an ISO).

For example, suppose there is a template based on a particular operating system, and the OS vendor releases a software patch. The administrator or user naturally wants to apply the patch and then make sure existing VMs start using it. Whether a software update is involved or not, it's also possible to simply switch a VM from its current template to any other desired template.

To change a VM's base image, call the restoreVirtualMachine API command and pass in the virtual machine ID and a new template ID. The template ID parameter may refer to either a template or an ISO, depending on which type of base image the VM was already using (it must match the previous type of image). When this call occurs, the VM's root disk is first destroyed, then a new root disk is created from the source designated in the template ID parameter. The new root disk is attached to the VM, and now the VM is based on the new template.

You can also omit the template ID parameter from the restoreVirtualMachine call. In this case, the VM's root disk is destroyed and recreated, but from the same template or ISO that was already in use by the VM.

6.1.16 Using SSH Keys for Authentication

In addition to the username and password authentication, CloudStack supports using SSH keys to log in to the cloud infrastructure for additional security. You can use the createSSHKeyPair API to generate the SSH keys.

Because each cloud user has their own SSH key, one cloud user cannot log in to another cloud user's instances unless they share their SSH key files. Using a single SSH key pair, you can manage multiple instances.

Creating an Instance Template that Supports SSH Keys

Create an instance template that supports SSH Keys.

1. Create a new instance by using the template provided by cloudstack.

   For more information on creating a new instance, see

2. Download the cloudstack script from The SSH Key Gen Script to the instance you have created.

```
wget http://downloads.sourceforge.net/project/cloudstack/SSH%20Key%20Gen%20Script/c
```

3. Copy the file to /etc/init.d.

```
cp cloud-set-guest-sshkey.in /etc/init.d/
```

4. Give the necessary permissions on the script:

```
chmod +x /etc/init.d/cloud-set-guest-sshkey.in
```

5. Run the script while starting up the operating system:

```
chkconfig --add cloud-set-guest-sshkey.in
```

6. Stop the instance.

Creating the SSH Keypair

You must make a call to the createSSHKeyPair api method. You can either use the CloudStack Python API library or the curl commands to make the call to the cloudstack api.

For example, make a call from the cloudstack server to create a SSH keypair called "keypair-doc" for the admin account in the root domain:

Note: Ensure that you adjust these values to meet your needs. If you are making the API call from a different server, your URL/PORT will be different, and you will need to use the API keys.

1. Run the following curl command:

```
curl --globoff "http://localhost:8096/?command=createSSHKeyPair&name=keypair-doc&ac
```

The output is something similar to what is given below:

```
<?xml version="1.0" encoding="ISO-8859-1"?><createsshkeypairresponse cloud-stack-ve
MIICXQIBAAKBgQCSydmnQ67jP6lNoXdX3noZjQdrMAWNQZ7y5SrEu4wDxplvhYci
dXYBeZVwakDVsU2MLGl/K+wefwefwefwefwefJyKJaogMKn7BperPD6n1wIDAQAB
AoGAdXaJ7uyZKeRDoy6wA0UmF0kSPbMZCR+UTIHNkS/E0/4U+6lhMokmFSHtu
mfDZ1kGGDYhMsdytjDBztljawfawfeawefawfawfawQQDCjEsoRdgkduTy
QpbSGDIal1Jsc+XNDx2fgRinDsxXI/zJYXTKRhSl/LIPHBw/brW8vzxhOlSOrwm7
VvemkkgpAkEAwSeEw394LYZiEVv395ar9MLRVTVLwpo54jC4tsOxQCBlloocK
lYaocpk0yBqqOUSBawfIiDCuLXSdvBolXz5ICTM19vgvEp/+kMuECQBzm
nVo8b2Gvyagqt/KEQo8wzH2THghZ1qQ1QRhIeJG2aissEacF6bGB2oZ7Igim5L14
4KR7OeEToyCLC2k+02UCQQCrniSnWKtDVoVqeK/zbB32JhW3Wullv5p5zUEcd
KfEEuzcCUIxtJYTahJ1pvlFkQ8anpuxjSEDp8x/18bq3
-----END RSA PRIVATE KEY-----
</privatekey></keypair></createsshkeypairresponse>
```

2. Copy the key data into a file. The file looks like this:

```
-----BEGIN RSA PRIVATE KEY-----
MIICXQIBAAKBgQCSydmnQ67jP6lNoXdX3noZjQdrMAWNQZ7y5SrEu4wDxplvhYci
dXYBeZVwakDVsU2MLGl/K+wefwefwefwefwefJyKJaogMKn7BperPD6n1wIDAQAB
AoGAdXaJ7uyZKeRDoy6wA0UmF0kSPbMZCR+UTIHNkS/E0/4U+6lhMokmFSHtu
mfDZ1kGGDYhMsdytjDBztljawfawfeawefawfawfawQQDCjEsoRdgkduTy
QpbSGDIal1Jsc+XNDx2fgRinDsxXI/zJYXTKRhSl/LIPHBw/brW8vzxhOlSOrwm7
VvemkkgpAkEAwSeEw394LYZiEVv395ar9MLRVTVLwpo54jC4tsOxQCBlloocK
lYaocpk0yBqqOUSBawfIiDCuLXSdvBolXz5ICTM19vgvEp/+kMuECQBzm
nVo8b2Gvyagqt/KEQo8wzH2THghZ1qQ1QRhIeJG2aissEacF6bGB2oZ7Igim5L14
4KR7OeEToyCLC2k+02UCQQCrniSnWKtDVoVqeK/zbB32JhW3Wullv5p5zUEcd
KfEEuzcCUIxtJYTahJ1pvlFkQ8anpuxjSEDp8x/18bq3
-----END RSA PRIVATE KEY-----
```

3. Save the file.

Creating an Instance

After you save the SSH keypair file, you must create an instance by using the template that you created at *Section 5.2.1, " Creating an Instance Template that Supports SSH Keys"*. Ensure that you use the same SSH key name that you created at *Section 5.2.2, "Creating the SSH Keypair"*.

Note: You cannot create the instance by using the GUI at this time and associate the instance with the newly created SSH keypair.

A sample curl command to create a new instance is:

```
curl --globoff http://localhost:<port number>/?command=deployVirtualMachine\&zoneId=1\&
```

Substitute the template, service offering and security group IDs (if you are using the security group feature) that are in your cloud environment.

Logging In Using the SSH Keypair

To test your SSH key generation is successful, check whether you can log in to the cloud setup.

For example, from a Linux OS, run:

```
ssh -i ~/.ssh/keypair-doc <ip address>
```

The -i parameter tells the ssh client to use a ssh key found at ~/.ssh/keypair-doc.

Resetting SSH Keys

With the API command resetSSHKeyForVirtualMachine, a user can set or reset the SSH keypair assigned to a virtual machine. A lost or compromised SSH keypair can be changed, and the user can access the VM by using the new keypair. Just create or register a new keypair, then call resetSSHKeyForVirtualMachine.

6.1.17 User-Data and Meta-Data

CloudStack provides API access to attach up to 2KB of data after base64 encoding to a deployed VM. Using HTTP POST(via POST body), you can send up to 32K of data after base64 encoding. Deployed VMs also have access to instance metadata via the virtual router.

Create virtual machine thru the API: deployVirtualMachine using the parameter userdata= to include user-data formated in base64.

Accessed user-data from VM. Once the IP address of the virtual router is known, use the following steps to retrieve user-data:

1. Run the following command to find the virtual router.

```
# cat /var/lib/dhclient/dhclient-eth0.leases | grep dhcp-server-identifier | tail -
```

2. Access user-data by running the following command using the result of the above command

```
# curl http://10.1.1.1/latest/user-data
```

Meta Data can be accessed similarly, using a URL of the form http://10.1.1.1/latest/meta-data/{metac type}. (For backwards compatibility, the previous URL http://10.1.1.1/latest/{metadata type} is also supported.) For metadata type, use one of the following:

- `service-offering`. A description of the VMs service offering

- `availability-zone`. The Zone name

- `local-ipv4`. The guest IP of the VM

- `local-hostname`. The hostname of the VM

- `public-ipv4`. The first public IP for the router. (E.g. the first IP of eth2)

- `public-hostname`. This is the same as public-ipv4

- `instance-id`. The instance name of the VM

Using Cloud-Init

Cloud-Init can be use to access an interpret user-data from virtual machines. Cloud-Init be installed into templates and also require CloudStack password and sshkey scripts (adding-password-management-to-templates and using ssh keys). User password management and `resetSSHKeyForVirtualMachine` API are not yet supported by cloud-init.

1. Install cloud-init package into a template:

```
# yum install cloud-init
  or
$ sudo apt-get install cloud-init
```

2. Create datasource configuration file: `/etc/cloud/cloud.cfg.d/99_cloudstack.cfg`

```
datasource:
  CloudStack: {}
  None: {}
datasource_list:
  - CloudStack
```

user-data example

This example use cloud-init to Upgrade Operating-System of the newly created VM:

```
#cloud-config

# Upgrade the instance on first boot
# (ie run apt-get upgrade)
#
# Default: false
# Aliases: apt_upgrade
package_upgrade: true
```

base64 formated:

I2Nsb3VkLWNvbmZpZw0KDQojIFVwZ3JhZGUgdGhlIGluc3RhbmNlIG9uIGZpcnN0IGJvb3QNCiMgKGllIHJ1biBh

Refer to Cloud-Init CloudStack datasource documentation for latest capabilities. Cloud-Init and Cloud-Init CloudStack datasource are not supported by Apache CloudStack community.

6.1.18 Assigning GPU/vGPU to Guest VMs

CloudStack can deploy guest VMs with Graphics Processing Unit (GPU) or Virtual Graphics Processing Unit (vGPU) capabilities on XenServer hosts. At the time of VM deployment or at a later stage, you can assign a physical GPU

(known as GPU-passthrough) or a portion of a physical GPU card (vGPU) to a guest VM by changing the Service Offering. With this capability, the VMs running on CloudStack meet the intensive graphical processing requirement by means of the high computation power of GPU/vGPU, and CloudStack users can run multimedia rich applications, such as Auto-CAD, that they otherwise enjoy at their desk on a virtualized environment. CloudStack leverages the XenServer support for NVIDIA GRID Kepler 1 and 2 series to run GPU/vGPU enabled VMs. NVIDIA GRID cards allows sharing a single GPU cards among multiple VMs by creating vGPUs for each VM. With vGPU technology, the graphics commands from each VM are passed directly to the underlying dedicated GPU, without the intervention of the hypervisor. This allows the GPU hardware to be time-sliced and shared across multiple VMs. XenServer hosts use the GPU cards in following ways:

GPU passthrough: GPU passthrough represents a physical GPU which can be directly assigned to a VM. GPU passthrough can be used on a hypervisor alongside GRID vGPU, with some restrictions: A GRID physical GPU can either host GRID vGPUs or be used as passthrough, but not both at the same time.

GRID vGPU: GRID vGPU enables multiple VMs to share a single physical GPU. The VMs run an NVIDIA driver stack and get direct access to the GPU. GRID physical GPUs are capable of supporting multiple virtual GPU devices (vGPUs) that can be assigned directly to guest VMs. Guest VMs use GRID virtual GPUs in the same manner as a physical GPU that has been passed through by the hypervisor: an NVIDIA driver loaded in the guest VM provides direct access to the GPU for performance-critical fast paths, and a paravirtualized interface to the GRID Virtual GPU Manager, which is used for nonperformant management operations. NVIDIA GRID Virtual GPU Manager for XenServer runs in dom0. CloudStack provides you with the following capabilities:

- Adding XenServer hosts with GPU/vGPU capability provisioned by the administrator.
- Creating a Compute Offering with GPU/vGPU capability.
- Deploying a VM with GPU/vGPU capability.
- Destroying a VM with GPU/vGPU capability.
- Allowing an user to add GPU/vGPU support to a VM without GPU/vGPU support by changing the Service Offering and vice-versa.
- Migrating VMs (cold migration) with GPU/vGPU capability.
- Managing GPU cards capacity.
- Querying hosts to obtain information about the GPU cards, supported vGPU types in case of GRID cards, and capacity of the cards.

Prerequisites and System Requirements

Before proceeding, ensure that you have these prerequisites:

- The vGPU-enabled XenServer 6.2 and later versions. For more information, see Citrix 3D Graphics Pack.
- GPU/vPGU functionality is supported for following HVM guest operating systems: For more information, see Citrix 3D Graphics Pack.
- Windows 7 (x86 and x64)
- Windows Server 2008 R2
- Windows Server 2012
- Windows 8 (x86 and x64)
- Windows 8.1 ("Blue") (x86 and x64)
- Windows Server 2012 R2 (server equivalent of "Blue")

- CloudStack does not restrict the deployment of GPU-enabled VMs with guest OS types that are not supported by XenServer for GPU/vGPU functionality. The deployment would be successful and a GPU/vGPU will also get allocated for VMs; however, due to missing guest OS drivers, VM would not be able to leverage GPU resources. Therefore, it is recommended to use GPU-enabled service offering only with supported guest OS.

- NVIDIA GRID K1 (16 GiB video RAM) AND K2 (8 GiB of video RAM) cards supports homogeneous virtual GPUs, implies that at any given time, the vGPUs resident on a single physical GPU must be all of the same type. However, this restriction doesn't extend across physical GPUs on the same card. Each physical GPU on a K1 or K2 may host different types of virtual GPU at the same time. For example, a GRID K2 card has two physical GPUs, and supports four types of virtual GPU; GRID K200, GRID K220Q, GRID K240Q, AND GRID K260Q.

- NVIDIA driver must be installed to enable vGPU operation as for a physical NVIDIA GPU.

- XenServer tools are installed in the VM to get maximum performance on XenServer, regardless of type of vGPU you are using. Without the optimized networking and storage drivers that the XenServer tools provide, remote graphics applications running on GRID vGPU will not deliver maximum performance.

- To deliver high frames from multiple heads on vGPU, install XenDesktop with HDX 3D Pro remote graphics.

Before continuing with configuration, consider the following:

- Deploying VMs GPU/vGPU capability is not supported if hosts are not available with enough GPU capacity.

- A Service Offering cannot be created with the GPU values that are not supported by CloudStack UI. However, you can make an API call to achieve this.

- Dynamic scaling is not supported. However, you can choose to deploy a VM without GPU support, and at a later point, you can change the system offering to upgrade to the one with vGPU. You can achieve this by offline upgrade: stop the VM, upgrade the Service Offering to the one with vGPU, then start the VM.

- Live migration of GPU/vGPU enabled VM is not supported.

- Limiting GPU resources per Account/Domain is not supported.

- Disabling GPU at Cluster level is not supported.

- Notification thresholds for GPU resource is not supported.

Supported GPU Devices

Device	Type
GPU	- Group of NVIDIA Corporation GK107GL [GRID K1] GPUs - Group of NVIDIA Corporation GK104GL [GRID K2] GPUs - Any other GPU Group
vGPU	- GRID K100 - GRID K120Q - GRID K140Q - GRID K200 - GRID K220Q - GRID K240Q - GRID K260Q

GPU/vGPU Assignment Workflow

CloudStack follows the below sequence of operations to provide GPU/vGPU support for VMs:

1. Ensure that XenServer host is ready with GPU installed and configured. For more information, see Citrix 3D Graphics Pack.

2. Add the host to CloudStack. CloudStack checks if the host is GPU-enabled or not. CloudStack queries the host and detect if it's GPU enabled.

3. Create a compute offering with GPU/vGPU support: For more information, see *Creating a New Compute Offering.*.

4. Continue with any of the following operations:

   • Deploy a VM.

   Deploy a VM with GPU/vGPU support by selecting appropriate Service Offering. CloudStack decide which host to choose for VM deployment based on following criteria:

   – Host has GPU cards in it. In case of vGPU, CloudStack checks if cards have the required vGPU type support and enough capacity available. Having no appropriate hosts results in an InsufficientServerCapacity exception.

   – Alternately, you can choose to deploy a VM without GPU support, and at a later point, you can change the system offering. You can achieve this by offline upgrade: stop the VM, upgrade the Service Offering to the one with vGPU, then start the VM.

   In this case, CloudStack gets a list of hosts which have enough capacity to host the VM. If there is a GPU-enabled host, CloudStack reorders this host list and place the GPU-enabled hosts at the bottom of the list.

   • Migrate a VM.

   CloudStack searches for hosts available for VM migration, which satisfies GPU requirement. If the host is available, stop the VM in the current host and perform the VM migration task. If the VM migration is successful, the remaining GPU capacity is updated for both the hosts accordingly.

   • Destroy a VM.

   GPU resources are released automatically when you stop a VM. Once the destroy VM is successful, CloudStack will make a resource call to the host to get the remaining GPU capacity in the card and update the database accordingly.

## CHAPTER 7

Working with Templates

7.1 Working with Templates

A template is a reusable configuration for virtual machines. When users launch VMs, they can choose from a list of templates in CloudStack.

Specifically, a template is a virtual disk image that includes one of a variety of operating systems, optional additional software such as office applications, and settings such as access control to determine who can use the template. Each template is associated with a particular type of hypervisor, which is specified when the template is added to CloudStack.

CloudStack ships with a default template. In order to present more choices to users, CloudStack administrators and users can create templates and add them to CloudStack.

7.1.1 Creating Templates: Overview

CloudStack ships with a default template for the CentOS operating system. There are a variety of ways to add more templates. Administrators and end users can add templates. The typical sequence of events is:

1. Launch a VM instance that has the operating system you want. Make any other desired configuration changes to the VM.

2. Stop the VM.

3. Convert the volume into a template.

There are other ways to add templates to CloudStack. For example, you can take a snapshot of the VM's volume and create a template from the snapshot, or import a VHD from another system into CloudStack.

The various techniques for creating templates are described in the next few sections.

7.1.2 Requirements for Templates

- For XenServer, install PV drivers / Xen tools on each template that you create. This will enable live migration and clean guest shutdown.

- For vSphere, install VMware Tools on each template that you create. This will enable console view to work properly.

7.1.3 Best Practices for Templates

If you plan to use large templates (100 GB or larger), be sure you have a 10-gigabit network to support the large templates. A slower network can lead to timeouts and other errors when large templates are used.

7.1.4 The Default Template

CloudStack includes a CentOS template. This template is downloaded by the Secondary Storage VM after the primary and secondary storage are configured. You can use this template in your production deployment or you can delete it and use custom templates.

The root password for the default template is "password".

A default template is provided for each of XenServer, KVM, and vSphere. The templates that are downloaded depend on the hypervisor type that is available in your cloud. Each template is approximately 2.5 GB physical size.

The default template includes the standard iptables rules, which will block most access to the template excluding ssh.

```
# iptables --list
Chain INPUT (policy ACCEPT)
target      prot opt source               destination
RH-Firewall-1-INPUT  all  --  anywhere              anywhere

Chain FORWARD (policy ACCEPT)
target      prot opt source               destination
RH-Firewall-1-INPUT  all  --  anywhere              anywhere

Chain OUTPUT (policy ACCEPT)
target      prot opt source               destination

Chain RH-Firewall-1-INPUT (2 references)
target      prot opt source               destination
ACCEPT      all  --  anywhere              anywhere
ACCEPT      icmp --  anywhere         anywhere          icmp any
ACCEPT      esp  --  anywhere         anywhere
ACCEPT      ah   --  anywhere         anywhere
ACCEPT      udp  --  anywhere         224.0.0.251       udp dpt:mdns
ACCEPT      udp  --  anywhere         anywhere          udp dpt:ipp
ACCEPT      tcp  --  anywhere         anywhere          tcp dpt:ipp
ACCEPT      all  --  anywhere         anywhere          state RELATED,ESTABLISHED
ACCEPT      tcp  --  anywhere         anywhere          state NEW tcp dpt:ssh
REJECT      all  --  anywhere         anywhere          reject-with icmp-host-
```

7.1.5 Private and Public Templates

When a user creates a template, it can be designated private or public.

Private templates are only available to the user who created them. By default, an uploaded template is private.

When a user marks a template as "public," the template becomes available to all users in all accounts in the user's domain, as well as users in any other domains that have access to the Zone where the template is stored. This depends on whether the Zone, in turn, was defined as private or public. A private Zone is assigned to a single domain, and a public Zone is accessible to any domain. If a public template is created in a private Zone, it is available only to users in the domain assigned to that Zone. If a public template is created in a public Zone, it is available to all users in all domains.

7.1.6 Creating a Template from an Existing Virtual Machine

Once you have at least one VM set up in the way you want, you can use it as the prototype for other VMs.

1. Create and start a virtual machine using any of the techniques given in "Creating VMs".

2. Make any desired configuration changes on the running VM, then click Stop.

3. Wait for the VM to stop. When the status shows Stopped, go to the next step.

4. Go into "View Volumes" and select the Volume having the type "ROOT".

5. Click Create Template and provide the following:

   - **Name and Display Text**. These will be shown in the UI, so choose something descriptive.

   - **OS Type**. This helps CloudStack and the hypervisor perform certain operations and make assumptions that improve the performance of the guest. Select one of the following.

     - If the operating system of the stopped VM is listed, choose it.

     - If the OS type of the stopped VM is not listed, choose Other.

     - If you want to boot from this template in PV mode, choose Other PV (32-bit) or Other PV (64-bit). This choice is available only for XenServere:

       Note: Generally you should not choose an older version of the OS than the version in the image. For example, choosing CentOS 5.4 to support a CentOS 6.2 image will in general not work. In those cases you should choose Other.

   - **Public**. Choose Yes to make this template accessible to all users of this CloudStack installation. The template will appear in the Community Templates list. See *"Private and Public Templates"*.

   - **Password Enabled**. Choose Yes if your template has the CloudStack password change script installed. See adding-password-management-to-templates.

6. Click Add.

The new template will be visible in the Templates section when the template creation process has been completed. The template is then available when creating a new VM.

7.1.7 Creating a Template from a Snapshot

If you do not want to stop the VM in order to use the Create Template menu item (as described in *"Creating a Template from an Existing Virtual Machine"*), you can create a template directly from any snapshot through the CloudStack UI.

7.1.8 Uploading Templates

7.1.9 vSphere Templates and ISOs

If you are uploading a template that was created using vSphere Client, be sure the OVA file does not contain an ISO. If it does, the deployment of VMs from the template will fail.

Templates are uploaded based on a URL. HTTP is the supported access protocol. Templates are frequently large files. You can optionally gzip them to decrease upload times.

To upload a template:

1. In the left navigation bar, click Templates.

2. Click Register Template.

3. Provide the following:

  - **Name and Description**. These will be shown in the UI, so choose something descriptive.

  - **URL**. The Management Server will download the file from the specified URL, such as `http://my.web.server/filename.vhd.gz`.

  - **Zone**. Choose the zone where you want the template to be available, or All Zones to make it available throughout CloudStack.

  - **OS Type**: This helps CloudStack and the hypervisor perform certain operations and make assumptions that improve the performance of the guest. Select one of the following:

    - If the operating system of the stopped VM is listed, choose it.

    - If the OS type of the stopped VM is not listed, choose Other.

    Note: You should not choose an older version of the OS than the version in the image. For example, choosing CentOS 5.4 to support a CentOS 6.2 image will in general not work. In those cases you should choose Other.

  - **Hypervisor**: The supported hypervisors are listed. Select the desired one.

  - **Format**. The format of the template upload file, such as VHD or OVA.

  - **Password Enabled**. Choose Yes if your template has the CloudStack password change script installed. See adding-password-management-to-templates.

  - **Extractable**. Choose Yes if the template is available for extraction. If this option is selected, end users can download a full image of a template.

  - **Public**. Choose Yes to make this template accessible to all users of this CloudStack installation. The template will appear in the Community Templates list. See *"Private and Public Templates"*.

  - **Featured**. Choose Yes if you would like this template to be more prominent for users to select. The template will appear in the Featured Templates list. Only an administrator can make a template Featured.

7.1.10 Exporting Templates

End users and Administrators may export templates from the CloudStack. Navigate to the template in the UI and choose the Download function from the Actions menu.

7.1.11 Creating a Linux Template

Linux templates should be prepared using this documentation in order to prepare your linux VMs for template deployment. For ease of documentation, the VM which you are configuring the template on will be referred to as "Template Master". This guide currently covers legacy setups which do not take advantage of UserData and cloud-init and assumes openssh-server is installed during installation.

An overview of the procedure is as follow:

1. Upload your Linux ISO.

   For more information, see "Adding an ISO".

2. Create a VM Instance with this ISO.

   For more information, see "Creating VMs".

3. Prepare the Linux VM

4. Create a template from the VM.

   For more information, see *"Creating a Template from an Existing Virtual Machine"*.

System preparation for Linux

The following steps will prepare a basic Linux installation for templating.

1. **Installation**

   It is good practice to name your VM something generic during installation, this will ensure components such as LVM do not appear unique to a machine. It is recommended that the name of "localhost" is used for installation.

   > **Warning:** For CentOS, it is necessary to take unique identification out of the interface configuration file, for this edit /etc/sysconfig/network-scripts/ifcfg-eth0 and change the content to the following.

   ```
   DEVICE=eth0
   TYPE=Ethernet
   BOOTPROTO=dhcp
   ONBOOT=yes
   ```

   The next steps updates the packages on the Template Master.

   - Ubuntu

   ```
   sudo -i
   apt-get update
   apt-get upgrade -y
   apt-get install -y acpid ntp
   reboot
   ```

   - CentOS

   ```
   ifup eth0
   yum update -y
   reboot
   ```

2. **Password management**

   > **Note:** If preferred, custom users (such as ones created during the Ubuntu installation) should be removed. First ensure the root user account is enabled by giving it a password and then login as root to continue.

   ```
   sudo passwd root
   logout
   ```

   As root, remove any custom user accounts created during the installation process.

   ```
   deluser myuser --remove-home
   ```

   See adding-password-management-to-templates for instructions to setup the password management script, this will allow CloudStack to change your root password from the web interface.

3. **Hostname Management**

   CentOS configures the hostname by default on boot. Unfortunately Ubuntu does not have this functionality, for Ubuntu installations use the following steps.

- Ubuntu

The hostname of a Templated VM is set by a custom script in */etc/dhcp/dhclient-exit-hooks.d*, this script first checks if the current hostname is localhost, if true, it will get the host-name, domain-name and fixed-ip from the DHCP lease file and use those values to set the hostname and append the */etc/hosts* file for local hostname resolution. Once this script, or a user has changed the hostname from localhost, it will no longer adjust system files regardless of its new hostname. The script also recreates openssh-server keys, which should have been deleted before templating (shown below). Save the following script to */etc/dhcp/dhclient-exit-hooks.d/sethostname*, and adjust the permissions.

```
#!/bin/sh
# dhclient change hostname script for Ubuntu
oldhostname=$(hostname -s)
if [ $oldhostname = 'localhost' ]
then
    sleep 10 # Wait for configuration to be written to disk
    hostname=$(cat /var/lib/dhcp/dhclient.eth0.leases  |  awk ' /host-name/ { h
    fqdn="$hostname.$(cat /var/lib/dhcp/dhclient.eth0.leases  |  awk ' /domain-
    ip=$(cat /var/lib/dhcp/dhclient.eth0.leases  |  awk ' /fixed-address/ { lea
    echo "cloudstack-hostname: Hostname _localhost_ detected. Changing hostname
    printf " Hostname: $hostname\n FQDN: $fqdn\n IP: $ip"
    # Update /etc/hosts
    awk -v i="$ip" -v f="$fqdn" -v h="$hostname" "/^127/{x=1} !/^127/ && x { x=
    mv /etc/hosts /etc/hosts.dhcp.bak
    mv /etc/hosts.dhcp.tmp /etc/hosts
    # Rename Host
    echo $hostname > /etc/hostname
    hostname -b -F /etc/hostname
    echo $hostname > /proc/sys/kernel/hostname
    # Recreate SSH2
    export DEBIAN_FRONTEND=noninteractive
    dpkg-reconfigure openssh-server
fi
### End of Script ###

chmod 774  /etc/dhcp/dhclient-exit-hooks.d/sethostname
```

Warning: The following steps should be run when you are ready to template your Template Master. If the Template Master is rebooted during these steps you will have to run all the steps again. At the end of this process the Template Master should be shutdown and the template created in order to create and deploy the final template.

4. **Remove the udev persistent device rules**

This step removes information unique to your Template Master such as network MAC addresses, lease files and CD block devices, the files are automatically generated on next boot.

- Ubuntu

```
rm -f /etc/udev/rules.d/70*
rm -f /var/lib/dhcp/dhclient.*
```

- CentOS

```
rm -f /etc/udev/rules.d/70*
rm -f /var/lib/dhclient/*
```

5. **Remove SSH Keys**

This step is to ensure all your Templated VMs do not have the same SSH keys, which would decrease the security of the machines dramatically.

```
rm -f /etc/ssh/*key*
```

6. **Cleaning log files**

   It is good practice to remove old logs from the Template Master.

```
cat /dev/null > /var/log/audit/audit.log 2>/dev/null
cat /dev/null > /var/log/wtmp 2>/dev/null
logrotate -f /etc/logrotate.conf 2>/dev/null
rm -f /var/log/*-* /var/log/*.gz 2>/dev/null
```

7. **Setting hostname**

   In order for the Ubuntu DHCP script to function and the CentOS dhclient to set the VM hostname they both require the Template Master's hostname to be "localhost", run the following commands to change the hostname.

```
hostname localhost
echo "localhost" > /etc/hostname
```

8. **Set user password to expire**

   This step forces the user to change the password of the VM after the template has been deployed.

```
passwd --expire root
```

9. **Clearing User History**

   The next step clears the bash commands you have just run.

```
history -c
unset HISTFILE
```

10. **Shutdown the VM**

    Your now ready to shutdown your Template Master and create a template!

```
halt -p
```

11. **Create the template!**

    You are now ready to create the template, for more information see *"Creating a Template from an Existing Virtual Machine"*.

Note: Templated VMs for both Ubuntu and CentOS may require a reboot after provisioning in order to pickup the hostname.

7.1.12 Creating a Windows Template

Windows templates must be prepared with Sysprep before they can be provisioned on multiple machines. Sysprep allows you to create a generic Windows template and avoid any possible SID conflicts.

Note: (XenServer) Windows VMs running on XenServer require PV drivers, which may be provided in the template or added after the VM is created. The PV drivers are necessary for essential management functions such as mounting additional volumes and ISO images, live migration, and graceful shutdown.

An overview of the procedure is as follows:

1. Upload your Windows ISO.

   For more information, see "Adding an ISO".

2. Create a VM Instance with this ISO.

   For more information, see "Creating VMs".

3. Follow the steps in Sysprep for Windows Server 2008 R2 (below) or Sysprep for Windows Server 2003 R2, depending on your version of Windows Server

4. The preparation steps are complete. Now you can actually create the template as described in Creating the Windows Template.

System Preparation for Windows Server 2008 R2

For Windows 2008 R2, you run Windows System Image Manager to create a custom sysprep response XML file. Windows System Image Manager is installed as part of the Windows Automated Installation Kit (AIK). Windows AIK can be downloaded from Microsoft Download Center.

Use the following steps to run sysprep for Windows 2008 R2:

Note: The steps outlined here are derived from the excellent guide by Charity Shelbourne, originally published at Windows Server 2008 Sysprep Mini-Setup.

---

1. Download and install the Windows AIK

   Note: Windows AIK should not be installed on the Windows 2008 R2 VM you just created. Windows AIK should not be part of the template you create. It is only used to create the sysprep answer file.

   ---

2. Copy the install.wim file in the \sources directory of the Windows 2008 R2 installation DVD to the hard disk. This is a very large file and may take a long time to copy. Windows AIK requires the WIM file to be writable.

3. Start the Windows System Image Manager, which is part of the Windows AIK.

4. In the Windows Image pane, right click the Select a Windows image or catalog file option to load the install.wim file you just copied.

5. Select the Windows 2008 R2 Edition.

   You may be prompted with a warning that the catalog file cannot be opened. Click Yes to create a new catalog file.

6. In the Answer File pane, right click to create a new answer file.

7. Generate the answer file from the Windows System Image Manager using the following steps:

   (a) The first page you need to automate is the Language and Country or Region Selection page. To automate this, expand Components in your Windows Image pane, right-click and add the Microsoft-Windows-International-Core setting to Pass 7 oobeSystem. In your Answer File pane, configure the InputLocale, SystemLocale, UILanguage, and UserLocale with the appropriate settings for your language and country or region. Should you have a question about any of these settings, you can right-click on the specific setting and select Help. This will open the appropriate CHM help file with more information, including examples on the setting you are attempting to configure.

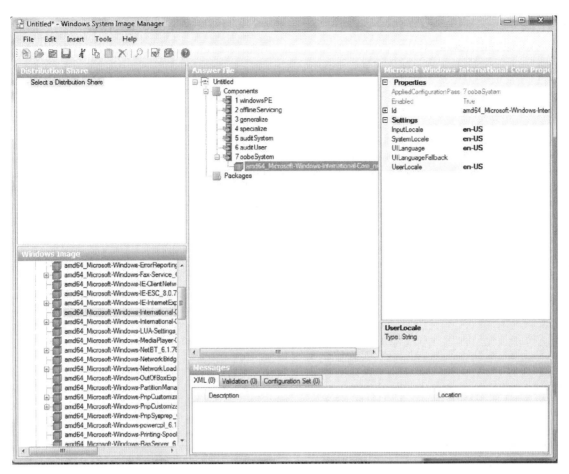

(b) You need to automate the Software License Terms Selection page, otherwise known as the End-User License Agreement (EULA). To do this, expand the Microsoft-Windows-Shell-Setup component. Highlight the OOBE setting, and add the setting to the Pass 7 oobeSystem. In Settings, set HideEULAPage true.

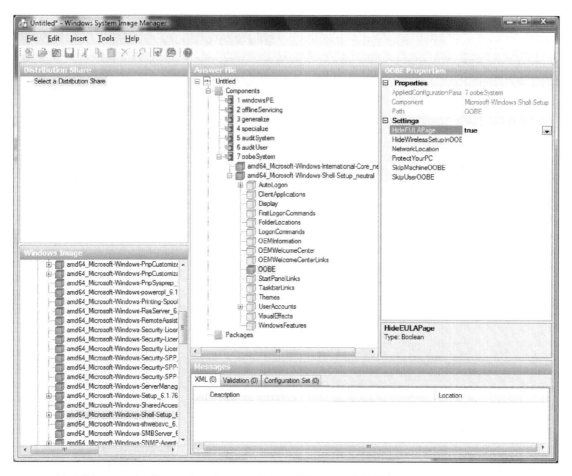

(c) Make sure the license key is properly set. If you use MAK key, you can just enter the MAK key on the Windows 2008 R2 VM. You need not input the MAK into the Windows System Image Manager. If you use KMS host for activation you need not enter the Product Key. Details of Windows Volume Activation can be found at http://technet.microsoft.com/en-us/library/bb892849.aspx

(d) You need to automate is the Change Administrator Password page. Expand the Microsoft-Windows-Shell-Setup component (if it is not still expanded), expand UserAccounts, right-click on AdministratorPassword, and add the setting to the Pass 7 oobeSystem configuration pass of your answer file. Under Settings, specify a password next to Value.

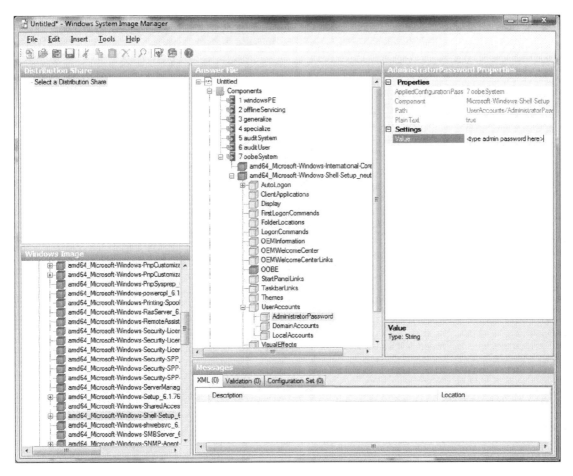

You may read the AIK documentation and set many more options that suit your deployment. The steps above are the minimum needed to make Windows unattended setup work.

8. Save the answer file as unattend.xml. You can ignore the warning messages that appear in the validation window.

9. Copy the unattend.xml file into the c:\windows\system32\sysprep directory of the Windows 2008 R2 Virtual Machine

10. Once you place the unattend.xml file in c:\windows\system32\sysprep directory, you run the sysprep tool as follows:

```
cd c:\Windows\System32\sysprep
sysprep.exe /oobe /generalize /shutdown
```

The Windows 2008 R2 VM will automatically shut down after sysprep is complete.

System Preparation for Windows Server 2003 R2

Earlier versions of Windows have a different sysprep tool. Follow these steps for Windows Server 2003 R2.

1. Extract the content of \support\tools\deploy.cab on the Windows installation CD into a directory called c:\sysprep on the Windows 2003 R2 VM.

2. Run c:\sysprep\setupmgr.exe to create the sysprep.inf file.

   (a) Select Create New to create a new Answer File.

   (b) Enter "Sysprep setup" for the Type of Setup.

(c) Select the appropriate OS version and edition.

(d) On the License Agreement screen, select "Yes fully automate the installation".

(e) Provide your name and organization.

(f) Leave display settings at default.

(g) Set the appropriate time zone.

(h) Provide your product key.

(i) Select an appropriate license mode for your deployment

(j) Select "Automatically generate computer name".

(k) Type a default administrator password. If you enable the password reset feature, the users will not actually use this password. This password will be reset by the instance manager after the guest boots up.

(l) Leave Network Components at "Typical Settings".

(m) Select the "WORKGROUP" option.

(n) Leave Telephony options at default.

(o) Select appropriate Regional Settings.

(p) Select appropriate language settings.

(q) Do not install printers.

(r) Do not specify "Run Once commands".

(s) You need not specify an identification string.

(t) Save the Answer File as c:\sysprep\sysprep.inf.

3. Run the following command to sysprep the image:

```
c:\sysprep\sysprep.exe -reseal -mini -activated
```

After this step the machine will automatically shut down

7.1.13 Importing Amazon Machine Images

The following procedures describe how to import an Amazon Machine Image (AMI) into CloudStack when using the XenServer hypervisor.

Assume you have an AMI file and this file is called CentOS_6.2_x64. Assume further that you are working on a CentOS host. If the AMI is a Fedora image, you need to be working on a Fedora host initially.

You need to have a XenServer host with a file-based storage repository (either a local ext3 SR or an NFS SR) to convert to a VHD once the image file has been customized on the Centos/Fedora host.

Note: When copying and pasting a command, be sure the command has pasted as a single line before executing. Some document viewers may introduce unwanted line breaks in copied text.

To import an AMI:

1. Set up loopback on image file:

```
# mkdir -p /mnt/loop/centos62
# mount -o loop  CentOS_6.2_x64 /mnt/loop/centos54
```

2. Install the kernel-xen package into the image. This downloads the PV kernel and ramdisk to the image.

```
# yum -c /mnt/loop/centos54/etc/yum.conf --installroot=/mnt/loop/centos62/ -y insta
```

3. Create a grub entry in /boot/grub/grub.conf.

```
# mkdir -p /mnt/loop/centos62/boot/grub
# touch /mnt/loop/centos62/boot/grub/grub.conf
# echo "" > /mnt/loop/centos62/boot/grub/grub.conf
```

4. Determine the name of the PV kernel that has been installed into the image.

```
# cd /mnt/loop/centos62
# ls lib/modules/
2.6.16.33-xenU  2.6.16-xenU  2.6.18-164.15.1.el5xen  2.6.18-164.6.1.el5.centos.plus
# ls boot/initrd*
boot/initrd-2.6.18-164.6.1.el5.centos.plus.img boot/initrd-2.6.18-164.15.1.el5xen.i
# ls boot/vmlinuz*
boot/vmlinuz-2.6.18-164.15.1.el5xen  boot/vmlinuz-2.6.18-164.6.1.el5.centos.plus  b
```

Xen kernels/ramdisk always end with "xen". For the kernel version you choose, there has to be an entry for that version under lib/modules, there has to be an initrd and vmlinuz corresponding to that. Above, the only kernel that satisfies this condition is 2.6.18-164.15.1.el5xen.

5. Based on your findings, create an entry in the grub.conf file. Below is an example entry.

```
default=0
timeout=5
hiddenmenu
title CentOS (2.6.18-164.15.1.el5xen)
    root (hd0,0)
    kernel /boot/vmlinuz-2.6.18-164.15.1.el5xen ro root=/dev/xvda
    initrd /boot/initrd-2.6.18-164.15.1.el5xen.img
```

6. Edit etc/fstab, changing "sda1" to "xvda" and changing "sdb" to "xvdb".

```
# cat etc/fstab
/dev/xvda    /           ext3     defaults        1 1
/dev/xvdb    /mnt        ext3     defaults        0 0
none         /dev/pts    devpts   gid=5,mode=620  0 0
none         /proc       proc     defaults        0 0
none         /sys        sysfs    defaults        0 0
```

7. Enable login via the console. The default console device in a XenServer system is xvc0. Ensure that etc/inittab and etc/securetty have the following lines respectively:

```
# grep xvc0 etc/inittab
co:2345:respawn:/sbin/agetty xvc0 9600 vt100-nav
# grep xvc0 etc/securetty
xvc0
```

8. Ensure the ramdisk supports PV disk and PV network. Customize this for the kernel version you have determined above.

```
# chroot /mnt/loop/centos54
# cd /boot/
# mv initrd-2.6.18-164.15.1.el5xen.img initrd-2.6.18-164.15.1.el5xen.img.bak
# mkinitrd -f /boot/initrd-2.6.18-164.15.1.el5xen.img --with=xennet --preload=xenbl
```

9. Change the password.

```
# passwd
Changing password for user root.
New UNIX password:
Retype new UNIX password:
passwd: all authentication tokens updated successfully.
```

10. Exit out of chroot.

```
# exit
```

11. Check *etc/ssh/sshd_config* for lines allowing ssh login using a password.

```
# egrep "PermitRootLogin|PasswordAuthentication" /mnt/loop/centos54/etc/ssh/sshd_co
PermitRootLogin yes
PasswordAuthentication yes
```

12. If you need the template to be enabled to reset passwords from the CloudStack UI or API, install the password change script into the image at this point. See adding-password-management-to-templates.

13. Unmount and delete loopback mount.

```
# umount /mnt/loop/centos54
# losetup -d /dev/loop0
```

14. Copy the image file to your XenServer host's file-based storage repository. In the example below, the Xenserver is "xenhost". This XenServer has an NFS repository whose uuid is a9c5b8c8-536b-a193-a6dc-51af3e5ff799.

```
# scp CentOS_6.2_x64 xenhost:/var/run/sr-mount/a9c5b8c8-536b-a193-a6dc-51af3e5ff799
```

15. Log in to the Xenserver and create a VDI the same size as the image.

```
[root@xenhost ~]# cd /var/run/sr-mount/a9c5b8c8-536b-a193-a6dc-51af3e5ff799
[root@xenhost a9c5b8c8-536b-a193-a6dc-51af3e5ff799]# ls -lh CentOS_6.2_x64
-rw-r--r-- 1 root root 10G Mar 16 16:49 CentOS_6.2_x64
[root@xenhost a9c5b8c8-536b-a193-a6dc-51af3e5ff799]# xe vdi-create virtual-size=10G
cad7317c-258b-4ef7-b207-cdf0283a7923
```

16. Import the image file into the VDI. This may take 10–20 minutes.

```
[root@xenhost a9c5b8c8-536b-a193-a6dc-51af3e5ff799]# xe vdi-import filename=CentOS_
```

17. Locate a the VHD file. This is the file with the VDI's UUID as its name. Compress it and upload it to your web server.

```
[root@xenhost a9c5b8c8-536b-a193-a6dc-51af3e5ff799]# bzip2 -c cad7317c-258b-4ef7-b2
[root@xenhost a9c5b8c8-536b-a193-a6dc-51af3e5ff799]# scp CentOS_6.2_x64.vhd.bz2 web
```

7.1.14 Converting a Hyper-V VM to a Template

To convert a Hyper-V VM to a XenServer-compatible CloudStack template, you will need a standalone XenServer host with an attached NFS VHD SR. Use whatever XenServer version you are using with CloudStack, but use XenCenter 5.6 FP1 or SP2 (it is backwards compatible to 5.6). Additionally, it may help to have an attached NFS ISO SR.

For Linux VMs, you may need to do some preparation in Hyper-V before trying to get the VM to work in XenServer. Clone the VM and work on the clone if you still want to use the VM in Hyper-V. Uninstall Hyper-V Integration Components and check for any references to device names in /etc/fstab:

1. From the linux_ic/drivers/dist directory, run make uninstall (where "linux_ic" is the path to the copied Hyper-V Integration Components files).

2. Restore the original initrd from backup in /boot/ (the backup is named *.backup0).

3. Remove the "hdX=noprobe" entries from /boot/grub/menu.lst.

4. Check /etc/fstab for any partitions mounted by device name. Change those entries (if any) to mount by LABEL or UUID. You can get that information with the blkid command.

The next step is make sure the VM is not running in Hyper-V, then get the VHD into XenServer. There are two options for doing this.

Option one:

1. Import the VHD using XenCenter. In XenCenter, go to Tools>Virtual Appliance Tools>Disk Image Import.

2. Choose the VHD, then click Next.

3. Name the VM, choose the NFS VHD SR under Storage, enable "Run Operating System Fixups" and choose the NFS ISO SR.

4. Click Next, then Finish. A VM should be created.

Option two:

1. Run XenConvert, under From choose VHD, under To choose XenServer. Click Next.

2. Choose the VHD, then click Next.

3. Input the XenServer host info, then click Next.

4. Name the VM, then click Next, then Convert. A VM should be created.

Once you have a VM created from the Hyper-V VHD, prepare it using the following steps:

1. Boot the VM, uninstall Hyper-V Integration Services, and reboot.

2. Install XenServer Tools, then reboot.

3. Prepare the VM as desired. For example, run sysprep on Windows VMs. See *"Creating a Windows Template"*.

Either option above will create a VM in HVM mode. This is fine for Windows VMs, but Linux VMs may not perform optimally. Converting a Linux VM to PV mode will require additional steps and will vary by distribution.

1. Shut down the VM and copy the VHD from the NFS storage to a web server; for example, mount the NFS share on the web server and copy it, or from the XenServer host use sftp or scp to upload it to the web server.

2. In CloudStack, create a new template using the following values:

   - URL. Give the URL for the VHD

   - OS Type. Use the appropriate OS. For PV mode on CentOS, choose Other PV (32-bit) or Other PV (64-bit). This choice is available only for XenServer.

   - Hypervisor. XenServer

   - Format. VHD

The template will be created, and you can create instances from it.

7.1.15 Adding Password Management to Your Templates

CloudStack provides an optional password reset feature that allows users to set a temporary admin or root password as well as reset the existing admin or root password from the CloudStack UI.

To enable the Reset Password feature, you will need to download an additional script to patch your template. When you later upload the template into CloudStack, you can specify whether reset admin/root password feature should be enabled for this template.

The password management feature works always resets the account password on instance boot. The script does an HTTP call to the virtual router to retrieve the account password that should be set. As long as the virtual router is accessible the guest will have access to the account password that should be used. When the user requests a password reset the management server generates and sends a new password to the virtual router for the account. Thus an instance reboot is necessary to effect any password changes.

If the script is unable to contact the virtual router during instance boot it will not set the password but boot will continue normally.

Linux OS Installation

Use the following steps to begin the Linux OS installation:

1. Download the script file cloud-set-guest-password:

   - http://download.cloud.com/templates/4.2/bindir/cloud-set-guest-password.in

2. Rename the file:

```
mv cloud-set-guest-password.in cloud-set-guest-password
```

3. Copy this file to /etc/init.d.

   On some Linux distributions, copy the file to `/etc/rc.d/init.d`.

4. Run the following command to make the script executable:

```
chmod +x /etc/init.d/cloud-set-guest-password
```

5. Depending on the Linux distribution, continue with the appropriate step.

   On Fedora, CentOS/RHEL, and Debian, run:

```
chkconfig --add cloud-set-guest-password
```

Windows OS Installation

Download the installer, CloudInstanceManager.msi, from the Download page and run the installer in the newly created Windows VM.

7.1.16 Deleting Templates

Templates may be deleted. In general, when a template spans multiple Zones, only the copy that is selected for deletion will be deleted; the same template in other Zones will not be deleted. The provided CentOS template is an exception to this. If the provided CentOS template is deleted, it will be deleted from all Zones.

When templates are deleted, the VMs instantiated from them will continue to run. However, new VMs cannot be created based on the deleted template.

## CHAPTER 8

Working with Hosts

8.1 Working with Hosts

8.1.1 Adding Hosts

Additional hosts can be added at any time to provide more capacity for guest VMs. For requirements and instructions, see "Adding a Host".

8.1.2 Scheduled Maintenance and Maintenance Mode for Hosts

You can place a host into maintenance mode. When maintenance mode is activated, the host becomes unavailable to receive new guest VMs, and the guest VMs already running on the host are seamlessly migrated to another host not in maintenance mode. This migration uses live migration technology and does not interrupt the execution of the guest.

vCenter and Maintenance Mode

To enter maintenance mode on a vCenter host, both vCenter and CloudStack must be used in concert. CloudStack and vCenter have separate maintenance modes that work closely together.

1. Place the host into CloudStack's "scheduled maintenance" mode. This does not invoke the vCenter maintenance mode, but only causes VMs to be migrated off the host

   When the CloudStack maintenance mode is requested, the host first moves into the Prepare for Maintenance state. In this state it cannot be the target of new guest VM starts. Then all VMs will be migrated off the server. Live migration will be used to move VMs off the host. This allows the guests to be migrated to other hosts with no disruption to the guests. After this migration is completed, the host will enter the Ready for Maintenance mode.

2. Wait for the "Ready for Maintenance" indicator to appear in the UI.

3. Now use vCenter to perform whatever actions are necessary to maintain the host. During this time, the host cannot be the target of new VM allocations.

4. When the maintenance tasks are complete, take the host out of maintenance mode as follows:

   (a) First use vCenter to exit the vCenter maintenance mode.

       This makes the host ready for CloudStack to reactivate it.

   (b) Then use CloudStack's administrator UI to cancel the CloudStack maintenance mode

When the host comes back online, the VMs that were migrated off of it may be migrated back to it manually and new VMs can be added.

XenServer and Maintenance Mode

For XenServer, you can take a server offline temporarily by using the Maintenance Mode feature in XenCenter. When you place a server into Maintenance Mode, all running VMs are automatically migrated from it to another host in the same pool. If the server is the pool master, a new master will also be selected for the pool. While a server is Maintenance Mode, you cannot create or start any VMs on it.

To place a server in Maintenance Mode:

1. In the Resources pane, select the server, then do one of the following:

   - Right-click, then click Enter Maintenance Mode on the shortcut menu.

   - On the Server menu, click Enter Maintenance Mode.

2. Click Enter Maintenance Mode.

The server's status in the Resources pane shows when all running VMs have been successfully migrated off the server.

To take a server out of Maintenance Mode:

1. In the Resources pane, select the server, then do one of the following:

   - Right-click, then click Exit Maintenance Mode on the shortcut menu.

   - On the Server menu, click Exit Maintenance Mode.

2. Click Exit Maintenance Mode.

8.1.3 Disabling and Enabling Zones, Pods, and Clusters

You can enable or disable a zone, pod, or cluster without permanently removing it from the cloud. This is useful for maintenance or when there are problems that make a portion of the cloud infrastructure unreliable. No new allocations will be made to a disabled zone, pod, or cluster until its state is returned to Enabled. When a zone, pod, or cluster is first added to the cloud, it is Disabled by default.

To disable and enable a zone, pod, or cluster:

1. Log in to the CloudStack UI as administrator

2. In the left navigation bar, click Infrastructure.

3. In Zones, click View More.

4. If you are disabling or enabling a zone, find the name of the zone in the list, and click the Enable/Disable button.

5. If you are disabling or enabling a pod or cluster, click the name of the zone that contains the pod or cluster.

6. Click the Compute tab.

7. In the Pods or Clusters node of the diagram, click View All.

8. Click the pod or cluster name in the list.

9. Click the Enable/Disable button.

8.1.4 Removing Hosts

Hosts can be removed from the cloud as needed. The procedure to remove a host depends on the hypervisor type.

Removing XenServer and KVM Hosts

A node cannot be removed from a cluster until it has been placed in maintenance mode. This will ensure that all of the VMs on it have been migrated to other Hosts. To remove a Host from the cloud:

1. Place the node in maintenance mode.

   See *"Scheduled Maintenance and Maintenance Mode for Hosts"*.

2. For KVM, stop the cloud-agent service.

3. Use the UI option to remove the node.

   Then you may power down the Host, re-use its IP address, re-install it, etc

Removing vSphere Hosts

To remove this type of host, first place it in maintenance mode, as described in *"Scheduled Maintenance and Maintenance Mode for Hosts"*. Then use CloudStack to remove the host. CloudStack will not direct commands to a host that has been removed using CloudStack. However, the host may still exist in the vCenter cluster.

8.1.5 Re-Installing Hosts

You can re-install a host after placing it in maintenance mode and then removing it. If a host is down and cannot be placed in maintenance mode, it should still be removed before the re-install.

8.1.6 Maintaining Hypervisors on Hosts

When running hypervisor software on hosts, be sure all the hotfixes provided by the hypervisor vendor are applied. Track the release of hypervisor patches through your hypervisor vendor's support channel, and apply patches as soon as possible after they are released. CloudStack will not track or notify you of required hypervisor patches. It is essential that your hosts are completely up to date with the provided hypervisor patches. The hypervisor vendor is likely to refuse to support any system that is not up to date with patches.

Note: The lack of up-do-date hotfixes can lead to data corruption and lost VMs.

(XenServer) For more information, see Highly Recommended Hotfixes for XenServer in the CloudStack Knowledge Base.

8.1.7 Changing Host Password

The password for a XenServer Node, KVM Node, or vSphere Node may be changed in the database. Note that all Nodes in a Cluster must have the same password.

To change a Node's password:

1. Identify all hosts in the cluster.

2. Change the password on all hosts in the cluster. Now the password for the host and the password known to CloudStack will not match. Operations on the cluster will fail until the two passwords match.

3. if the password in the database is encrypted, it is (likely) necessary to encrypt the new password using the database key before adding it to the database.

```
java -classpath /usr/share/cloudstack-common/lib/jasypt-1.9.0.jar \
org.jasypt.intf.cli.JasyptPBEStringEncryptionCLI \
encrypt.sh input="newrootpassword" \
password="databasekey" \
verbose=false
```

4. Get the list of host IDs for the host in the cluster where you are changing the password. You will need to access the database to determine these host IDs. For each hostname "h" (or vSphere cluster) that you are changing the password for, execute:

```
mysql> SELECT id FROM cloud.host WHERE name like '%h%';
```

5. This should return a single ID. Record the set of such IDs for these hosts. Now retrieve the host_details row id for the host

```
mysql> SELECT * FROM cloud.host_details WHERE name='password' AND host_id={previous
```

6. Update the passwords for the host in the database. In this example, we change the passwords for hosts with host IDs 5 and 12 and host_details IDs 8 and 22 to "password".

```
mysql> UPDATE cloud.host_details SET value='password' WHERE id=8 OR id=22;
```

8.1.8 Over-Provisioning and Service Offering Limits

(Supported for XenServer, KVM, and VMware)

CPU and memory (RAM) over-provisioning factors can be set for each cluster to change the number of VMs that can run on each host in the cluster. This helps optimize the use of resources. By increasing the over-provisioning ratio, more resource capacity will be used. If the ratio is set to 1, no over-provisioning is done.

The administrator can also set global default over-provisioning ratios in the cpu.overprovisioning.factor and mem.overprovisioning.factor global configuration variables. The default value of these variables is 1: over-provisioning is turned off by default.

Over-provisioning ratios are dynamically substituted in CloudStack's capacity calculations. For example:

Capacity = 2 GB Over-provisioning factor = 2 Capacity after over-provisioning = 4 GB

With this configuration, suppose you deploy 3 VMs of 1 GB each:

Used = 3 GB Free = 1 GB

The administrator can specify a memory over-provisioning ratio, and can specify both CPU and memory over-provisioning ratios on a per-cluster basis.

In any given cloud, the optimum number of VMs for each host is affected by such things as the hypervisor, storage, and hardware configuration. These may be different for each cluster in the same cloud. A single global over-provisioning setting can not provide the best utilization for all the different clusters in the cloud. It has to be set for the lowest common denominator. The per-cluster setting provides a finer granularity for better utilization of resources, no matter where the CloudStack placement algorithm decides to place a VM.

The overprovisioning settings can be used along with dedicated resources (assigning a specific cluster to an account) to effectively offer different levels of service to different accounts. For example, an account paying for a more expensive level of service could be assigned to a dedicated cluster with an over-provisioning ratio of 1, and a lower-paying account to a cluster with a ratio of 2.

When a new host is added to a cluster, CloudStack will assume the host has the capability to perform the CPU and RAM over-provisioning which is configured for that cluster. It is up to the administrator to be sure the host is actually suitable for the level of over-provisioning which has been set.

Limitations on Over-Provisioning in XenServer and KVM

- In XenServer, due to a constraint of this hypervisor, you can not use an over-provisioning factor greater than 4.
- The KVM hypervisor can not manage memory allocation to VMs dynamically. CloudStack sets the minimum and maximum amount of memory that a VM can use. The hypervisor adjusts the memory within the set limits based on the memory contention.

Requirements for Over-Provisioning

Several prerequisites are required in order for over-provisioning to function properly. The feature is dependent on the OS type, hypervisor capabilities, and certain scripts. It is the administrator's responsibility to ensure that these requirements are met.

Balloon Driver

All VMs should have a balloon driver installed in them. The hypervisor communicates with the balloon driver to free up and make the memory available to a VM.

XenServer The balloon driver can be found as a part of xen pv or PVHVM drivers. The xen pvhvm drivers are included in upstream linux kernels 2.6.36+.

VMware The balloon driver can be found as a part of the VMware tools. All the VMs that are deployed in a over-provisioned cluster should have the VMware tools installed.

KVM All VMs are required to support the virtio drivers. These drivers are installed in all Linux kernel versions 2.6.25 and greater. The administrator must set CONFIG_VIRTIO_BALLOON=y in the virtio configuration.

Hypervisor capabilities

The hypervisor must be capable of using the memory ballooning.

XenServer The DMC (Dynamic Memory Control) capability of the hypervisor should be enabled. Only XenServer Advanced and above versions have this feature.

VMware, KVM Memory ballooning is supported by default.

Setting Over-Provisioning Ratios

There are two ways the root admin can set CPU and RAM over-provisioning ratios. First, the global configuration settings cpu.overprovisioning.factor and mem.overprovisioning.factor will be applied when a new cluster is created. Later, the ratios can be modified for an existing cluster.

Only VMs deployed after the change are affected by the new setting. If you want VMs deployed before the change to adopt the new over-provisioning ratio, you must stop and restart the VMs. When this is done, CloudStack recalculates or scales the used and reserved capacities based on the new over-provisioning ratios, to ensure that CloudStack is correctly tracking the amount of free capacity.

Note: It is safer not to deploy additional new VMs while the capacity recalculation is underway, in case the new values for available capacity are not high enough to accommodate the new VMs. Just wait for the new used/available values to become available, to be sure there is room for all the new VMs you want.

To change the over-provisioning ratios for an existing cluster:

1. Log in as administrator to the CloudStack UI.
2. In the left navigation bar, click Infrastructure.
3. Under Clusters, click View All.
4. Select the cluster you want to work with, and click the Edit button.
5. Fill in your desired over-provisioning multipliers in the fields CPU overcommit ratio and RAM overcommit ratio. The value which is intially shown in these fields is the default value inherited from the global configuration settings.

Note: In XenServer, due to a constraint of this hypervisor, you can not use an over-provisioning factor greater than 4.

Service Offering Limits and Over-Provisioning

Service offering limits (e.g. 1 GHz, 1 core) are strictly enforced for core count. For example, a guest with a service offering of one core will have only one core available to it regardless of other activity on the Host.

Service offering limits for gigahertz are enforced only in the presence of contention for CPU resources. For example, suppose that a guest was created with a service offering of 1 GHz on a Host that has 2 GHz cores, and that guest is the only guest running on the Host. The guest will have the full 2 GHz available to it. When multiple guests are attempting to use the CPU a weighting factor is used to schedule CPU resources. The weight is based on the clock speed in the service offering. Guests receive a CPU allocation that is proportionate to the GHz in the service offering. For example, a guest created from a 2 GHz service offering will receive twice the CPU allocation as a guest created from a 1 GHz service offering. CloudStack does not perform memory over-provisioning.

8.1.9 VLAN Provisioning

CloudStack automatically creates and destroys interfaces bridged to VLANs on the hosts. In general the administrator does not need to manage this process.

CloudStack manages VLANs differently based on hypervisor type. For XenServer or KVM, the VLANs are created on only the hosts where they will be used and then they are destroyed when all guests that require them have been terminated or moved to another host.

For vSphere the VLANs are provisioned on all hosts in the cluster even if there is no guest running on a particular Host that requires the VLAN. This allows the administrator to perform live migration and other functions in vCenter without having to create the VLAN on the destination Host. Additionally, the VLANs are not removed from the Hosts when they are no longer needed.

You can use the same VLANs on different physical networks provided that each physical network has its own underlying layer-2 infrastructure, such as switches. For example, you can specify VLAN range 500 to 1000 while deploying physical networks A and B in an Advanced zone setup. This capability allows you to set up an additional layer-2 physical infrastructure on a different physical NIC and use the same set of VLANs if you run out of VLANs. Another advantage is that you can use the same set of IPs for different customers, each one with their own routers and the guest networks on different physical NICs.

VLAN Allocation Example

VLANs are required for public and guest traffic. The following is an example of a VLAN allocation scheme:

VLAN IDs	Traffic type	Scope
less than 500	Management traffic.	Reserved for administrative purposes. CloudStack software can access this, hypervisors, system VMs.
500-599	VLAN carrying public traffic.	CloudStack accounts.
600-799	VLANs carrying guest traffic.	CloudStack accounts. Account-specific VLAN is chosen from this pool.
800-899	VLANs carrying guest traffic.	CloudStack accounts. Account-specific VLAN chosen by CloudStack admin to assign to that account.
900-999	VLAN carrying guest traffic	CloudStack accounts. Can be scoped by project, domain, or all accounts.
greater than 1000	Reserved for future use	

Adding Non Contiguous VLAN Ranges

CloudStack provides you with the flexibility to add non contiguous VLAN ranges to your network. The administrator can either update an existing VLAN range or add multiple non contiguous VLAN ranges while creating a zone. You can also use the UpdatephysicalNetwork API to extend the VLAN range.

1. Log in to the CloudStack UI as an administrator or end user.

2. Ensure that the VLAN range does not already exist.

3. In the left navigation, choose Infrastructure.

4. On Zones, click View More, then click the zone to which you want to work with.

5. Click Physical Network.

6. In the Guest node of the diagram, click Configure.

7. Click Edit.

   The VLAN Ranges field now is editable.

8. Specify the start and end of the VLAN range in comma-separated list.

   Specify all the VLANs you want to use, VLANs not specified will be removed if you are adding new ranges to the existing list.

9. Click Apply.

Assigning VLANs to Isolated Networks

CloudStack provides you the ability to control VLAN assignment to Isolated networks. As a Root admin, you can assign a VLAN ID when a network is created, just the way it's done for Shared networks.

The former behaviour also is supported — VLAN is randomly allocated to a network from the VNET range of the physical network when the network turns to Implemented state. The VLAN is released back to the VNET pool when the network shuts down as a part of the Network Garbage Collection. The VLAN can be re-used either by the same network when it is implemented again, or by any other network. On each subsequent implementation of a network, a new VLAN can be assigned.

Only the Root admin can assign VLANs because the regular users or domain admin are not aware of the physical network topology. They cannot even view what VLAN is assigned to a network.

To enable you to assign VLANs to Isolated networks,

1. Create a network offering by specifying the following:

   - **Guest Type**: Select Isolated.

   - **Specify VLAN**: Select the option.

   For more information, see the CloudStack Installation Guide.

2. Using this network offering, create a network.

   You can create a VPC tier or an Isolated network.

3. Specify the VLAN when you create the network.

   When VLAN is specified, a CIDR and gateway are assigned to this network and the state is changed to Setup. In this state, the network will not be garbage collected.

Note: You cannot change a VLAN once it's assigned to the network. The VLAN remains with the network for its entire life cycle.

## CHAPTER 9

Working with Storage

9.1 Working with Storage

9.1.1 Storage Overview

CloudStack defines two types of storage: primary and secondary. Primary storage can be accessed by either iSCSI or NFS. Additionally, direct attached storage may be used for primary storage. Secondary storage is always accessed using NFS.

There is no ephemeral storage in CloudStack. All volumes on all nodes are persistent.

9.1.2 Primary Storage

This section gives concepts and technical details about CloudStack primary storage. For information about how to install and configure primary storage through the CloudStack UI, see the Installation Guide.

"About Primary Storage"

Best Practices for Primary Storage

- The speed of primary storage will impact guest performance. If possible, choose smaller, higher RPM drives or SSDs for primary storage.

- There are two ways CloudStack can leverage primary storage:

  Static: This is CloudStack's traditional way of handling storage. In this model, a preallocated amount of storage (ex. a volume from a SAN) is given to CloudStack. CloudStack then permits many of its volumes to be created on this storage (can be root and/or data disks). If using this technique, ensure that nothing is stored on the storage. Adding the storage to CloudStack will destroy any existing data.

  Dynamic: This is a newer way for CloudStack to manage storage. In this model, a storage system (rather than a preallocated amount of storage) is given to CloudStack. CloudStack, working in concert with a storage plug-in, dynamically creates volumes on the storage system and each volume on the storage system maps to a single CloudStack volume. This is highly useful for features such as storage Quality of Service. Currently this feature is supported for data disks (Disk Offerings).

Runtime Behavior of Primary Storage

Root volumes are created automatically when a virtual machine is created. Root volumes are deleted when the VM is destroyed. Data volumes can be created and dynamically attached to VMs. Data volumes are not deleted when VMs are destroyed.

Administrators should monitor the capacity of primary storage devices and add additional primary storage as needed. See the Advanced Installation Guide.

Administrators add primary storage to the system by creating a CloudStack storage pool. Each storage pool is associated with a cluster or a zone.

With regards to data disks, when a user executes a Disk Offering to create a data disk, the information is initially written to the CloudStack database only. Upon the first request that the data disk be attached to a VM, CloudStack determines what storage to place the volume on and space is taken from that storage (either from preallocated storage or from a storage system (ex. a SAN), depending on how the primary storage was added to CloudStack).

Hypervisor Support for Primary Storage

The following table shows storage options and parameters for different hypervisors.

Storage media \ hypervisor	VMware vSphere	Citrix XenServer	KVM	Hyper-V
Format for Disks, Templates, and Snapshots	VMDK	VHD	QCOW2	VHD Snapshots are not supported.
iSCSI support	VMFS	Clustered LVM	Yes, via Shared Mountpoint	No
Fiber Channel support	VMFS	Yes, via Existing SR	Yes, via Shared Mountpoint	No
NFS support	Yes	Yes	Yes	No
Local storage support	Yes	Yes	Yes	Yes
Storage over-provisioning	NFS and iSCSI	NFS	NFS	No
SMB/CIFS	No	No	No	Yes
Ceph/RBD	No	No	Yes	No

XenServer uses a clustered LVM system to store VM images on iSCSI and Fiber Channel volumes and does not support over-provisioning in the hypervisor. The storage server itself, however, can support thin-provisioning. As a result the CloudStack can still support storage over-provisioning by running on thin-provisioned storage volumes.

KVM supports "Shared Mountpoint" storage. A shared mountpoint is a file system path local to each server in a given cluster. The path must be the same across all Hosts in the cluster, for example /mnt/primary1. This shared mountpoint is assumed to be a clustered filesystem such as OCFS2. In this case the CloudStack does not attempt to mount or unmount the storage as is done with NFS. The CloudStack requires that the administrator insure that the storage is available

With NFS storage, CloudStack manages the overprovisioning. In this case the global configuration parameter storage.overprovisioning.factor controls the degree of overprovisioning. This is independent of hypervisor type.

Local storage is an option for primary storage for vSphere, XenServer, and KVM. When the local disk option is enabled, a local disk storage pool is automatically created on each host. To use local storage for the System Virtual Machines (such as the Virtual Router), set system.vm.use.local.storage to true in global configuration.

CloudStack supports multiple primary storage pools in a Cluster. For example, you could provision 2 NFS servers in primary storage. Or you could provision 1 iSCSI LUN initially and then add a second iSCSI LUN when the first approaches capacity.

Storage Tags

Storage may be "tagged". A tag is a text string attribute associated with primary storage, a Disk Offering, or a Service Offering. Tags allow administrators to provide additional information about the storage. For example, that is a "SSD" or it is "slow". Tags are not interpreted by CloudStack. They are matched against tags placed on service and disk offerings. CloudStack requires all tags on service and disk offerings to exist on the primary storage before it allocates root or data disks on the primary storage. Service and disk offering tags are used to identify the requirements of the storage that those offerings have. For example, the high end service offering may require "fast" for its root disk volume.

The interaction between tags, allocation, and volume copying across clusters and pods can be complex. To simplify the situation, use the same set of tags on the primary storage for all clusters in a pod. Even if different devices are used to present those tags, the set of exposed tags can be the same.

Maintenance Mode for Primary Storage

Primary storage may be placed into maintenance mode. This is useful, for example, to replace faulty RAM in a storage device. Maintenance mode for a storage device will first stop any new guests from being provisioned on the storage device. Then it will stop all guests that have any volume on that storage device. When all such guests are stopped the storage device is in maintenance mode and may be shut down. When the storage device is online again you may cancel maintenance mode for the device. The CloudStack will bring the device back online and attempt to start all guests that were running at the time of the entry into maintenance mode.

9.1.3 Secondary Storage

This section gives concepts and technical details about CloudStack secondary storage. For information about how to install and configure secondary storage through the CloudStack UI, see the Advanced Installation Guide.

"About Secondary Storage"

9.1.4 Working With Volumes

A volume provides storage to a guest VM. The volume can provide for a root disk or an additional data disk. Cloud-Stack supports additional volumes for guest VMs.

Volumes are created for a specific hypervisor type. A volume that has been attached to guest using one hypervisor type (e.g, XenServer) may not be attached to a guest that is using another hypervisor type, for example:vSphere, KVM. This is because the different hypervisors use different disk image formats.

CloudStack defines a volume as a unit of storage available to a guest VM. Volumes are either root disks or data disks. The root disk has "/" in the file system and is usually the boot device. Data disks provide for additional storage, for example: "/opt" or "D:". Every guest VM has a root disk, and VMs can also optionally have a data disk. End users can mount multiple data disks to guest VMs. Users choose data disks from the disk offerings created by administrators. The user can create a template from a volume as well; this is the standard procedure for private template creation. Volumes are hypervisor-specific: a volume from one hypervisor type may not be used on a guest of another hypervisor type.

Note: CloudStack supports attaching up to

- 13 data disks on XenServer hypervisor versions 6.0 and above, And all versions of VMware.

- 64 data disks on Hyper-V.

- 6 data disks on other hypervisor types.

Creating a New Volume

You can add more data disk volumes to a guest VM at any time, up to the limits of your storage capacity. Both CloudStack administrators and users can add volumes to VM instances. When you create a new volume, it is stored as an entity in CloudStack, but the actual storage resources are not allocated on the physical storage device until you attach the volume. This optimization allows the CloudStack to provision the volume nearest to the guest that will use it when the first attachment is made.

Using Local Storage for Data Volumes

You can create data volumes on local storage (supported with XenServer, KVM, and VMware). The data volume is placed on the same host as the VM instance that is attached to the data volume. These local data volumes can be attached to virtual machines, detached, re-attached, and deleted just as with the other types of data volume.

Local storage is ideal for scenarios where persistence of data volumes and HA is not required. Some of the benefits include reduced disk I/O latency and cost reduction from using inexpensive local disks.

In order for local volumes to be used, the feature must be enabled for the zone.

You can create a data disk offering for local storage. When a user creates a new VM, they can select this disk offering in order to cause the data disk volume to be placed in local storage.

You can not migrate a VM that has a volume in local storage to a different host, nor migrate the volume itself away to a different host. If you want to put a host into maintenance mode, you must first stop any VMs with local data volumes on that host.

To Create a New Volume

1. Log in to the CloudStack UI as a user or admin.

2. In the left navigation bar, click Storage.

3. In Select View, choose Volumes.

4. To create a new volume, click Add Volume, provide the following details, and click OK.

    • Name. Give the volume a unique name so you can find it later.

    • Availability Zone. Where do you want the storage to reside? This should be close to the VM that will use the volume.

    • Disk Offering. Choose the characteristics of the storage.

    The new volume appears in the list of volumes with the state "Allocated." The volume data is stored in Cloud-Stack, but the volume is not yet ready for use

5. To start using the volume, continue to Attaching a Volume

Uploading an Existing Volume to a Virtual Machine

Existing data can be made accessible to a virtual machine. This is called uploading a volume to the VM. For example, this is useful to upload data from a local file system and attach it to a VM. Root administrators, domain administrators, and end users can all upload existing volumes to VMs.

The upload is performed using HTTP. The uploaded volume is placed in the zone's secondary storage

You cannot upload a volume if the preconfigured volume limit has already been reached. The default limit for the cloud is set in the global configuration parameter max.account.volumes, but administrators can also set per-domain limits that are different from the global default. See Setting Usage Limits

To upload a volume:

1. (Optional) Create an MD5 hash (checksum) of the disk image file that you are going to upload. After uploading the data disk, CloudStack will use this value to verify that no data corruption has occurred.

2. Log in to the CloudStack UI as an administrator or user

3. In the left navigation bar, click Storage.

4. Click Upload Volume.

5. Provide the following:

   - Name and Description. Any desired name and a brief description that can be shown in the UI.

   - Availability Zone. Choose the zone where you want to store the volume. VMs running on hosts in this zone can attach the volume.

   - Format. Choose one of the following to indicate the disk image format of the volume.

Hypervisor	Disk Image Format
XenServer	VHD
VMware	OVA
KVM	QCOW2

   - URL. The secure HTTP or HTTPS URL that CloudStack can use to access your disk. The type of file at the URL must match the value chosen in Format. For example, if Format is VHD, the URL might look like the following:

     ```
     http://yourFileServerIP/userdata/myDataDisk.vhd
     ```

   - MD5 checksum. (Optional) Use the hash that you created in step 1.

6. Wait until the status of the volume shows that the upload is complete. Click Instances - Volumes, find the name you specified in step 5, and make sure the status is Uploaded.

Attaching a Volume

You can attach a volume to a guest VM to provide extra disk storage. Attach a volume when you first create a new volume, when you are moving an existing volume from one VM to another, or after you have migrated a volume from one storage pool to another.

1. Log in to the CloudStack UI as a user or admin.

2. In the left navigation, click Storage.

3. In Select View, choose Volumes.

4. Click the volume name in the Volumes list, then click the Attach Disk button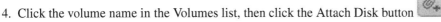

5. In the Instance popup, choose the VM to which you want to attach the volume. You will only see instances to which you are allowed to attach volumes; for example, a user will see only instances created by that user, but the administrator will have more choices.

6. When the volume has been attached, you should be able to see it by clicking Instances, the instance name, and View Volumes.

Detaching and Moving Volumes

Note: This procedure is different from moving volumes from one storage pool to another as described in *"VM Storage Migration"*.

A volume can be detached from a guest VM and attached to another guest. Both CloudStack administrators and users can detach volumes from VMs and move them to other VMs.

If the two VMs are in different clusters, and the volume is large, it may take several minutes for the volume to be moved to the new VM.

1. Log in to the CloudStack UI as a user or admin.

2. In the left navigation bar, click Storage, and choose Volumes in Select View. Alternatively, if you know which VM the volume is attached to, you can click Instances, click the VM name, and click View Volumes.

3. Click the name of the volume you want to detach, then click the Detach Disk button.

4. To move the volume to another VM, follow the steps in *"Attaching a Volume"*.

VM Storage Migration

Supported in XenServer, KVM, and VMware.

Note: This procedure is different from moving disk volumes from one VM to another as described in *"Detaching and Moving Volumes"*.

You can migrate a virtual machine's root disk volume or any additional data disk volume from one storage pool to another in the same zone.

You can use the storage migration feature to achieve some commonly desired administration goals, such as balancing the load on storage pools and increasing the reliability of virtual machines by moving them away from any storage pool that is experiencing issues.

On XenServer and VMware, live migration of VM storage is enabled through CloudStack support for XenMotion and vMotion. Live storage migration allows VMs to be moved from one host to another, where the VMs are not located on storage shared between the two hosts. It provides the option to live migrate a VM's disks along with the VM itself. It is possible to migrate a VM from one XenServer resource pool / VMware cluster to another, or to migrate a VM whose disks are on local storage, or even to migrate a VM's disks from one storage repository to another, all while the VM is running.

Note: Because of a limitation in VMware, live migration of storage for a VM is allowed only if the source and target storage pool are accessible to the source host; that is, the host where the VM is running when the live migration operation is requested.

Migrating a Data Volume to a New Storage Pool

There are two situations when you might want to migrate a disk:

- Move the disk to new storage, but leave it attached to the same running VM.

- Detach the disk from its current VM, move it to new storage, and attach it to a new VM.

Migrating Storage For a Running VM   (Supported on XenServer and VMware)

1. Log in to the CloudStack UI as a user or admin.

2. In the left navigation bar, click Instances, click the VM name, and click View Volumes.

3. Click the volume you want to migrate.

4. Detach the disk from the VM. See *"Detaching and Moving Volumes"* but skip the "reattach" step at the end. You will do that after migrating to new storage.

5. Click the Migrate Volume button [+] and choose the destination from the dropdown list.

6. Watch for the volume status to change to Migrating, then back to Ready.

Migrating Storage and Attaching to a Different VM

1. Log in to the CloudStack UI as a user or admin.

2. Detach the disk from the VM. See *"Detaching and Moving Volumes"* but skip the "reattach" step at the end. You will do that after migrating to new storage.

3. Click the Migrate Volume button [+] and choose the destination from the dropdown list.

4. Watch for the volume status to change to Migrating, then back to Ready. You can find the volume by clicking Storage in the left navigation bar. Make sure that Volumes is displayed at the top of the window, in the Select View dropdown.

5. Attach the volume to any desired VM running in the same cluster as the new storage server. See *"Attaching a Volume"*

Migrating a VM Root Volume to a New Storage Pool

(XenServer, VMware) You can live migrate a VM's root disk from one storage pool to another, without stopping the VM first.

(KVM) When migrating the root disk volume, the VM must first be stopped, and users can not access the VM. After migration is complete, the VM can be restarted.

1. Log in to the CloudStack UI as a user or admin.

2. In the left navigation bar, click Instances, and click the VM name.

3. (KVM only) Stop the VM.

4. Click the Migrate button [+] and choose the destination from the dropdown list.

Note: If the VM's storage has to be migrated along with the VM, this will be noted in the host list. CloudStack will take care of the storage migration for you.

5. Watch for the volume status to change to Migrating, then back to Running (or Stopped, in the case of KVM). This can take some time.

6. (KVM only) Restart the VM.

Resizing Volumes

CloudStack provides the ability to resize data disks; CloudStack controls volume size by using disk offerings. This provides CloudStack administrators with the flexibility to choose how much space they want to make available to the end users. Volumes within the disk offerings with the same storage tag can be resized. For example, if you only want to offer 10, 50, and 100 GB offerings, the allowed resize should stay within those limits. That implies if you define a 10 GB, a 50 GB and a 100 GB disk offerings, a user can upgrade from 10 GB to 50 GB, or 50 GB to 100 GB. If you create a custom-sized disk offering, then you have the option to resize the volume by specifying a new, larger size.

Additionally, using the resizeVolume API, a data volume can be moved from a static disk offering to a custom disk offering with the size specified. This functionality allows those who might be billing by certain volume sizes or disk offerings to stick to that model, while providing the flexibility to migrate to whatever custom size necessary.

This feature is supported on KVM, XenServer, and VMware hosts. However, shrinking volumes is not supported on VMware hosts.

Before you try to resize a volume, consider the following:

- The VMs associated with the volume are stopped.
- The data disks associated with the volume are removed.
- When a volume is shrunk, the disk associated with it is simply truncated, and doing so would put its content at risk of data loss. Therefore, resize any partitions or file systems before you shrink a data disk so that all the data is moved off from that disk.

To resize a volume:

1. Log in to the CloudStack UI as a user or admin.
2. In the left navigation bar, click Storage.
3. In Select View, choose Volumes.
4. Select the volume name in the Volumes list, then click the Resize Volume button
5. In the Resize Volume pop-up, choose desired characteristics for the storage.

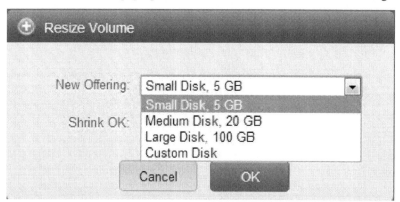

   (a) If you select Custom Disk, specify a custom size.
   (b) Click Shrink OK to confirm that you are reducing the size of a volume.

       This parameter protects against inadvertent shrinking of a disk, which might lead to the risk of data loss. You must sign off that you know what you are doing.

6. Click OK.

Reset VM to New Root Disk on Reboot

You can specify that you want to discard the root disk and create a new one whenever a given VM is rebooted. This is useful for secure environments that need a fresh start on every boot and for desktops that should not retain state. The IP address of the VM will not change due to this operation.

To enable root disk reset on VM reboot:

When creating a new service offering, set the parameter isVolatile to True. VMs created from this service offering will have their disks reset upon reboot. See "Creating a New Compute Offering".

Volume Deletion and Garbage Collection

The deletion of a volume does not delete the snapshots that have been created from the volume

When a VM is destroyed, data disk volumes that are attached to the VM are not deleted.

Volumes are permanently destroyed using a garbage collection process. The global configuration variables expunge.delay and expunge.interval determine when the physical deletion of volumes will occur.

- *expunge.delay*: determines how old the volume must be before it is destroyed, in seconds
- *expunge.interval*: determines how often to run the garbage collection check

Administrators should adjust these values depending on site policies around data retention.

9.1.5 Working with Volume Snapshots

(Supported for the following hypervisors: **XenServer**, **VMware vSphere**, and **KVM**)

CloudStack supports snapshots of disk volumes. Snapshots are a point-in-time capture of virtual machine disks. Memory and CPU states are not captured. If you are using the Oracle VM hypervisor, you can not take snapshots, since OVM does not support them.

Snapshots may be taken for volumes, including both root and data disks (except when the Oracle VM hypervisor is used, which does not support snapshots). The administrator places a limit on the number of stored snapshots per user. Users can create new volumes from the snapshot for recovery of particular files and they can create templates from snapshots to boot from a restored disk.

Users can create snapshots manually or by setting up automatic recurring snapshot policies. Users can also create disk volumes from snapshots, which may be attached to a VM like any other disk volume. Snapshots of both root disks and data disks are supported. However, CloudStack does not currently support booting a VM from a recovered root disk. A disk recovered from snapshot of a root disk is treated as a regular data disk; the data on recovered disk can be accessed by attaching the disk to a VM.

A completed snapshot is copied from primary storage to secondary storage, where it is stored until deleted or purged by newer snapshot.

How to Snapshot a Volume

1. Log in to the CloudStack UI as a user or administrator.
2. In the left navigation bar, click Storage.
3. In Select View, be sure Volumes is selected.
4. Click the name of the volume you want to snapshot.

5. Click the Snapshot button.

Automatic Snapshot Creation and Retention

(Supported for the following hypervisors: **XenServer**, **VMware vSphere**, and **KVM**)

Users can set up a recurring snapshot policy to automatically create multiple snapshots of a disk at regular intervals. Snapshots can be created on an hourly, daily, weekly, or monthly interval. One snapshot policy can be set up per disk volume. For example, a user can set up a daily snapshot at 02:30.

With each snapshot schedule, users can also specify the number of scheduled snapshots to be retained. Older snapshots that exceed the retention limit are automatically deleted. This user-defined limit must be equal to or lower than the global limit set by the CloudStack administrator. See "Globally Configured Limits". The limit applies only to those snapshots that are taken as part of an automatic recurring snapshot policy. Additional manual snapshots can be created and retained.

Incremental Snapshots and Backup

Snapshots are created on primary storage where a disk resides. After a snapshot is created, it is immediately backed up to secondary storage and removed from primary storage for optimal utilization of space on primary storage.

CloudStack does incremental backups for some hypervisors. When incremental backups are supported, every N backup is a full backup.

	VMware vSphere	Citrix XenServer	KVM
Support incremental backup	No	Yes	No

Volume Status

When a snapshot operation is triggered by means of a recurring snapshot policy, a snapshot is skipped if a volume has remained inactive since its last snapshot was taken. A volume is considered to be inactive if it is either detached or attached to a VM that is not running. CloudStack ensures that at least one snapshot is taken since the volume last became inactive.

When a snapshot is taken manually, a snapshot is always created regardless of whether a volume has been active or not.

Snapshot Restore

There are two paths to restoring snapshots. Users can create a volume from the snapshot. The volume can then be mounted to a VM and files recovered as needed. Alternatively, a template may be created from the snapshot of a root disk. The user can then boot a VM from this template to effect recovery of the root disk.

Snapshot Job Throttling

When a snapshot of a virtual machine is requested, the snapshot job runs on the same host where the VM is running or, in the case of a stopped VM, the host where it ran last. If many snapshots are requested for VMs on a single host, this can lead to problems with too many snapshot jobs overwhelming the resources of the host.

To address this situation, the cloud's root administrator can throttle how many snapshot jobs are executed simultaneously on the hosts in the cloud by using the global configuration setting concurrent.snapshots.threshold.perhost. By using this setting, the administrator can better ensure that snapshot jobs do not time out and hypervisor hosts do not experience performance issues due to hosts being overloaded with too many snapshot requests.

Set concurrent.snapshots.threshold.perhost to a value that represents a best guess about how many snapshot jobs the hypervisor hosts can execute at one time, given the current resources of the hosts and the number of VMs running on the hosts. If a given host has more snapshot requests, the additional requests are placed in a waiting queue. No new snapshot jobs will start until the number of currently executing snapshot jobs falls below the configured limit.

The admin can also set job.expire.minutes to place a maximum on how long a snapshot request will wait in the queue. If this limit is reached, the snapshot request fails and returns an error message.

VMware Volume Snapshot Performance

When you take a snapshot of a data or root volume on VMware, CloudStack uses an efficient storage technique to improve performance.

A snapshot is not immediately exported from vCenter to a mounted NFS share and packaged into an OVA file format. This operation would consume time and resources. Instead, the original file formats (e.g., VMDK) provided by vCenter are retained. An OVA file will only be created as needed, on demand. To generate the OVA, CloudStack uses information in a properties file (*.ova.meta) which it stored along with the original snapshot data.

Note: For upgrading customers: This process applies only to newly created snapshots after upgrade to CloudStack 4.2. Snapshots that have already been taken and stored in OVA format will continue to exist in that format, and will continue to work as expected.

## CHAPTER 10

Working with System Virtual Machines

10.1 Working with System Virtual Machines

CloudStack uses several types of system virtual machines to perform tasks in the cloud. In general CloudStack manages these system VMs and creates, starts, and stops them as needed based on scale and immediate needs. However, the administrator should be aware of them and their roles to assist in debugging issues.

10.1.1 The System VM Template

The System VMs come from a single template. The System VM has the following characteristics:

- Debian 7.8 ("wheezy"), 3.2.0 kernel with the latest security patches from the Debian security APT repository

- Has a minimal set of packages installed thereby reducing the attack surface

- 64-bit for enhanced performance on Xen/VMWare

- pvops kernel with Xen PV drivers, KVM virtio drivers, and VMware tools for optimum performance on all hypervisors

- Xen tools inclusion allows performance monitoring

- Latest versions of HAProxy, iptables, IPsec, and Apache from debian repository ensures improved security and speed

- Latest version of JRE from Sun/Oracle ensures improved security and speed

10.1.2 Changing the Default System VM Template

Using the 64-bit template should be use with a System Offering of at least 512MB of memory.

1. Based on the hypervisor you use, download the 64-bit template from the following location:

Hypervisor	Download Location
XenServer	http://cloudstack.apt-get.eu/systemvm/4.5/systemvm64template-4.5-xen.vhd.bz2
KVM	http://cloudstack.apt-get.eu/systemvm/4.5/systemvm64template-4.5-kvm.qcow2.bz2
VMware	http://cloudstack.apt-get.eu/systemvm/4.5/systemvm64template-4.5-vmware.ova
Hyper-V	http://cloudstack.apt-get.eu/systemvm/4.5/systemvm64template-4.5-hyperv.vhd.zip

2. As an administrator, log in to the CloudStack UI

3. Register the 64 bit template.

   For example: KVM64bitTemplate

4. While registering the template, select Routing.

5. Navigate to Infrastructure > Zone > Settings.

6. Set the name of the 64-bit template, KVM64bitTemplate, in the *"router.template.kvm"* global parameter.

   If you are using a XenServer 64-bit template, set the name in the *"router.template.xen"* global parameter.

   Any new virtual router created in this Zone automatically picks up this template.

7. Restart the Management Server.

10.1.3 Multiple System VM Support for VMware

Every CloudStack zone has single System VM for template processing tasks such as downloading templates, uploading templates, and uploading ISOs. In a zone where VMware is being used, additional System VMs can be launched to process VMware-specific tasks such as taking snapshots and creating private templates. The CloudStack management server launches additional System VMs for VMware-specific tasks as the load increases. The management server monitors and weights all commands sent to these System VMs and performs dynamic load balancing and scaling-up of more System VMs.

10.1.4 Console Proxy

The Console Proxy is a type of System Virtual Machine that has a role in presenting a console view via the web UI. It connects the user's browser to the VNC port made available via the hypervisor for the console of the guest. Both the administrator and end user web UIs offer a console connection.

Clicking a console icon brings up a new window. The AJAX code downloaded into that window refers to the public IP address of a console proxy VM. There is exactly one public IP address allocated per console proxy VM. The AJAX application connects to this IP. The console proxy then proxies the connection to the VNC port for the requested VM on the Host hosting the guest.

Note: The hypervisors will have many ports assigned to VNC usage so that multiple VNC sessions can occur simultaneously.

There is never any traffic to the guest virtual IP, and there is no need to enable VNC within the guest.

The console proxy VM will periodically report its active session count to the Management Server. The default reporting interval is five seconds. This can be changed through standard Management Server configuration with the parameter consoleproxy.loadscan.interval.

Assignment of guest VM to console proxy is determined by first determining if the guest VM has a previous session associated with a console proxy. If it does, the Management Server will assign the guest VM to the target Console Proxy VM regardless of the load on the proxy VM. Failing that, the first available running Console Proxy VM that has the capacity to handle new sessions is used.

Console proxies can be restarted by administrators but this will interrupt existing console sessions for users.

Using a SSL Certificate for the Console Proxy

By default, the console viewing functionality uses plaintext HTTP. In any production environment, the console proxy connection should be encrypted via SSL at the mininum.

A CloudStack administrator has 2 ways to secure the console proxy communication with SSL:

- Set up a SSL wild-card certificate and domain name resolution

- Set up SSL certificate for specific FQDN and configure load-balancer

Changing the Console Proxy SSL Certificate and Domain

The administrator can configure SSL encryption by selecting a domain and uploading a new SSL certificate and private key. The domain must run a DNS service that is capable of resolving queries for addresses of the form aaa-bbb-ccc-ddd.your.domain to an IPv4 IP address in the form aaa.bbb.ccc.ddd, for example, 202.8.44.1. To change the console proxy domain, SSL certificate, and private key:

1. Set up dynamic name resolution or populate all possible DNS names in your public IP range into your existing DNS server with the format aaa-bbb-ccc-ddd.consoleproxy.company.com -> aaa.bbb.ccc.ddd.

Note: In these steps you will notice *consoleproxy.company.com* -For security best practices, we recommend creating a wildcard SSL certificate on a separate subdomain so in the event that the certificate is compromised, a malicious user cannot impersonate a company.com domain.

---

2. Generate the private key and certificate signing request (CSR). When you are using openssl to generate private/public key pairs and CSRs, for the private key that you are going to paste into the CloudStack UI, be sure to convert it into PKCS#8 format.

    (a) Generate a new 2048-bit private key

```
openssl genrsa -des3 -out yourprivate.key 2048
```

    (b) Generate a new certificate CSR. Ensure the creation of a wildcard certificate, eg *.consoleproxy.company.com

```
openssl req -new -key yourprivate.key -out yourcertificate.csr
```

    (c) Head to the website of your favorite trusted Certificate Authority, purchase an SSL certificate, and submit the CSR. You should receive a valid certificate in return

    (d) Convert your private key format into PKCS#8 encrypted format.

```
openssl pkcs8 -topk8 -in yourprivate.key -out yourprivate.pkcs8.encrypted.key
```

    (e) Convert your PKCS#8 encrypted private key into the PKCS#8 format that is compliant with CloudStack

```
openssl pkcs8 -in yourprivate.pkcs8.encrypted.key -out yourprivate.pkcs8.key
```

3. In the Update SSL Certificate screen of the CloudStack UI, paste the following:

    - The certificate you've just generated.
    - The private key you've just generated.
    - The desired domain name, prefixed with *.; for example, *.consoleproxy.company.com

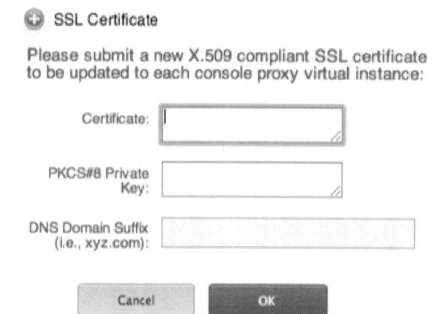

4. This stops all currently running console proxy VMs, then restarts them with the new certificate and key. Users might notice a brief interruption in console availability.

The Management Server generates URLs of the form "aaa-bbb-ccc-ddd.consoleproxy.company.com" after this change is made. The new console requests will be served with the new DNS domain name, certificate, and key.

Uploading ROOT CA and Intermediate CA

If you need to upload custom certificate with ROOT CA and intermediate CA, you can find more details here: https://cwiki.apache.org/confluence/display/CLOUDSTACK/Procedure+to+Replace+realhostip.com+with+Your+Own

IMPORTANT NOTES:

In order to avoid errors and problems while uploading custom certificates, please check following:

1. While doing URL encoding of ROOT CA and any Intermediate CA, be sure that the plus signs ("+") inside certificates are not replaced by space (" "), because some URL/string encoding tools tend to do that.

2. If you are renewing certificates it might happen you need to upload new ROOT CA and Intermediate CA, together with new Server Certificate and key. In this case please be sure to use same names for certificates during API upload of certificate, example:

http://123.123.123.123:8080/client/api?command=uploadCustomCertificate&...&name=root1...
http://123.123.123.123:8080/client/api?command=uploadCustomCertificate&...&name=intermed1...

Here names are "root1" and "intermed1". If you used other names previously, please check the cloud.keystore table to obtain used names.

If you still have problems and folowing errors in management.log while destroying CPVM:

- Unable to build keystore for CPVMCertificate due to CertificateException

- Cold not find and construct a valid SSL certificate

that means that still some of the Root/intermediate/server certificates or the key is not in a good format, or incorrectly encoded or multiply Root CA/Intemediate CA present in database by mistake.

Other way to renew Certificates (Root,Intermediates,Server certificates and key) - although not recommended unless you fill comfortable - is to directly edit the database, while still respect the main requirement that the private key is PKCS8 encoded, while Root CA, Intemediate and Server certificates are still in default PEM format (no URL encoding needed here). After editing the database, please restart management server, and destroy SSVM and CPVM after that, so the new SSVM and CPVM with new certificates are created.

Load-balancing Console Proxies

An alternative to using dynamic DNS or creating a range of DNS entries as described in the last section would be to create a SSL certificate for a specific domain name, configure CloudStack to use that particular FQDN, and then configure a load balancer to load balance the console proxy's IP address behind the FQDN. As the functionality for this is still new, please see https://cwiki.apache.org/confluence/display/CLOUDSTACK/Realhost+IP+changes for more details.

10.1.5 Virtual Router

The virtual router is a type of System Virtual Machine. The virtual router is one of the most frequently used service providers in CloudStack. The end user has no direct access to the virtual router. Users can ping the virtual router and take actions that affect it (such as setting up port forwarding), but users do not have SSH access into the virtual router.

There is no mechanism for the administrator to log in to the virtual router. Virtual routers can be restarted by administrators, but this will interrupt public network access and other services for end users. A basic test in debugging networking issues is to attempt to ping the virtual router from a guest VM. Some of the characteristics of the virtual router are determined by its associated system service offering.

Configuring the Virtual Router

You can set the following:

- IP range
- Supported network services
- Default domain name for the network serviced by the virtual router
- Gateway IP address
- How often CloudStack fetches network usage statistics from CloudStack virtual routers. If you want to collect traffic metering data from the virtual router, set the global configuration parameter router.stats.interval. If you are not using the virtual router to gather network usage statistics, set it to 0.

Upgrading a Virtual Router with System Service Offerings

When CloudStack creates a virtual router, it uses default settings which are defined in a default system service offering. See *"System Service Offerings"*. All the virtual routers in a single guest network use the same system service offering. You can upgrade the capabilities of the virtual router by creating and applying a custom system service offering.

1. Define your custom system service offering. See *"Creating a New System Service Offering"*. In System VM Type, choose Domain Router.

2. Associate the system service offering with a network offering. See "Creating a New Network Offering".

3. Apply the network offering to the network where you want the virtual routers to use the new system service offering. If this is a new network, follow the steps in Adding an Additional Guest Network on page 66. To change the service offering for existing virtual routers, follow the steps in "Changing the Network Offering on a Guest Network".

Best Practices for Virtual Routers

- WARNING: Restarting a virtual router from a hypervisor console deletes all the iptables rules. To work around this issue, stop the virtual router and start it from the CloudStack UI.

-
> **Warning:** Do not use the destroyRouter API when only one router is available in the network, because restartNetwork API with the cleanup=false parameter can't recreate it later. If you want to destroy and recreate the single router available in the network, use the restartNetwork API with the cleanup=true parameter.

Service Monitoring Tool for Virtual Router

Various services running on the CloudStack virtual routers can be monitored by using a Service Monitoring tool. The tool ensures that services are successfully running until CloudStack deliberately disables them. If a service goes down, the tool automatically restarts the service, and if that does not help bringing up the service, an alert as well as an event is generated indicating the failure. A new global parameter, `network.router.enableservicemonitoring`, has been introduced to control this feature. The default value is false, implies, monitoring is disabled. When you enable, ensure that the Management Server and the router are restarted.

Monitoring tool can help to start a VR service, which is crashed due to an unexpected reason. For example:

- The services crashed due to defects in the source code.

- The services that are terminated by the OS when memory or CPU is not sufficiently available for the service.

Note: Only those services with daemons are monitored. The services that are failed due to errors in the service/daemon configuration file cannot be restarted by the Monitoring tool. VPC networks are not supported.

The following services are monitored in a VR:

- DNS
- HA Proxy
- SSH
- Apache Web Server

The following networks are supported:

- Isolated Networks
- Shared Networks in both Advanced and Basic zone

Note: VPC networks are not supported

This feature is supported on the following hypervisors: XenServer, VMware, and KVM.

Enhanced Upgrade for Virtual Routers

Upgrading VR is made flexible. The CloudStack administrators will be able to control the sequence of the VR upgrades. The sequencing is based on Infrastructure hierarchy, such as by Cluster, Pod, or Zone, and Administrative

(Account) hierarchy, such as by Tenant or Domain. As an administrator, you can also determine when a particular customer service, such as VR, is upgraded within a specified upgrade interval. Upgrade operation is enhanced to increase the upgrade speed by allowing as many upgrade operations in parallel as possible.

During the entire duration of the upgrade, users cannot launch new services or make changes to an existing service.

Additionally, using multiple versions of VRs in a single instance is supported. In the Details tab of a VR, you can view the version and whether it requires upgrade. During the Management Server upgrade, CloudStack checks whether VR is at the latest version before performing any operation on the VR. To support this, a new global parameter, *"router.version.check"*, has been added. This parameter is set to true by default, which implies minimum required version is checked before performing any operation. No operation is performed if the VR is not at the required version. Services of the older version VR continue to be available, but no further operations can be performed on the VR until it is upgraded to the latest version. This will be a transient state until the VR is upgraded. This will ensure that the availability of VR services and VR state is not impacted due to the Management Server upgrade.

The following service will be available even if the VR is not upgraded. However, no changes for any of the services can be sent to the VR, until it is upgraded:

- SecurityGroup
- UserData
- DHCP
- DNS
- LB
- Port Forwarding
- VPN
- Static NAT
- Source NAT
- Firewall
- Gateway
- NetworkACL

Supported Virtual Routers

- VR
- VPC VR
- Redundant VR

Upgrading Virtual Routers

1. Download the latest System VM template.
2. Download the latest System VM to all the primary storage pools.
3. Upgrade the Management Server.
4. Upgrade CPVM and SSVM either from the UI or by using the following script:

```
# cloudstack-sysvmadm -d <IP address> -u cloud -p -s
```

Even when the VRs are still on older versions, existing services will continue to be available to the VMs. The Management Server cannot perform any operations on the VRs until they are upgraded.

5. Selectively upgrade the VRs:

    (a) Log in to the CloudStack UI as the root administrator.

    (b) In the left navigation, choose Infrastructure.

    (c) On Virtual Routers, click View More.

    All the VRs are listed in the Virtual Routers page.

    (d) In Select View drop-down, select desired grouping based on your requirement.

    You can use either of the following:

    - Group by zone

    - Group by pod

    - Group by cluster

    - Group by account

    (e) Click the group which has the VRs to be upgraded.

    For example, if you have selected Group by zone, select the name of the desired zone.

    (f) Click the Upgrade button to upgrade all the VRs.

    (g) Click OK to confirm.

10.1.6 Secondary Storage VM

In addition to the hosts, CloudStack's Secondary Storage VM mounts and writes to secondary storage.

Submissions to secondary storage go through the Secondary Storage VM. The Secondary Storage VM can retrieve templates and ISO images from URLs using a variety of protocols.

The secondary storage VM provides a background task that takes care of a variety of secondary storage activities: downloading a new template to a Zone, copying templates between Zones, and snapshot backups.

The administrator can log in to the secondary storage VM if needed.

## CHAPTER 11

Working with Usage

11.1 Working with Usage

The Usage Server is an optional, separately-installed part of CloudStack that provides aggregated usage records which you can use to create billing integration for CloudStack. The Usage Server works by taking data from the events log and creating summary usage records that you can access using the listUsageRecords API call.

The usage records show the amount of resources, such as VM run time or template storage space, consumed by guest instances.

The Usage Server runs at least once per day. It can be configured to run multiple times per day.

11.1.1 Configuring the Usage Server

To configure the usage server:

1. Be sure the Usage Server has been installed. This requires extra steps beyond just installing the CloudStack software. See Installing the Usage Server (Optional) in the Advanced Installation Guide.

2. Log in to the CloudStack UI as administrator.

3. Click Global Settings.

4. In Search, type usage. Find the configuration parameter that controls the behavior you want to set. See the table below for a description of the available parameters.

5. In Actions, click the Edit icon.

6. Type the desired value and click the Save icon.

7. Restart the Management Server (as usual with any global configuration change) and also the Usage Server:

```
# service cloudstack-management restart
# service cloudstack-usage restart
```

The following table shows the global configuration settings that control the behavior of the Usage Server.

Parameter Name Description

enable.usage.server Whether the Usage Server is active.

usage.aggregation.timezone

Time zone of usage records. Set this if the usage records and daily job execution are in different time zones. For example, with the following settings, the usage job will run at PST 00:15 and generate usage records for the 24 hours from 00:00:00 GMT to 23:59:59 GMT:

```
usage.stats.job.exec.time = 00:15
usage.execution.timezone = PST
usage.aggregation.timezone = GMT
```

Valid values for the time zone are specified in Appendix A, *Time Zones*

Default: GMT

usage.execution.timezone

The time zone of usage.stats.job.exec.time. Valid values for the time zone are specified in Appendix A, *Time Zones*

Default: The time zone of the management server.

usage.sanity.check.interval

The number of days between sanity checks. Set this in order to periodically search for records with erroneous data before issuing customer invoices. For example, this checks for VM usage records created after the VM was destroyed, and similar checks for templates, volumes, and so on. It also checks for usage times longer than the aggregation range. If any issue is found, the alert ALERT_TYPE_USAGE_SANITY_RESULT = 21 is sent.

usage.stats.job.aggregation.range

The time period in minutes between Usage Server processing jobs. For example, if you set it to 1440, the Usage Server will run once per day. If you set it to 600, it will run every ten hours. In general, when a Usage Server job runs, it processes all events generated since usage was last run.

There is special handling for the case of 1440 (once per day). In this case the Usage Server does not necessarily process all records since Usage was last run. CloudStack assumes that you require processing once per day for the previous, complete day's records. For example, if the current day is October 7, then it is assumed you would like to process records for October 6, from midnight to midnight. CloudStack assumes this "midnight to midnight" is relative to the usage.execution.timezone.

Default: 1440

usage.stats.job.exec.time

The time when the Usage Server processing will start. It is specified in 24-hour format (HH:MM) in the time zone of the server, which should be GMT. For example, to start the Usage job at 10:30 GMT, enter "10:30".

If usage.stats.job.aggregation.range is also set, and its value is not 1440, then its value will be added to usage.stats.job.exec.time to get the time to run the Usage Server job again. This is repeated until 24 hours have elapsed, and the next day's processing begins again at usage.stats.job.exec.time.

Default: 00:15.

For example, suppose that your server is in GMT, your user population is predominantly in the East Coast of the United States, and you would like to process usage records every night at 2 AM local (EST) time. Choose these settings:

- enable.usage.server = true

- usage.execution.timezone = America/New_York

- usage.stats.job.exec.time = 07:00. This will run the Usage job at 2:00 AM EST. Note that this will shift by an hour as the East Coast of the U.S. enters and exits Daylight Savings Time.

- usage.stats.job.aggregation.range = 1440

With this configuration, the Usage job will run every night at 2 AM EST and will process records for the previous day's midnight-midnight as defined by the EST (America/New_York) time zone.

Note: Because the special value 1440 has been used for usage.stats.job.aggregation.range, the Usage Server will ignore the data between midnight and 2 AM. That data will be included in the next day's run.

11.1.2 Setting Usage Limits

CloudStack provides several administrator control points for capping resource usage by users. Some of these limits are global configuration parameters. Others are applied at the ROOT domain and may be overridden on a per-account basis.

Globally Configured Limits

In a zone, the guest virtual network has a 24 bit CIDR by default. This limits the guest virtual network to 254 running instances. It can be adjusted as needed, but this must be done before any instances are created in the zone. For example, 10.1.1.0/22 would provide for ~1000 addresses.

The following table lists limits set in the Global Configuration:

Parameter Name	Definition
max.account.public	Number of public IP addresses that can be owned by an account
max.account.snapshots	Number of snapshots that can exist for an account
max.account.templates	Number of templates that can exist for an account
max.account.user	Number of virtual machine instances that can exist for an account
max.account.vol	Number of disk volumes that can exist for an account
max.template.iso	Maximum size for a downloaded template or ISO in GB
max.volume.size	Maximum size for a volume in GB
network.throttling.rate	Default data transfer rate in megabits per second allowed per user (supported on XenServer)
snapshot.max.hourly	Maximum recurring hourly snapshots to be retained for a volume. If the limit is reached, early snapshots from the start of the hour are deleted so that newer ones can be saved. This limit does not apply to manual snapshots. If set to 0, recurring hourly snapshots can not be scheduled
snapshot.max.daily	Maximum recurring daily snapshots to be retained for a volume. If the limit is reached, snapshots from the start of the day are deleted so that newer ones can be saved. This limit does not apply to manual snapshots. If set to 0, recurring daily snapshots can not be scheduled
snapshot.max.weekly	Maximum recurring weekly snapshots to be retained for a volume. If the limit is reached, snapshots from the beginning of the week are deleted so that newer ones can be saved. This limit does not apply to manual snapshots. If set to 0, recurring weekly snapshots can not be scheduled
snapshot.max.monthly	Maximum recurring monthly snapshots to be retained for a volume. If the limit is reached, snapshots from the beginning of the month are deleted so that newer ones can be saved. This limit does not apply to manual snapshots. If set to 0, recurring monthly snapshots can not be scheduled.

To modify global configuration parameters, use the global configuration screen in the CloudStack UI. See Setting Global Configuration Parameters

Limiting Resource Usage

CloudStack allows you to control resource usage based on the types of resources, such as CPU, RAM, Primary storage, and Secondary storage. A new set of resource types has been added to the existing pool of resources to support the new customization model—need-basis usage, such as large VM or small VM. The new resource types are now broadly classified as CPU, RAM, Primary storage, and Secondary storage. The root administrator is able to impose resource usage limit by the following resource types for Domain, Project, and Accounts.

- CPUs
- Memory (RAM)
- Primary Storage (Volumes)
- Secondary Storage (Snapshots, Templates, ISOs)

To control the behaviour of this feature, the following configuration parameters have been added:

Parameter Name	Description
max.account.cpus	Maximum number of CPU cores that can be used for an account. Default is 40.
max.account.ram (MB)	Maximum RAM that can be used for an account. Default is 40960.
max.account.primary.storage (GB)	Maximum primary storage space that can be used for an account. Default is 200.
max.account.secondary.storage (GB)	Maximum secondary storage space that can be used for an account. Default is 400.
max.project.cpus	Maximum number of CPU cores that can be used for an account. Default is 40.
max.project.ram (MB)	Maximum RAM that can be used for an account. Default is 40960.
max.project.primary.storage (GB)	Maximum primary storage space that can be used for an account. Default is 200.
max.project.secondary.storage (GB)	Maximum secondary storage space that can be used for an account. Default is 400.

User Permission

The root administrator, domain administrators and users are able to list resources. Ensure that proper logs are maintained in the vmops.log and api.log files.

- The root admin will have the privilege to list and update resource limits.

- The domain administrators are allowed to list and change these resource limits only for the sub-domains and accounts under their own domain or the sub-domains.

- The end users will the privilege to list resource limits. Use the listResourceLimits API.

Limit Usage Considerations

- Primary or Secondary storage space refers to the stated size of the volume and not the physical size— the actual consumed size on disk in case of thin provisioning.

- If the admin reduces the resource limit for an account and set it to less than the resources that are currently being consumed, the existing VMs/templates/volumes are not destroyed. Limits are imposed only if the user under that account tries to execute a new operation using any of these resources. For example, the existing behavior in the case of a VM are:

    - migrateVirtualMachine: The users under that account will be able to migrate the running VM into any other host without facing any limit issue.

    - recoverVirtualMachine: Destroyed VMs cannot be recovered.

- For any resource type, if a domain has limit X, sub-domains or accounts under that domain can have there own limits. However, the sum of resource allocated to a sub-domain or accounts under the domain at any point of time should not exceed the value X.

    For example, if a domain has the CPU limit of 40 and the sub-domain D1 and account A1 can have limits of 30 each, but at any point of time the resource allocated to D1 and A1 should not exceed the limit of 40.

- If any operation needs to pass through two of more resource limit check, then the lower of 2 limits will be enforced, For example: if an account has the VM limit of 10 and CPU limit of 20, and a user under that account requests 5 VMs of 4 CPUs each. The user can deploy 5 more VMs because VM limit is 10. However, the user cannot deploy any more instances because the CPU limit has been exhausted.

Limiting Resource Usage in a Domain

CloudStack allows the configuration of limits on a domain basis. With a domain limit in place, all users still have their account limits. They are additionally limited, as a group, to not exceed the resource limits set on their domain. Domain limits aggregate the usage of all accounts in the domain as well as all the accounts in all the sub-domains of that domain. Limits set at the root domain level apply to the sum of resource usage by the accounts in all the domains and sub-domains below that root domain.

To set a domain limit:

1. Log in to the CloudStack UI.

2. In the left navigation tree, click Domains.

3. Select the domain you want to modify. The current domain limits are displayed.

   A value of -1 shows that there is no limit in place.

4. Click the Edit button

5. Edit the following as per your requirement:

   - Parameter Name

   - Description

   - Instance Limits

     The number of instances that can be used in a domain.

   - Public IP Limits

     The number of public IP addresses that can be used in a domain.

   - Volume Limits

     The number of disk volumes that can be created in a domain.

   - Snapshot Limits

     The number of snapshots that can be created in a domain.

   - Template Limits

     The number of templates that can be registered in a domain.

   - VPC limits

     The number of VPCs that can be created in a domain.

   - CPU limits

     The number of CPU cores that can be used for a domain.

   - Memory limits (MB)

     The number of RAM that can be used for a domain.

   - Primary Storage limits (GB)

     The primary storage space that can be used for a domain.

   - Secondary Storage limits (GB)

     The secondary storage space that can be used for a domain.

6. Click Apply.

Default Account Resource Limits

You can limit resource use by accounts. The default limits are set by using Global configuration parameters, and they affect all accounts within a cloud. The relevant parameters are those beginning with max.account, for example: max.account.snapshots.

To override a default limit for a particular account, set a per-account resource limit.

1. Log in to the CloudStack UI.

2. In the left navigation tree, click Accounts.

3. Select the account you want to modify. The current limits are displayed.

   A value of -1 shows that there is no limit in place.

4. Click the Edit button.

5. Edit the following as per your requirement:

   - Parameter Name

   - Description

   - Instance Limits

     The number of instances that can be used in an account.

     The default is 20.

   - Public IP Limits

     The number of public IP addresses that can be used in an account.

     The default is 20.

   - Volume Limits

     The number of disk volumes that can be created in an account.

     The default is 20.

   - Snapshot Limits

     The number of snapshots that can be created in an account.

     The default is 20.

   - Template Limits

     The number of templates that can be registered in an account.

     The default is 20.

   - VPC limits

     The number of VPCs that can be created in an account.

     The default is 20.

   - CPU limits

     The number of CPU cores that can be used for an account.

     The default is 40.

- Memory limits (MB)

  The number of RAM that can be used for an account.

  The default is 40960.
- Primary Storage limits (GB)

  The primary storage space that can be used for an account.

  The default is 200.
- Secondary Storage limits (GB)

  The secondary storage space that can be used for an account.

  The default is 400.

6. Click Apply.

11.1.3 Usage Record Format

Virtual Machine Usage Record Format

For running and allocated virtual machine usage, the following fields exist in a usage record:

- account – name of the account
- accountid – ID of the account
- domainid – ID of the domain in which this account resides
- zoneid – Zone where the usage occurred
- description – A string describing what the usage record is tracking
- usage – String representation of the usage, including the units of usage (e.g. 'Hrs' for VM running time)
- usagetype – A number representing the usage type (see Usage Types)
- rawusage – A number representing the actual usage in hours
- virtualMachineId – The ID of the virtual machine
- name – The name of the virtual machine
- offeringid – The ID of the service offering
- templateid – The ID of the template or the ID of the parent template. The parent template value is present when the current template was created from a volume.
- usageid – Virtual machine
- type – Hypervisor
- startdate, enddate – The range of time for which the usage is aggregated; see Dates in the Usage Record

Network Usage Record Format

For network usage (bytes sent/received), the following fields exist in a usage record.

- account – name of the account
- accountid – ID of the account
- domainid – ID of the domain in which this account resides

- zoneid – Zone where the usage occurred
- description – A string describing what the usage record is tracking
- usagetype – A number representing the usage type (see Usage Types)
- rawusage – A number representing the actual usage in hours
- usageid – Device ID (virtual router ID or external device ID)
- type – Device type (domain router, external load balancer, etc.)
- startdate, enddate – The range of time for which the usage is aggregated; see Dates in the Usage Record

IP Address Usage Record Format

For IP address usage the following fields exist in a usage record.

- account - name of the account
- accountid - ID of the account
- domainid - ID of the domain in which this account resides
- zoneid - Zone where the usage occurred
- description - A string describing what the usage record is tracking
- usage - String representation of the usage, including the units of usage
- usagetype - A number representing the usage type (see Usage Types)
- rawusage - A number representing the actual usage in hours
- usageid - IP address ID
- startdate, enddate - The range of time for which the usage is aggregated; see Dates in the Usage Record
- issourcenat - Whether source NAT is enabled for the IP address
- iselastic - True if the IP address is elastic.

Disk Volume Usage Record Format

For disk volumes, the following fields exist in a usage record.

- account – name of the account
- accountid – ID of the account
- domainid – ID of the domain in which this account resides
- zoneid – Zone where the usage occurred
- description – A string describing what the usage record is tracking
- usage – String representation of the usage, including the units of usage (e.g. 'Hrs' for hours)
- usagetype – A number representing the usage type (see Usage Types)
- rawusage – A number representing the actual usage in hours
- usageid – The volume ID
- offeringid – The ID of the disk offering
- type – Hypervisor

- templateid – ROOT template ID
- size – The amount of storage allocated
- startdate, enddate – The range of time for which the usage is aggregated; see Dates in the Usage Record

Template, ISO, and Snapshot Usage Record Format

- account – name of the account
- accountid – ID of the account
- domainid – ID of the domain in which this account resides
- zoneid – Zone where the usage occurred
- description – A string describing what the usage record is tracking
- usage – String representation of the usage, including the units of usage (e.g. 'Hrs' for hours)
- usagetype – A number representing the usage type (see Usage Types)
- rawusage – A number representing the actual usage in hours
- usageid – The ID of the the the template, ISO, or snapshot
- offeringid – The ID of the disk offering
- templateid – – Included only for templates (usage type 7). Source template ID.
- size – Size of the template, ISO, or snapshot
- startdate, enddate – The range of time for which the usage is aggregated; see Dates in the Usage Record

Load Balancer Policy or Port Forwarding Rule Usage Record Format

- account - name of the account
- accountid - ID of the account
- domainid - ID of the domain in which this account resides
- zoneid - Zone where the usage occurred
- description - A string describing what the usage record is tracking
- usage - String representation of the usage, including the units of usage (e.g. 'Hrs' for hours)
- usagetype - A number representing the usage type (see Usage Types)
- rawusage - A number representing the actual usage in hours
- usageid - ID of the load balancer policy or port forwarding rule
- usagetype - A number representing the usage type (see Usage Types)
- startdate, enddate - The range of time for which the usage is aggregated; see Dates in the Usage Record

Network Offering Usage Record Format

- account – name of the account
- accountid – ID of the account
- domainid – ID of the domain in which this account resides

- zoneid – Zone where the usage occurred
- description – A string describing what the usage record is tracking
- usage – String representation of the usage, including the units of usage (e.g. 'Hrs' for hours)
- usagetype – A number representing the usage type (see Usage Types)
- rawusage – A number representing the actual usage in hours
- usageid – ID of the network offering
- usagetype – A number representing the usage type (see Usage Types)
- offeringid – Network offering ID
- virtualMachineId – The ID of the virtual machine
- virtualMachineId – The ID of the virtual machine
- startdate, enddate – The range of time for which the usage is aggregated; see Dates in the Usage Record

VPN User Usage Record Format

- account – name of the account
- accountid – ID of the account
- domainid – ID of the domain in which this account resides
- zoneid – Zone where the usage occurred
- description – A string describing what the usage record is tracking
- usage – String representation of the usage, including the units of usage (e.g. 'Hrs' for hours)
- usagetype – A number representing the usage type (see Usage Types)
- rawusage – A number representing the actual usage in hours
- usageid – VPN user ID
- usagetype – A number representing the usage type (see Usage Types)
- startdate, enddate – The range of time for which the usage is aggregated; see Dates in the Usage Record

11.1.4 Usage Types

The following table shows all usage types.

Type ID	Type Name	Description
1	RUNNING_VM	Tracks the total running time of a VM per usage record period. If the VM is upgraded during the usage period, you will get a separate Usage Record for the new upgraded VM.
2	ALLO-CATED_VM	Tracks the total time the VM has been created to the time when it has been destroyed. This usage type is also useful in determining usage for specific templates such as Windows-based templates.
3	IP_ADDRESS	Tracks the public IP address owned by the account.
4	NET-WORK_BYTES_SENT	Tracks the total number of bytes sent by all the VMs for an account. Cloud.com does not currently track network traffic per VM.
5	NET-WORK_BYTES_RECEIVED	Tracks the total number of bytes received by all the VMs for an account. Cloud.com does not currently track network traffic per VM.
6	VOLUME	Tracks the total time a disk volume has been created to the time when it has been destroyed.
7	TEMPLATE	Tracks the total time a template (either created from a snapshot or uploaded to the cloud) has been created to the time it has been destroyed. The size of the template is also returned.
8	ISO	Tracks the total time an ISO has been uploaded to the time it has been removed from the cloud. The size of the ISO is also returned.
9	SNAPSHOT	Tracks the total time from when a snapshot has been created to the time it have been destroyed.
11	LOAD_BALANCER_POLICY	Tracks the total time a load balancer policy has been created to the time it has been removed. Cloud.com does not track whether a VM has been assigned to a policy.
12	PORT_FORWARDING_RULE	Tracks the time from when a port forwarding rule was created until the time it was removed.
13	NET-WORK_OFFERING	The time from when a network offering was assigned to a VM until it is removed.
14	VPN_USERS	The time from when a VPN user is created until it is removed.

11.1.5 Example response from listUsageRecords

All CloudStack API requests are submitted in the form of a HTTP GET/POST with an associated command and any parameters. A request is composed of the following whether in HTTP or HTTPS:

```
<listusagerecordsresponse>
   <count>1816</count>
   <usagerecord>
      <account>user5</account>
      <accountid>10004</accountid>
      <domainid>1</domainid>
      <zoneid>1</zoneid>
      <description>i-3-4-WC running time (ServiceOffering: 1) (Template: 3)</description>
      <usage>2.95288 Hrs</usage>
      <usagetype>1</usagetype>
      <rawusage>2.95288</rawusage>
      <virtualmachineid>4</virtualmachineid>
      <name>i-3-4-WC</name>
      <offeringid>1</offeringid>
      <templateid>3</templateid>
      <usageid>245554</usageid>
      <type>XenServer</type>
      <startdate>2009-09-15T00:00:00-0700</startdate>
      <enddate>2009-09-18T16:14:26-0700</enddate>
   </usagerecord>
```

```
    ... (1,815 more usage records)
</listusagerecordsresponse>
```

11.1.6 Dates in the Usage Record

Usage records include a start date and an end date. These dates define the period of time for which the raw usage number was calculated. If daily aggregation is used, the start date is midnight on the day in question and the end date is 23:59:59 on the day in question (with one exception; see below). A virtual machine could have been deployed at noon on that day, stopped at 6pm on that day, then started up again at 11pm. When usage is calculated on that day, there will be 7 hours of running VM usage (usage type 1) and 12 hours of allocated VM usage (usage type 2). If the same virtual machine runs for the entire next day, there will 24 hours of both running VM usage (type 1) and allocated VM usage (type 2).

Note: The start date is not the time a virtual machine was started, and the end date is not the time when a virtual machine was stopped. The start and end dates give the time range within which usage was calculated.

For network usage, the start date and end date again define the range in which the number of bytes transferred was calculated. If a user downloads 10 MB and uploads 1 MB in one day, there will be two records, one showing the 10 megabytes received and one showing the 1 megabyte sent.

There is one case where the start date and end date do not correspond to midnight and 11:59:59pm when daily aggregation is used. This occurs only for network usage records. When the usage server has more than one day's worth of unprocessed data, the old data will be included in the aggregation period. The start date in the usage record will show the date and time of the earliest event. For other types of usage, such as IP addresses and VMs, the old unprocessed data is not included in daily aggregation.

## CHAPTER 12

Managing Networks and Traffic

12.1 Managing Networks and Traffic

In a CloudStack, guest VMs can communicate with each other using shared infrastructure with the security and user perception that the guests have a private LAN. The CloudStack virtual router is the main component providing networking features for guest traffic.

12.1.1 Guest Traffic

A network can carry guest traffic only between VMs within one zone. Virtual machines in different zones cannot communicate with each other using their IP addresses; they must communicate with each other by routing through a public IP address.

See a typical guest traffic setup given below:

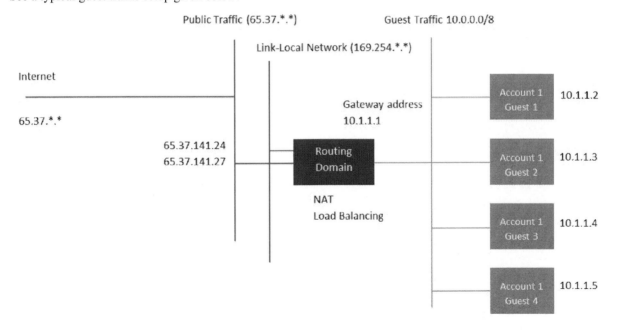

Guest Traffic Setup

Typically, the Management Server automatically creates a virtual router for each network. A virtual router is a special virtual machine that runs on the hosts. Each virtual router in an isolated network has three network interfaces. If multiple public VLAN is used, the router will have multiple public interfaces. Its eth0 interface serves as the gateway for the guest traffic and has the IP address of 10.1.1.1. Its eth1 interface is used by the system to configure the virtual router. Its eth2 interface is assigned a public IP address for public traffic. If multiple public VLAN is used, the router will have multiple public interfaces.

The virtual router provides DHCP and will automatically assign an IP address for each guest VM within the IP range assigned for the network. The user can manually reconfigure guest VMs to assume different IP addresses.

Source NAT is automatically configured in the virtual router to forward outbound traffic for all guest VMs

12.1.2 Networking in a Pod

The figure below illustrates network setup within a single pod. The hosts are connected to a pod-level switch. At a minimum, the hosts should have one physical uplink to each switch. Bonded NICs are supported as well. The pod-level switch is a pair of redundant gigabit switches with 10 G uplinks.

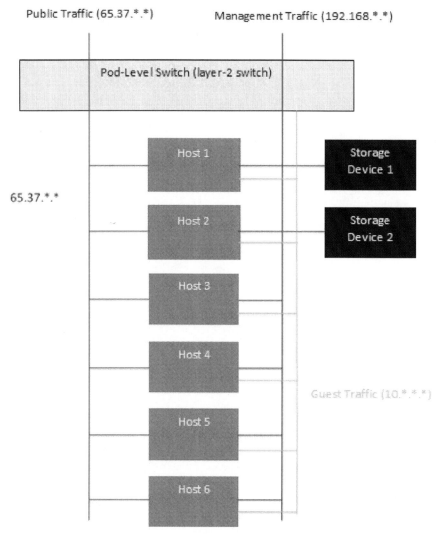

Network Setup within a Single Pod – Logical View

Servers are connected as follows:

- Storage devices are connected to only the network that carries management traffic.

- Hosts are connected to networks for both management traffic and public traffic.

- Hosts are also connected to one or more networks carrying guest traffic.

We recommend the use of multiple physical Ethernet cards to implement each network interface as well as redundant switch fabric in order to maximize throughput and improve reliability.

12.1.3 Networking in a Zone

The following figure illustrates the network setup within a single zone.

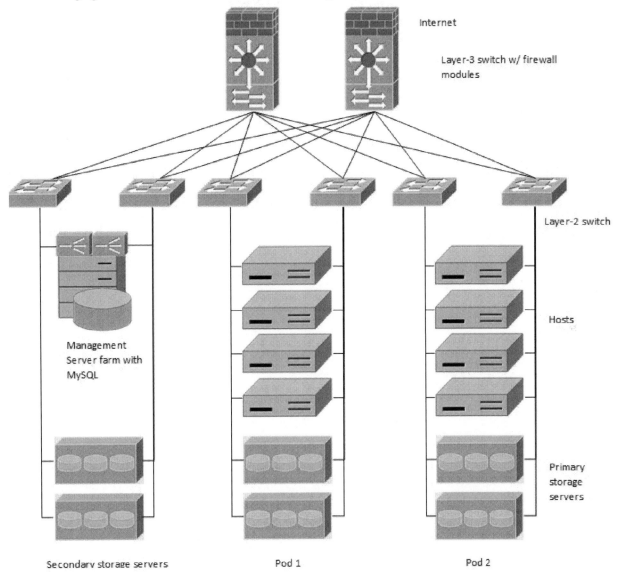

A firewall for management traffic operates in the NAT mode. The network typically is assigned IP addresses in the 192.168.0.0/16 Class B private address space. Each pod is assigned IP addresses in the 192.168.*.0/24 Class C private address space.

Each zone has its own set of public IP addresses. Public IP addresses from different zones do not overlap.

12.1.4 Basic Zone Physical Network Configuration

In a basic network, configuring the physical network is fairly straightforward. You only need to configure one guest network to carry traffic that is generated by guest VMs. When you first add a zone to CloudStack, you set up the guest network through the Add Zone screens.

12.1.5 Advanced Zone Physical Network Configuration

Within a zone that uses advanced networking, you need to tell the Management Server how the physical network is set up to carry different kinds of traffic in isolation.

Configure Guest Traffic in an Advanced Zone

These steps assume you have already logged in to the CloudStack UI. To configure the base guest network:

1. In the left navigation, choose Infrastructure. On Zones, click View More, then click the zone to which you want to add a network.

2. Click the Network tab.

3. Click Add guest network.

   The Add guest network window is displayed:

   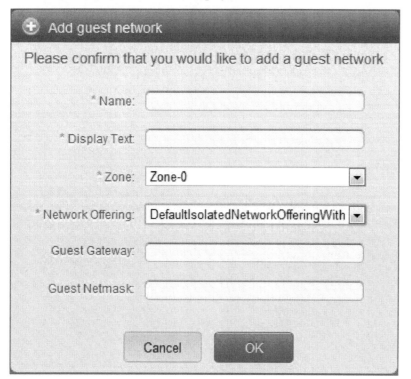

4. Provide the following information:

   - **Name**: The name of the network. This will be user-visible

   - **Display Text**: The description of the network. This will be user-visible

   - **Zone**: The zone in which you are configuring the guest network.

- **Network offering**: If the administrator has configured multiple network offerings, select the one you want to use for this network
- **Guest Gateway**: The gateway that the guests should use
- **Guest Netmask**: The netmask in use on the subnet the guests will use

5. Click OK.

Configure Public Traffic in an Advanced Zone

In a zone that uses advanced networking, you need to configure at least one range of IP addresses for Internet traffic.

Configuring a Shared Guest Network

1. Log in to the CloudStack UI as administrator.
2. In the left navigation, choose Infrastructure.
3. On Zones, click View More.
4. Click the zone to which you want to add a guest network.
5. Click the Physical Network tab.
6. Click the physical network you want to work with.
7. On the Guest node of the diagram, click Configure.
8. Click the Network tab.
9. Click Add guest network.

    The Add guest network window is displayed.

10. Specify the following:

    - **Name**: The name of the network. This will be visible to the user.
    - **Description**: The short description of the network that can be displayed to users.
    - **VLAN ID**: The unique ID of the VLAN.
    - **Isolated VLAN ID**: The unique ID of the Secondary Isolated VLAN.
    - **Scope**: The available scopes are Domain, Account, Project, and All.

        - **Domain**: Selecting Domain limits the scope of this guest network to the domain you specify. The network will not be available for other domains. If you select Subdomain Access, the guest network is available to all the sub domains within the selected domain.
        - **Account**: The account for which the guest network is being created for. You must specify the domain the account belongs to.
        - **Project**: The project for which the guest network is being created for. You must specify the domain the project belongs to.
        - **All**: The guest network is available for all the domains, account, projects within the selected zone.

    - **Network Offering**: If the administrator has configured multiple network offerings, select the one you want to use for this network.
    - **Gateway**: The gateway that the guests should use.
    - **Netmask**: The netmask in use on the subnet the guests will use.

- **IP Range**: A range of IP addresses that are accessible from the Internet and are assigned to the guest VMs. If one NIC is used, these IPs should be in the same CIDR in the case of IPv6.

- **IPv6 CIDR**: The network prefix that defines the guest network subnet. This is the CIDR that describes the IPv6 addresses in use in the guest networks in this zone. To allot IP addresses from within a particular address block, enter a CIDR.

- **Network Domain**: A custom DNS suffix at the level of a network. If you want to assign a special domain name to the guest VM network, specify a DNS suffix.

11. Click OK to confirm.

12.1.6 Using Multiple Guest Networks

In zones that use advanced networking, additional networks for guest traffic may be added at any time after the initial installation. You can also customize the domain name associated with the network by specifying a DNS suffix for each network.

A VM's networks are defined at VM creation time. A VM cannot add or remove networks after it has been created, although the user can go into the guest and remove the IP address from the NIC on a particular network.

Each VM has just one default network. The virtual router's DHCP reply will set the guest's default gateway as that for the default network. Multiple non-default networks may be added to a guest in addition to the single, required default network. The administrator can control which networks are available as the default network.

Additional networks can either be available to all accounts or be assigned to a specific account. Networks that are available to all accounts are zone-wide. Any user with access to the zone can create a VM with access to that network. These zone-wide networks provide little or no isolation between guests.Networks that are assigned to a specific account provide strong isolation.

Adding an Additional Guest Network

1. Log in to the CloudStack UI as an administrator or end user.

2. In the left navigation, choose Network.

3. Click Add guest network. Provide the following information:

   - **Name**: The name of the network. This will be user-visible.

   - **Display Text**: The description of the network. This will be user-visible.

   - **Zone**. The name of the zone this network applies to. Each zone is a broadcast domain, and therefore each zone has a different IP range for the guest network. The administrator must configure the IP range for each zone.

   - **Network offering**: If the administrator has configured multiple network offerings, select the one you want to use for this network.

   - **Guest Gateway**: The gateway that the guests should use.

   - **Guest Netmask**: The netmask in use on the subnet the guests will use.

4. Click Create.

Reconfiguring Networks in VMs

CloudStack provides you the ability to move VMs between networks and reconfigure a VM's network. You can remove a VM from a network and add to a new network. You can also change the default network of a virtual machine. With this functionality, hybrid or traditional server loads can be accommodated with ease.

This feature is supported on XenServer, VMware, and KVM hypervisors.

Prerequisites

Ensure that vm-tools are running on guest VMs for adding or removing networks to work on VMware hypervisor.

Adding a Network

1. Log in to the CloudStack UI as an administrator or end user.

2. In the left navigation, click Instances.

3. Choose the VM that you want to work with.

4. Click the NICs tab.

5. Click Add network to VM.

   The Add network to VM dialog is displayed.

6. In the drop-down list, select the network that you would like to add this VM to.

   A new NIC is added for this network. You can view the following details in the NICs page:

   - ID
   - Network Name
   - Type
   - IP Address
   - Gateway
   - Netmask
   - Is default
   - CIDR (for IPv6)

Removing a Network

1. Log in to the CloudStack UI as an administrator or end user.

2. In the left navigation, click Instances.

3. Choose the VM that you want to work with.

4. Click the NICs tab.

5. Locate the NIC you want to remove.

6. Click Remove NIC button.

7. Click Yes to confirm.

Selecting the Default Network

1. Log in to the CloudStack UI as an administrator or end user.

2. In the left navigation, click Instances.

3. Choose the VM that you want to work with.

4. Click the NICs tab.

5. Locate the NIC you want to work with.

6. Click the Set default NIC button. .

7. Click Yes to confirm.

Changing the Network Offering on a Guest Network

A user or administrator can change the network offering that is associated with an existing guest network.

1. Log in to the CloudStack UI as an administrator or end user.

2. If you are changing from a network offering that uses the CloudStack virtual router to one that uses external devices as network service providers, you must first stop all the VMs on the network.

3. In the left navigation, choose Network.

4. Click the name of the network you want to modify.

5. In the Details tab, click Edit.

6. In Network Offering, choose the new network offering, then click Apply.

   A prompt is displayed asking whether you want to keep the existing CIDR. This is to let you know that if you change the network offering, the CIDR will be affected.

   If you upgrade between virtual router as a provider and an external network device as provider, acknowledge the change of CIDR to continue, so choose Yes.

7. Wait for the update to complete. Don't try to restart VMs until the network change is complete.

8. If you stopped any VMs, restart them.

12.1.7 IP Reservation in Isolated Guest Networks

In isolated guest networks, a part of the guest IP address space can be reserved for non-CloudStack VMs or physical servers. To do so, you configure a range of Reserved IP addresses by specifying the CIDR when a guest network is in Implemented state. If your customers wish to have non-CloudStack controlled VMs or physical servers on the same network, they can share a part of the IP address space that is primarily provided to the guest network.

In an Advanced zone, an IP address range or a CIDR is assigned to a network when the network is defined. The CloudStack virtual router acts as the DHCP server and uses CIDR for assigning IP addresses to the guest VMs. If you decide to reserve CIDR for non-CloudStack purposes, you can specify a part of the IP address range or the CIDR that should only be allocated by the DHCP service of the virtual router to the guest VMs created in CloudStack. The remaining IPs in that network are called Reserved IP Range. When IP reservation is configured, the administrator can add additional VMs or physical servers that are not part of CloudStack to the same network and assign them the Reserved IP addresses. CloudStack guest VMs cannot acquire IPs from the Reserved IP Range.

IP Reservation Considerations

Consider the following before you reserve an IP range for non-CloudStack machines:

- IP Reservation is supported only in Isolated networks.

- IP Reservation can be applied only when the network is in Implemented state.

- No IP Reservation is done by default.

- Guest VM CIDR you specify must be a subset of the network CIDR.

- Specify a valid Guest VM CIDR. IP Reservation is applied only if no active IPs exist outside the Guest VM CIDR.

  You cannot apply IP Reservation if any VM is alloted with an IP address that is outside the Guest VM CIDR.

- To reset an existing IP Reservation, apply IP reservation by specifying the value of network CIDR in the CIDR field.

  For example, the following table describes three scenarios of guest network creation:

Case	CIDR	Network CIDR	Reserved IP Range for Non-CloudStack VMs	Description
1	10.1.1.0/24	None	None	No IP Reservation.
2	10.1.1.0/24	10.1.1.0/26	10.1.1.64 to 10.1.1.254	IP Reservation configured by the UpdateNetwork API with guestvmcidr=10.1.1.0/26 or enter 10.1.1.0/26 in the CIDR field in the UI.
3	10.1.1.0/24	None	None	Removing IP Reservation by the UpdateNetwork API with guestvmcidr=10.1.1.0/24 or enter 10.1.1.0/24 in the CIDR field in the UI.

Limitations

- The IP Reservation is not supported if active IPs that are found outside the Guest VM CIDR.

- Upgrading network offering which causes a change in CIDR (such as upgrading an offering with no external devices to one with external devices) IP Reservation becomes void if any. Reconfigure IP Reservation in the new re-implemeted network.

Best Practices

Apply IP Reservation to the guest network as soon as the network state changes to Implemented. If you apply reservation soon after the first guest VM is deployed, lesser conflicts occurs while applying reservation.

Reserving an IP Range

1. Log in to the CloudStack UI as an administrator or end user.

2. In the left navigation, choose Network.

3. Click the name of the network you want to modify.

4. In the Details tab, click Edit.

   The CIDR field changes to editable one.

5. In CIDR, specify the Guest VM CIDR.

6. Click Apply.

    Wait for the update to complete. The Network CIDR and the Reserved IP Range are displayed on the Details page.

12.1.8 Reserving Public IP Addresses and VLANs for Accounts

CloudStack provides you the ability to reserve a set of public IP addresses and VLANs exclusively for an account. During zone creation, you can continue defining a set of VLANs and multiple public IP ranges. This feature extends the functionality to enable you to dedicate a fixed set of VLANs and guest IP addresses for a tenant.

Note that if an account has consumed all the VLANs and IPs dedicated to it, the account can acquire two more resources from the system. CloudStack provides the root admin with two configuration parameter to modify this default behavior: use.system.public.ips and use.system.guest.vlans. These global parameters enable the root admin to disallow an account from acquiring public IPs and guest VLANs from the system, if the account has dedicated resources and these dedicated resources have all been consumed. Both these configurations are configurable at the account level.

This feature provides you the following capabilities:

- Reserve a VLAN range and public IP address range from an Advanced zone and assign it to an account

- Disassociate a VLAN and public IP address range from an account

- View the number of public IP addresses allocated to an account

- Check whether the required range is available and is conforms to account limits.

    The maximum IPs per account limit cannot be superseded.

Dedicating IP Address Ranges to an Account

1. Log in to the CloudStack UI as administrator.

2. In the left navigation bar, click Infrastructure.

3. In Zones, click View All.

4. Choose the zone you want to work with.

5. Click the Physical Network tab.

6. In the Public node of the diagram, click Configure.

7. Click the IP Ranges tab.

    You can either assign an existing IP range to an account, or create a new IP range and assign to an account.

8. To assign an existing IP range to an account, perform the following:

    (a) Locate the IP range you want to work with.

    (b) Click Add Account ![icon] button.

        The Add Account dialog is displayed.

    (c) Specify the following:

        - **Account**: The account to which you want to assign the IP address range.

        - **Domain**: The domain associated with the account.

To create a new IP range and assign an account, perform the following:

i. Specify the following:

- **Gateway**
- **Netmask**
- **VLAN**
- **Start IP**
- **End IP**
- **Account**: Perform the following:

  A. Click Account.

     The Add Account page is displayed.

  B. Specify the following:

     – **Account**: The account to which you want to assign an IP address range.

     – **Domain**: The domain associated with the account.

  C. Click OK.

ii. Click Add.

Dedicating VLAN Ranges to an Account

1. After the CloudStack Management Server is installed, log in to the CloudStack UI as administrator.
2. In the left navigation bar, click Infrastructure.
3. In Zones, click View All.
4. Choose the zone you want to work with.
5. Click the Physical Network tab.
6. In the Guest node of the diagram, click Configure.
7. Select the Dedicated VLAN Ranges tab.
8. Click Dedicate VLAN Range.

   The Dedicate VLAN Range dialog is displayed.

9. Specify the following:

- **VLAN Range**: The VLAN range that you want to assign to an account.
- **Account**: The account to which you want to assign the selected VLAN range.
- **Domain**: The domain associated with the account.

12.1.9 Configuring Multiple IP Addresses on a Single NIC

CloudStack provides you the ability to associate multiple private IP addresses per guest VM NIC. In addition to the primary IP, you can assign additional IPs to the guest VM NIC. This feature is supported on all the network configurations: Basic, Advanced, and VPC. Security Groups, Static NAT and Port forwarding services are supported on these additional IPs.

As always, you can specify an IP from the guest subnet; if not specified, an IP is automatically picked up from the guest VM subnet. You can view the IPs associated with for each guest VM NICs on the UI. You can apply NAT on these additional guest IPs by using network configuration option in the CloudStack UI. You must specify the NIC to which the IP should be associated.

This feature is supported on XenServer, KVM, and VMware hypervisors. Note that Basic zone security groups are not supported on VMware.

Use Cases

Some of the use cases are described below:

- Network devices, such as firewalls and load balancers, generally work best when they have access to multiple IP addresses on the network interface.

- Moving private IP addresses between interfaces or instances. Applications that are bound to specific IP addresses can be moved between instances.

- Hosting multiple SSL Websites on a single instance. You can install multiple SSL certificates on a single instance, each associated with a distinct IP address.

Guidelines

To prevent IP conflict, configure different subnets when multiple networks are connected to the same VM.

Assigning Additional IPs to a VM

1. Log in to the CloudStack UI.

2. In the left navigation bar, click Instances.

3. Click the name of the instance you want to work with.

4. In the Details tab, click NICs.

5. Click View Secondary IPs.

6. Click Acquire New Secondary IP, and click Yes in the confirmation dialog.

   You need to configure the IP on the guest VM NIC manually. CloudStack will not automatically configure the acquired IP address on the VM. Ensure that the IP address configuration persist on VM reboot.

   Within a few moments, the new IP address should appear with the state Allocated. You can now use the IP address in Port Forwarding or StaticNAT rules.

Port Forwarding and StaticNAT Services Changes

Because multiple IPs can be associated per NIC, you are allowed to select a desired IP for the Port Forwarding and StaticNAT services. The default is the primary IP. To enable this functionality, an extra optional parameter 'vmguestip' is added to the Port forwarding and StaticNAT APIs (enableStaticNat, createIpForwardingRule) to indicate on what IP address NAT need to be configured. If vmguestip is passed, NAT is configured on the specified private IP of the VM. if not passed, NAT is configured on the primary IP of the VM.

12.1.10 About Multiple IP Ranges

Note: The feature can only be implemented on IPv4 addresses.

CloudStack provides you with the flexibility to add guest IP ranges from different subnets in Basic zones and security groups-enabled Advanced zones. For security groups-enabled Advanced zones, it implies multiple subnets can be added to the same VLAN. With the addition of this feature, you will be able to add IP address ranges from the same subnet or from a different one when IP address are exhausted. This would in turn allows you to employ higher number of subnets and thus reduce the address management overhead. To support this feature, the capability of createVlanIpRange API is extended to add IP ranges also from a different subnet.

Ensure that you manually configure the gateway of the new subnet before adding the IP range. Note that CloudStack supports only one gateway for a subnet; overlapping subnets are not currently supported.

Use the deleteVlanRange API to delete IP ranges. This operation fails if an IP from the remove range is in use. If the remove range contains the IP address on which the DHCP server is running, CloudStack acquires a new IP from the same subnet. If no IP is available in the subnet, the remove operation fails.

This feature is supported on KVM, xenServer, and VMware hypervisors.

12.1.11 About Elastic IPs

Elastic IP (EIP) addresses are the IP addresses that are associated with an account, and act as static IP addresses. The account owner has the complete control over the Elastic IP addresses that belong to the account. As an account owner, you can allocate an Elastic IP to a VM of your choice from the EIP pool of your account. Later if required you can reassign the IP address to a different VM. This feature is extremely helpful during VM failure. Instead of replacing the VM which is down, the IP address can be reassigned to a new VM in your account.

Similar to the public IP address, Elastic IP addresses are mapped to their associated private IP addresses by using StaticNAT. The EIP service is equipped with StaticNAT (1:1) service in an EIP-enabled basic zone. The default network offering, DefaultSharedNetscalerEIPandELBNetworkOffering, provides your network with EIP and ELB network services if a NetScaler device is deployed in your zone. Consider the following illustration for more details.

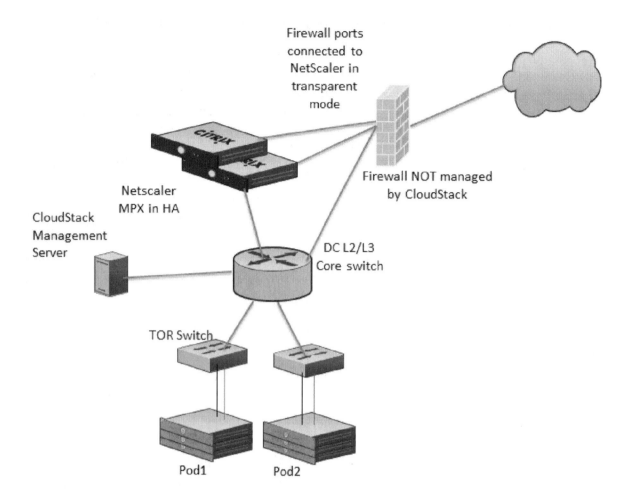

In the illustration, a NetScaler appliance is the default entry or exit point for the CloudStack instances, and firewall is the default entry or exit point for the rest of the data center. Netscaler provides LB services and staticNAT service to the guest networks. The guest traffic in the pods and the Management Server are on different subnets / VLANs. The policy-based routing in the data center core switch sends the public traffic through the NetScaler, whereas the rest of the data center goes through the firewall.

The EIP work flow is as follows:

- When a user VM is deployed, a public IP is automatically acquired from the pool of public IPs configured in the zone. This IP is owned by the VM's account.

- Each VM will have its own private IP. When the user VM starts, Static NAT is provisioned on the NetScaler device by using the Inbound Network Address Translation (INAT) and Reverse NAT (RNAT) rules between the public IP and the private IP.

Note: Inbound NAT (INAT) is a type of NAT supported by NetScaler, in which the destination IP address is replaced in the packets from the public network, such as the Internet, with the private IP address of a VM in the private network. Reverse NAT (RNAT) is a type of NAT supported by NetScaler, in which the source IP address is replaced in the packets generated by a VM in the private network with the public IP address.

- This default public IP will be released in two cases:

  - When the VM is stopped. When the VM starts, it again receives a new public IP, not necessarily the same one allocated initially, from the pool of Public IPs.

– The user acquires a public IP (Elastic IP). This public IP is associated with the account, but will not be mapped to any private IP. However, the user can enable Static NAT to associate this IP to the private IP of a VM in the account. The Static NAT rule for the public IP can be disabled at any time. When Static NAT is disabled, a new public IP is allocated from the pool, which is not necessarily be the same one allocated initially.

For the deployments where public IPs are limited resources, you have the flexibility to choose not to allocate a public IP by default. You can use the Associate Public IP option to turn on or off the automatic public IP assignment in the EIP-enabled Basic zones. If you turn off the automatic public IP assignment while creating a network offering, only a private IP is assigned to a VM when the VM is deployed with that network offering. Later, the user can acquire an IP for the VM and enable static NAT.

For more information on the Associate Public IP option, see "Creating a New Network Offering".

Note: The Associate Public IP feature is designed only for use with user VMs. The System VMs continue to get both public IP and private by default, irrespective of the network offering configuration.

New deployments which use the default shared network offering with EIP and ELB services to create a shared network in the Basic zone will continue allocating public IPs to each user VM.

12.1.12 Portable IPs

About Portable IP

Portable IPs in CloudStack are region-level pool of IPs, which are elastic in nature, that can be transferred across geographically separated zones. As an administrator, you can provision a pool of portable public IPs at region level and are available for user consumption. The users can acquire portable IPs if admin has provisioned portable IPs at the region level they are part of. These IPs can be use for any service within an advanced zone. You can also use portable IPs for EIP services in basic zones.

The salient features of Portable IP are as follows:

- IP is statically allocated
- IP need not be associated with a network
- IP association is transferable across networks
- IP is transferable across both Basic and Advanced zones
- IP is transferable across VPC, non-VPC isolated and shared networks
- Portable IP transfer is available only for static NAT.

Guidelines

Before transferring to another network, ensure that no network rules (Firewall, Static NAT, Port Forwarding, and so on) exist on that portable IP.

Configuring Portable IPs

1. Log in to the CloudStack UI as an administrator or end user.
2. In the left navigation, click Regions.
3. Choose the Regions that you want to work with.

4. Click View Portable IP.

5. Click Portable IP Range.

   The Add Portable IP Range window is displayed.

6. Specify the following:

   • **Start IP/ End IP**: A range of IP addresses that are accessible from the Internet and will be allocated to guest VMs. Enter the first and last IP addresses that define a range that CloudStack can assign to guest VMs.

   • **Gateway**: The gateway in use for the Portable IP addresses you are configuring.

   • **Netmask**: The netmask associated with the Portable IP range.

   • **VLAN**: The VLAN that will be used for public traffic.

7. Click OK.

Acquiring a Portable IP

1. Log in to the CloudStack UI as an administrator or end user.

2. In the left navigation, choose Network.

3. Click the name of the network where you want to work with.

4. Click View IP Addresses.

5. Click Acquire New IP.

   The Acquire New IP window is displayed.

6. Specify whether you want cross-zone IP or not.

7. Click Yes in the confirmation dialog.

   Within a few moments, the new IP address should appear with the state Allocated. You can now use the IP address in port forwarding or static NAT rules.

Transferring Portable IP

An IP can be transferred from one network to another only if Static NAT is enabled. However, when a portable IP is associated with a network, you can use it for any service in the network.

To transfer a portable IP across the networks, execute the following API:

```
http://localhost:8096/client/api?command=enableStaticNat&response=json&ipaddressid=a4bc
```

Replace the UUID with appropriate UUID. For example, if you want to transfer a portable IP to network X and VM Y in a network, execute the following:

```
http://localhost:8096/client/api?command=enableStaticNat&response=json&ipaddressid=a4bc
```

12.1.13 Multiple Subnets in Shared Network

CloudStack provides you with the flexibility to add guest IP ranges from different subnets in Basic zones and security groups-enabled Advanced zones. For security groups-enabled Advanced zones, it implies multiple subnets can be added to the same VLAN. With the addition of this feature, you will be able to add IP address ranges from the same subnet or from a different one when IP address are exhausted. This would in turn allows you to employ higher number of subnets and thus reduce the address management overhead. You can delete the IP ranges you have added.

Prerequisites and Guidelines

- This feature can only be implemented:
    - on IPv4 addresses
    - if virtual router is the DHCP provider
    - on KVM, xenServer, and VMware hypervisors
- Manually configure the gateway of the new subnet before adding the IP range.
- CloudStack supports only one gateway for a subnet; overlapping subnets are not currently supported

Adding Multiple Subnets to a Shared Network

1. Log in to the CloudStack UI as an administrator or end user.
2. In the left navigation, choose Infrastructure.
3. On Zones, click View More, then click the zone to which you want to work with..
4. Click Physical Network.
5. In the Guest node of the diagram, click Configure.
6. Click Networks.
7. Select the networks you want to work with.
8. Click View IP Ranges.
9. Click Add IP Range.

    The Add IP Range dialog is displayed, as follows:

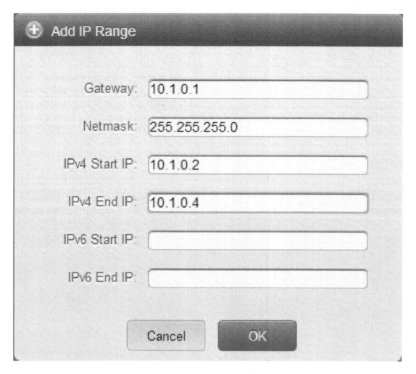

10. Specify the following:

    All the fields are mandatory.

    - **Gateway**: The gateway for the tier you create. Ensure that the gateway is within the Super CIDR range that you specified while creating the VPC, and is not overlapped with the CIDR of any existing tier within the VPC.

    - **Netmask**: The netmask for the tier you create.

      For example, if the VPC CIDR is 10.0.0.0/16 and the network tier CIDR is 10.0.1.0/24, the gateway of the tier is 10.0.1.1, and the netmask of the tier is 255.255.255.0.

    - **Start IP/ End IP**: A range of IP addresses that are accessible from the Internet and will be allocated to guest VMs. Enter the first and last IP addresses that define a range that CloudStack can assign to guest VMs .

11. Click OK.

12.1.14 Isolation in Advanced Zone Using Private VLAN

Isolation of guest traffic in shared networks can be achieved by using Private VLANs (PVLAN). PVLANs provide Layer 2 isolation between ports within the same VLAN. In a PVLAN-enabled shared network, a user VM cannot reach other user VM though they can reach the DHCP server and gateway, this would in turn allow users to control traffic within a network and help them deploy multiple applications without communication between application as well as prevent communication with other users' VMs.

- Isolate VMs in a shared networks by using Private VLANs.

- Supported on KVM, XenServer, and VMware hypervisors

- PVLAN-enabled shared network can be a part of multiple networks of a guest VM.

About Private VLAN

In an Ethernet switch, a VLAN is a broadcast domain where hosts can establish direct communication with each another at Layer 2. Private VLAN is designed as an extension of VLAN standard to add further segmentation of the logical broadcast domain. A regular VLAN is a single broadcast domain, whereas a private VLAN partitions a larger VLAN broadcast domain into smaller sub-domains. A sub-domain is represented by a pair of VLANs: a Primary VLAN and a Secondary VLAN. The original VLAN that is being divided into smaller groups is called Primary, which implies that all VLAN pairs in a private VLAN share the same Primary VLAN. All the secondary VLANs exist only inside the Primary. Each Secondary VLAN has a specific VLAN ID associated to it, which differentiates one sub-domain from another.

Three types of ports exist in a private VLAN domain, which essentially determine the behaviour of the participating hosts. Each ports will have its own unique set of rules, which regulate a connected host's ability to communicate with other connected host within the same private VLAN domain. Configure each host that is part of a PVLAN pair can be by using one of these three port designation:

- **Promiscuous**: A promiscuous port can communicate with all the interfaces, including the community and isolated host ports that belong to the secondary VLANs. In Promiscuous mode, hosts are connected to promiscuous ports and are able to communicate directly with resources on both primary and secondary VLAN. Routers, DHCP servers, and other trusted devices are typically attached to promiscuous ports.

- **Isolated VLANs**: The ports within an isolated VLAN cannot communicate with each other at the layer-2 level. The hosts that are connected to Isolated ports can directly communicate only with the Promiscuous resources. If your customer device needs to have access only to a gateway router, attach it to an isolated port.

- **Community VLANs**: The ports within a community VLAN can communicate with each other and with the promiscuous ports, but they cannot communicate with the ports in other communities at the layer-2 level. In a Community mode, direct communication is permitted only with the hosts in the same community and those that are connected to the Primary PVLAN in promiscuous mode. If your customer has two devices that need to be isolated from other customers' devices, but to be able to communicate among themselves, deploy them in community ports.

For further reading:

- Understanding Private VLANs

- Cisco Systems' Private VLANs: Scalable Security in a Multi-Client Environment

- Private VLAN (PVLAN) on vNetwork Distributed Switch - Concept Overview (1010691)

Prerequisites

- Use a PVLAN supported switch.

  See Private VLAN Catalyst Switch Support Matrix for more information.

- All the layer 2 switches, which are PVLAN-aware, are connected to each other, and one of them is connected to a router. All the ports connected to the host would be configured in trunk mode. Open Management VLAN, Primary VLAN (public) and Secondary Isolated VLAN ports. Configure the switch port connected to the router in PVLAN promiscuous trunk mode, which would translate an isolated VLAN to primary VLAN for the PVLAN-unaware router.

  Note that only Cisco Catalyst 4500 has the PVLAN promiscuous trunk mode to connect both normal VLAN and PVLAN to a PVLAN-unaware switch. For the other Catalyst PVLAN support switch, connect the switch to upper switch by using cables, one each for a PVLAN pair.

- Configure private VLAN on your physical switches out-of-band.

- Before you use PVLAN on XenServer and KVM, enable Open vSwitch (OVS).

> **Note:** OVS on XenServer and KVM does not support PVLAN natively. Therefore, CloudStack managed to simulate PVLAN on OVS for XenServer and KVM by modifying the flow table.

Creating a PVLAN-Enabled Guest Network

1. Log in to the CloudStack UI as administrator.

2. In the left navigation, choose Infrastructure.

3. On Zones, click View More.

4. Click the zone to which you want to add a guest network.

5. Click the Physical Network tab.

6. Click the physical network you want to work with.

7. On the Guest node of the diagram, click Configure.

8. Click the Network tab.

9. Click Add guest network.

   The Add guest network window is displayed.

10. Specify the following:

    - **Name**: The name of the network. This will be visible to the user.

    - **Description**: The short description of the network that can be displayed to users.

    - **VLAN ID**: The unique ID of the VLAN.

    - **Secondary Isolated VLAN ID**: The unique ID of the Secondary Isolated VLAN.

      For the description on Secondary Isolated VLAN, see *About Private VLAN"*.

    - **Scope**: The available scopes are Domain, Account, Project, and All.

      - **Domain**: Selecting Domain limits the scope of this guest network to the domain you specify. The network will not be available for other domains. If you select Subdomain Access, the guest network is available to all the sub domains within the selected domain.

      - **Account**: The account for which the guest network is being created for. You must specify the domain the account belongs to.

      - **Project**: The project for which the guest network is being created for. You must specify the domain the project belongs to.

      - **All**: The guest network is available for all the domains, account, projects within the selected zone.

    - **Network Offering**: If the administrator has configured multiple network offerings, select the one you want to use for this network.

    - **Gateway**: The gateway that the guests should use.

    - **Netmask**: The netmask in use on the subnet the guests will use.

    - **IP Range**: A range of IP addresses that are accessible from the Internet and are assigned to the guest VMs.

    - **Network Domain**: A custom DNS suffix at the level of a network. If you want to assign a special domain name to the guest VM network, specify a DNS suffix.

11. Click OK to confirm.

12.1.15 Security Groups

About Security Groups

Security groups provide a way to isolate traffic to VMs. A security group is a group of VMs that filter their incoming and outgoing traffic according to a set of rules, called ingress and egress rules. These rules filter network traffic according to the IP address that is attempting to communicate with the VM. Security groups are particularly useful in zones that use basic networking, because there is a single guest network for all guest VMs. In advanced zones, security groups are supported only on the KVM hypervisor.

Note: In a zone that uses advanced networking, you can instead define multiple guest networks to isolate traffic to VMs.

Each CloudStack account comes with a default security group that denies all inbound traffic and allows all outbound traffic. The default security group can be modified so that all new VMs inherit some other desired set of rules.

Any CloudStack user can set up any number of additional security groups. When a new VM is launched, it is assigned to the default security group unless another user-defined security group is specified. A VM can be a member of any number of security groups. Once a VM is assigned to a security group, it remains in that group for its entire lifetime; you can not move a running VM from one security group to another.

You can modify a security group by deleting or adding any number of ingress and egress rules. When you do, the new rules apply to all VMs in the group, whether running or stopped.

If no ingress rules are specified, then no traffic will be allowed in, except for responses to any traffic that has been allowed out through an egress rule.

Adding a Security Group

A user or administrator can define a new security group.

1. Log in to the CloudStack UI as an administrator or end user.

2. In the left navigation, choose Network.

3. In Select view, choose Security Groups.

4. Click Add Security Group.

5. Provide a name and description.

6. Click OK.

   The new security group appears in the Security Groups Details tab.

7. To make the security group useful, continue to Adding Ingress and Egress Rules to a Security Group.

Security Groups in Advanced Zones (KVM Only)

CloudStack provides the ability to use security groups to provide isolation between guests on a single shared, zone-wide network in an advanced zone where KVM is the hypervisor. Using security groups in advanced zones rather than multiple VLANs allows a greater range of options for setting up guest isolation in a cloud.

Limitations

The following are not supported for this feature:

- Two IP ranges with the same VLAN and different gateway or netmask in security group-enabled shared network.
- Two IP ranges with the same VLAN and different gateway or netmask in account-specific shared networks.
- Multiple VLAN ranges in security group-enabled shared network.
- Multiple VLAN ranges in account-specific shared networks.

Security groups must be enabled in the zone in order for this feature to be used.

Enabling Security Groups

In order for security groups to function in a zone, the security groups feature must first be enabled for the zone. The administrator can do this when creating a new zone, by selecting a network offering that includes security groups. The procedure is described in Basic Zone Configuration in the Advanced Installation Guide. The administrator can not enable security groups for an existing zone, only when creating a new zone.

Adding Ingress and Egress Rules to a Security Group

1. Log in to the CloudStack UI as an administrator or end user.

2. In the left navigation, choose Network

3. In Select view, choose Security Groups, then click the security group you want.

4. To add an ingress rule, click the Ingress Rules tab and fill out the following fields to specify what network traffic is allowed into VM instances in this security group. If no ingress rules are specified, then no traffic will be allowed in, except for responses to any traffic that has been allowed out through an egress rule.

   - **Add by CIDR/Account**. Indicate whether the source of the traffic will be defined by IP address (CIDR) or an existing security group in a CloudStack account (Account). Choose Account if you want to allow incoming traffic from all VMs in another security group

   - **Protocol**. The networking protocol that sources will use to send traffic to the security group. TCP and UDP are typically used for data exchange and end-user communications. ICMP is typically used to send error messages or network monitoring data.

   - **Start Port, End Port**. (TCP, UDP only) A range of listening ports that are the destination for the incoming traffic. If you are opening a single port, use the same number in both fields.

   - **ICMP Type, ICMP Code**. (ICMP only) The type of message and error code that will be accepted.

   - **CIDR**. (Add by CIDR only) To accept only traffic from IP addresses within a particular address block, enter a CIDR or a comma-separated list of CIDRs. The CIDR is the base IP address of the incoming traffic. For example, 192.168.0.0/22. To allow all CIDRs, set to 0.0.0.0/0.

   - **Account, Security Group**. (Add by Account only) To accept only traffic from another security group, enter the CloudStack account and name of a security group that has already been defined in that account. To allow traffic between VMs within the security group you are editing now, enter the same name you used in step 7.

   The following example allows inbound HTTP access from anywhere:

5. To add an egress rule, click the Egress Rules tab and fill out the following fields to specify what type of traffic is allowed to be sent out of VM instances in this security group. If no egress rules are specified, then all traffic will be allowed out. Once egress rules are specified, the following types of traffic are allowed out: traffic specified in egress rules; queries to DNS and DHCP servers; and responses to any traffic that has been allowed in through an ingress rule

   - **Add by CIDR/Account**. Indicate whether the destination of the traffic will be defined by IP address (CIDR) or an existing security group in a CloudStack account (Account). Choose Account if you want to allow outgoing traffic to all VMs in another security group.

   - **Protocol**. The networking protocol that VMs will use to send outgoing traffic. TCP and UDP are typically used for data exchange and end-user communications. ICMP is typically used to send error messages or network monitoring data.

   - **Start Port, End Port**. (TCP, UDP only) A range of listening ports that are the destination for the outgoing traffic. If you are opening a single port, use the same number in both fields.

   - **ICMP Type, ICMP Code**. (ICMP only) The type of message and error code that will be sent

   - **CIDR**. (Add by CIDR only) To send traffic only to IP addresses within a particular address block, enter a CIDR or a comma-separated list of CIDRs. The CIDR is the base IP address of the destination. For example, 192.168.0.0/22. To allow all CIDRs, set to 0.0.0.0/0.

   - **Account, Security Group**. (Add by Account only) To allow traffic to be sent to another security group, enter the CloudStack account and name of a security group that has already been defined in that account. To allow traffic between VMs within the security group you are editing now, enter its name.

6. Click Add.

12.1.16 External Firewalls and Load Balancers

CloudStack is capable of replacing its Virtual Router with an external Juniper SRX device and an optional external NetScaler or F5 load balancer for gateway and load balancing services. In this case, the VMs use the SRX as their gateway.

About Using a NetScaler Load Balancer

Citrix NetScaler is supported as an external network element for load balancing in zones that use isolated networking in advanced zones. Set up an external load balancer when you want to provide load balancing through means other than CloudStack's provided virtual router.

Note: In a Basic zone, load balancing service is supported only if Elastic IP or Elastic LB services are enabled.

When NetScaler load balancer is used to provide EIP or ELB services in a Basic zone, ensure that all guest VM traffic must enter and exit through the NetScaler device. When inbound traffic goes through the NetScaler device, traffic is routed by using the NAT protocol depending on the EIP/ELB configured on the public IP to the private IP. The traffic that is originated from the guest VMs usually goes through the layer 3 router. To ensure that outbound traffic goes through NetScaler device providing EIP/ELB, layer 3 router must have a policy-based routing. A policy-based route must be set up so that all traffic originated from the guest VM's are directed to NetScaler device. This is required to ensure that the outbound traffic from the guest VM's is routed to a public IP by using NAT.For more information on Elastic IP, see *"About Elastic IP"*.

The NetScaler can be set up in direct (outside the firewall) mode. It must be added before any load balancing rules are deployed on guest VMs in the zone.

The functional behavior of the NetScaler with CloudStack is the same as described in the CloudStack documentation for using an F5 external load balancer. The only exception is that the F5 supports routing domains, and NetScaler does not. NetScaler can not yet be used as a firewall.

To install and enable an external load balancer for CloudStack management, see External Guest Load Balancer Integration in the Installation Guide.

The Citrix NetScaler comes in three varieties. The following summarizes how these variants are treated in CloudStack.

MPX

- Physical appliance. Capable of deep packet inspection. Can act as application firewall and load balancer

- In advanced zones, load balancer functionality fully supported without limitation. In basic zones, static NAT, elastic IP (EIP), and elastic load balancing (ELB) are also provided.

VPX

- Virtual appliance. Can run as VM on XenServer, ESXi, and Hyper-V hypervisors. Same functionality as MPX

- Supported on ESXi and XenServer. Same functional support as for MPX. CloudStack will treat VPX and MPX as the same device type.

SDX

- Physical appliance. Can create multiple fully isolated VPX instances on a single appliance to support multi-tenant usage

- CloudStack will dynamically provision, configure, and manage the life cycle of VPX instances on the SDX. Provisioned instances are added into CloudStack automatically - no manual configuration by the administrator is required. Once a VPX instance is added into CloudStack, it is treated the same as a VPX on an ESXi host.

Configuring SNMP Community String on a RHEL Server

The SNMP Community string is similar to a user id or password that provides access to a network device, such as router. This string is sent along with all SNMP requests. If the community string is correct, the device responds with the requested information. If the community string is incorrect, the device discards the request and does not respond.

The NetScaler device uses SNMP to communicate with the VMs. You must install SNMP and configure SNMP Community string for a secure communication between the NetScaler device and the RHEL machine.

1. Ensure that you installed SNMP on RedHat. If not, run the following command:

```
yum install net-snmp-utils
```

2. Edit the /etc/snmp/snmpd.conf file to allow the SNMP polling from the NetScaler device.

   (a) Map the community name into a security name (local and mynetwork, depending on where the request is coming from):

Note: Use a strong password instead of public when you edit the following table.

```
#              sec.name    source          community
com2sec   local        localhost       public
com2sec   mynetwork   0.0.0.0          public
```

Note: Setting to 0.0.0.0 allows all IPs to poll the NetScaler server.

(b) Map the security names into group names:

```
#          group.name    sec.model   sec.name
group   MyRWGroup    v1          local
group   MyRWGroup    v2c         local
group   MyROGroup    v1          mynetwork
group   MyROGroup    v2c         mynetwork
```

(c) Create a view to allow the groups to have the permission to:

```
incl/excl subtree mask view all included .1
```

(d) Grant access with different write permissions to the two groups to the view you created.

```
# context    sec.model      sec.level      prefix    read    write   notif
   access     MyROGroup ""  any noauth    exact     all     none    none
   access     MyRWGroup ""  any noauth    exact     all     all     all
```

3. Unblock SNMP in iptables.

```
iptables -A INPUT -p udp --dport 161 -j ACCEPT
```

4. Start the SNMP service:

```
service snmpd start
```

5. Ensure that the SNMP service is started automatically during the system startup:

```
chkconfig snmpd on
```

Initial Setup of External Firewalls and Load Balancers

When the first VM is created for a new account, CloudStack programs the external firewall and load balancer to work with the VM. The following objects are created on the firewall:

- A new logical interface to connect to the account's private VLAN. The interface IP is always the first IP of the account's private subnet (e.g. 10.1.1.1).

- A source NAT rule that forwards all outgoing traffic from the account's private VLAN to the public Internet, using the account's public IP address as the source address

- A firewall filter counter that measures the number of bytes of outgoing traffic for the account

The following objects are created on the load balancer:

- A new VLAN that matches the account's provisioned Zone VLAN

- A self IP for the VLAN. This is always the second IP of the account's private subnet (e.g. 10.1.1.2).

Ongoing Configuration of External Firewalls and Load Balancers

Additional user actions (e.g. setting a port forward) will cause further programming of the firewall and load balancer. A user may request additional public IP addresses and forward traffic received at these IPs to specific VMs. This is accomplished by enabling static NAT for a public IP address, assigning the IP to a VM, and specifying a set of protocols and port ranges to open. When a static NAT rule is created, CloudStack programs the zone's external firewall with the following objects:

- A static NAT rule that maps the public IP address to the private IP address of a VM.

- A security policy that allows traffic within the set of protocols and port ranges that are specified.

- A firewall filter counter that measures the number of bytes of incoming traffic to the public IP.

The number of incoming and outgoing bytes through source NAT, static NAT, and load balancing rules is measured and saved on each external element. This data is collected on a regular basis and stored in the CloudStack database.

Load Balancer Rules

A CloudStack user or administrator may create load balancing rules that balance traffic received at a public IP to one or more VMs. A user creates a rule, specifies an algorithm, and assigns the rule to a set of VMs.

Note: If you create load balancing rules while using a network service offering that includes an external load balancer device such as NetScaler, and later change the network service offering to one that uses the CloudStack virtual router, you must create a firewall rule on the virtual router for each of your existing load balancing rules so that they continue to function.

Adding a Load Balancer Rule

1. Log in to the CloudStack UI as an administrator or end user.

2. In the left navigation, choose Network.

3. Click the name of the network where you want to load balance the traffic.

4. Click View IP Addresses.

5. Click the IP address for which you want to create the rule, then click the Configuration tab.

6. In the Load Balancing node of the diagram, click View All.

   In a Basic zone, you can also create a load balancing rule without acquiring or selecting an IP address. Cloud-Stack internally assign an IP when you create the load balancing rule, which is listed in the IP Addresses page when the rule is created.

   To do that, select the name of the network, then click Add Load Balancer tab. Continue with #7.

7. Fill in the following:

   - **Name**: A name for the load balancer rule.

   - **Public Port**: The port receiving incoming traffic to be balanced.

   - **Private Port**: The port that the VMs will use to receive the traffic.

   - **Algorithm**: Choose the load balancing algorithm you want CloudStack to use. CloudStack supports a variety of well-known algorithms. If you are not familiar with these choices, you will find plenty of information about them on the Internet.

- **Stickiness**: (Optional) Click Configure and choose the algorithm for the stickiness policy. See Sticky Session Policies for Load Balancer Rules.

- **AutoScale**: Click Configure and complete the AutoScale configuration as explained in *Configuring AutoScale*.

- **Health Check**: (Optional; NetScaler load balancers only) Click Configure and fill in the characteristics of the health check policy. See *Health Checks for Load Balancer Rules*.

  - **Ping path (Optional)**: Sequence of destinations to which to send health check queries. Default: / (all).

  - **Response time (Optional)**: How long to wait for a response from the health check (2 - 60 seconds). Default: 5 seconds.

  - **Interval time (Optional)**: Amount of time between health checks (1 second - 5 minutes). Default value is set in the global configuration parameter lbrule_health check_time_interval.

  - **Healthy threshold (Optional)**: Number of consecutive health check successes that are required before declaring an instance healthy. Default: 2.

  - **Unhealthy threshold (Optional)**: Number of consecutive health check failures that are required before declaring an instance unhealthy. Default: 10.

8. Click Add VMs, then select two or more VMs that will divide the load of incoming traffic, and click Apply.

   The new load balancer rule appears in the list. You can repeat these steps to add more load balancer rules for this IP address.

Sticky Session Policies for Load Balancer Rules

Sticky sessions are used in Web-based applications to ensure continued availability of information across the multiple requests in a user's session. For example, if a shopper is filling a cart, you need to remember what has been purchased so far. The concept of "stickiness" is also referred to as persistence or maintaining state.

Any load balancer rule defined in CloudStack can have a stickiness policy. The policy consists of a name, stickiness method, and parameters. The parameters are name-value pairs or flags, which are defined by the load balancer vendor. The stickiness method could be load balancer-generated cookie, application-generated cookie, or source-based. In the source-based method, the source IP address is used to identify the user and locate the user's stored data. In the other methods, cookies are used. The cookie generated by the load balancer or application is included in request and response URLs to create persistence. The cookie name can be specified by the administrator or automatically generated. A variety of options are provided to control the exact behavior of cookies, such as how they are generated and whether they are cached.

For the most up to date list of available stickiness methods, see the CloudStack UI or call listNetworks and check the SupportedStickinessMethods capability.

Health Checks for Load Balancer Rules

(NetScaler load balancer only; requires NetScaler version 10.0)

Health checks are used in load-balanced applications to ensure that requests are forwarded only to running, available services. When creating a load balancer rule, you can specify a health check policy. This is in addition to specifying the stickiness policy, algorithm, and other load balancer rule options. You can configure one health check policy per load balancer rule.

Any load balancer rule defined on a NetScaler load balancer in CloudStack can have a health check policy. The policy consists of a ping path, thresholds to define "healthy" and "unhealthy" states, health check frequency, and timeout wait interval.

When a health check policy is in effect, the load balancer will stop forwarding requests to any resources that are found to be unhealthy. If the resource later becomes available again, the periodic health check will discover it, and the resource will once again be added to the pool of resources that can receive requests from the load balancer. At any given time, the most recent result of the health check is displayed in the UI. For any VM that is attached to a load balancer rule with a health check configured, the state will be shown as UP or DOWN in the UI depending on the result of the most recent health check.

You can delete or modify existing health check policies.

To configure how often the health check is performed by default, use the global configuration setting healthcheck.update.interval (default value is 600 seconds). You can override this value for an individual health check policy.

For details on how to set a health check policy using the UI, see *Adding a Load Balancer Rule*.

Configuring AutoScale

AutoScaling allows you to scale your back-end services or application VMs up or down seamlessly and automatically according to the conditions you define. With AutoScaling enabled, you can ensure that the number of VMs you are using seamlessly scale up when demand increases, and automatically decreases when demand subsides. Thus it helps you save compute costs by terminating underused VMs automatically and launching new VMs when you need them, without the need for manual intervention.

NetScaler AutoScaling is designed to seamlessly launch or terminate VMs based on user-defined conditions. Conditions for triggering a scaleup or scaledown action can vary from a simple use case like monitoring the CPU usage of a server to a complex use case of monitoring a combination of server's responsiveness and its CPU usage. For example, you can configure AutoScaling to launch an additional VM whenever CPU usage exceeds 80 percent for 15 minutes, or to remove a VM whenever CPU usage is less than 20 percent for 30 minutes.

CloudStack uses the NetScaler load balancer to monitor all aspects of a system's health and work in unison with CloudStack to initiate scale-up or scale-down actions.

Note: AutoScale is supported on NetScaler Release 10 Build 74.4006.e and beyond.

Prerequisites

Before you configure an AutoScale rule, consider the following:

- Ensure that the necessary template is prepared before configuring AutoScale. When a VM is deployed by using a template and when it comes up, the application should be up and running.

  Note: If the application is not running, the NetScaler device considers the VM as ineffective and continues provisioning the VMs unconditionally until the resource limit is exhausted.

- Deploy the templates you prepared. Ensure that the applications come up on the first boot and is ready to take the traffic. Observe the time requires to deploy the template. Consider this time when you specify the quiet time while configuring AutoScale.

- The AutoScale feature supports the SNMP counters that can be used to define conditions for taking scale up or scale down actions. To monitor the SNMP-based counter, ensure that the SNMP agent is installed in the template used for creating the AutoScale VMs, and the SNMP operations work with the configured SNMP community and port by using standard SNMP managers. For example, see *"Configuring SNMP Community String on a RHELServer"* to configure SNMP on a RHEL machine.

- Ensure that the endpointe.url parameter present in the Global Settings is set to the Management Server API URL. For example, `http://10.102.102.22:8080/client/api`. In a multi-node Management Server deployment, use the virtual IP address configured in the load balancer for the management server's cluster. Additionally, ensure that the NetScaler device has access to this IP address to provide AutoScale support.

If you update the endpointe.url, disable the AutoScale functionality of the load balancer rules in the system, then enable them back to reflect the changes. For more information see *Updating an AutoScale Configuration*.

- If the API Key and Secret Key are regenerated for an AutoScale user, ensure that the AutoScale functionality of the load balancers that the user participates in are disabled and then enabled to reflect the configuration changes in the NetScaler.

- In an advanced Zone, ensure that at least one VM should be present before configuring a load balancer rule with AutoScale. Having one VM in the network ensures that the network is in implemented state for configuring AutoScale.

Configuration

Specify the following:

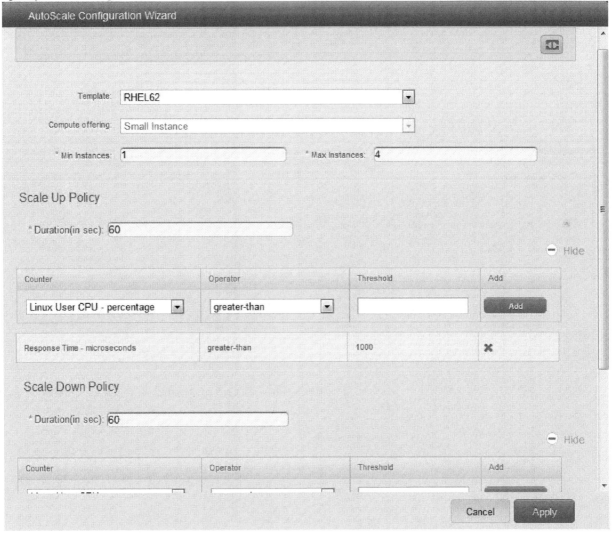

- **Template**: A template consists of a base OS image and application. A template is used to provision the new instance of an application on a scaleup action. When a VM is deployed from a template, the VM can start taking the traffic from the load balancer without any admin intervention. For example, if the VM is deployed for a Web service, it should have the Web server running, the database connected, and so on.

- **Compute offering**: A predefined set of virtual hardware attributes, including CPU speed, number of CPUs, and RAM size, that the user can select when creating a new virtual machine instance. Choose one of the compute offerings to be used while provisioning a VM instance as part of scaleup action.

- **Min Instance**: The minimum number of active VM instances that is assigned to a load balancing rule. The active VM instances are the application instances that are up and serving the traffic, and are being load balanced. This parameter ensures that a load balancing rule has at least the configured number of active VM instances are available to serve the traffic.

Note: If an application, such as SAP, running on a VM instance is down for some reason, the VM is then not counted as part of Min Instance parameter, and the AutoScale feature initiates a scaleup action if the number of active VM instances is below the configured value. Similarly, when an application instance comes up from its earlier down state, this application instance is counted as part of the active instance count and the AutoScale process initiates a scaledown action when the active instance count breaches the Max instance value.

- **Max Instance**: Maximum number of active VM instances that **should be assigned to** a load balancing rule. This parameter defines the upper limit of active VM instances that can be assigned to a load balancing rule.

  Specifying a large value for the maximum instance parameter might result in provisioning large number of VM instances, which in turn leads to a single load balancing rule exhausting the VM instances limit specified at the account or domain level.

Note: If an application, such as SAP, running on a VM instance is down for some reason, the VM is not counted as part of Max Instance parameter. So there may be scenarios where the number of VMs provisioned for a scaleup action might be more than the configured Max Instance value. Once the application instances in the VMs are up from an earlier down state, the AutoScale feature starts aligning to the configured Max Instance value.

Specify the following scale-up and scale-down policies:

- **Duration**: The duration, in seconds, for which the conditions you specify must be true to trigger a scaleup action. The conditions defined should hold true for the entire duration you specify for an AutoScale action to be invoked.

- **Counter**: The performance counters expose the state of the monitored instances. By default, CloudStack offers four performance counters: Three SNMP counters and one NetScaler counter. The SNMP counters are Linux User CPU, Linux System CPU, and Linux CPU Idle. The NetScaler counter is ResponseTime. The root administrator can add additional counters into CloudStack by using the CloudStack API.

- **Operator**: The following five relational operators are supported in AutoScale feature: Greater than, Less than, Less than or equal to, Greater than or equal to, and Equal to.

- **Threshold**: Threshold value to be used for the counter. Once the counter defined above breaches the threshold value, the AutoScale feature initiates a scaleup or scaledown action.

- **Add**: Click Add to add the condition.

Additionally, if you want to configure the advanced settings, click Show advanced settings, and specify the following:

- **Polling interval**: Frequency in which the conditions, combination of counter, operator and threshold, are to be evaluated before taking a scale up or down action. The default polling interval is 30 seconds.

- **Quiet Time**: This is the cool down period after an AutoScale action is initiated. The time includes the time taken to complete provisioning a VM instance from its template and the time taken by an application to be ready to serve traffic. This quiet time allows the fleet to come up to a stable state before any action can take place. The default is 300 seconds.

- **Destroy VM Grace Period**: The duration in seconds, after a scaledown action is initiated, to wait before the VM is destroyed as part of scaledown action. This is to ensure graceful close of any pending sessions or transactions being served by the VM marked for destroy. The default is 120 seconds.

- **Security Groups**: Security groups provide a way to isolate traffic to the VM instances. A security group is a group of VMs that filter their incoming and outgoing traffic according to a set of rules, called ingress and egress rules. These rules filter network traffic according to the IP address that is attempting to communicate with the VM.

- **Disk Offerings**: A predefined set of disk size for primary data storage.

- **SNMP Community**: The SNMP community string to be used by the NetScaler device to query the configured counter value from the provisioned VM instances. Default is public.

- **SNMP Port**: The port number on which the SNMP agent that run on the provisioned VMs is listening. Default port is 161.

- **User**: This is the user that the NetScaler device use to invoke scaleup and scaledown API calls to the cloud. If no option is specified, the user who configures AutoScaling is applied. Specify another user name to override.

- **Apply**: Click Apply to create the AutoScale configuration.

Disabling and Enabling an AutoScale Configuration

If you want to perform any maintenance operation on the AutoScale VM instances, disable the AutoScale configuration. When the AutoScale configuration is disabled, no scaleup or scaledown action is performed. You can use this downtime for the maintenance activities. To disable the AutoScale configuration, click the Disable AutoScale button.

The button toggles between enable and disable, depending on whether AutoScale is currently enabled or not. After the maintenance operations are done, you can enable the AutoScale configuration back. To enable, open the AutoScale configuration page again, then click the Enable AutoScale button.

Updating an AutoScale Configuration

You can update the various parameters and add or delete the conditions in a scaleup or scaledown rule. Before you update an AutoScale configuration, ensure that you disable the AutoScale load balancer rule by clicking the Disable AutoScale button.

After you modify the required AutoScale parameters, click Apply. To apply the new AutoScale policies, open the AutoScale configuration page again, then click the Enable AutoScale button.

Runtime Considerations

- An administrator should not assign a VM to a load balancing rule which is configured for AutoScale.

- Before a VM provisioning is completed if NetScaler is shutdown or restarted, the provisioned VM cannot be a part of the load balancing rule though the intent was to assign it to a load balancing rule. To workaround, rename the AutoScale provisioned VMs based on the rule name or ID so at any point of time the VMs can be reconciled to its load balancing rule.

- Making API calls outside the context of AutoScale, such as destroyVM, on an autoscaled VM leaves the load balancing configuration in an inconsistent state. Though VM is destroyed from the load balancer rule, NetScaler continues to show the VM as a service assigned to a rule.

12.1.17 Global Server Load Balancing Support

CloudStack supports Global Server Load Balancing (GSLB) functionalities to provide business continuity, and enable seamless resource movement within a CloudStack environment. CloudStack achieve this by extending its functionality of integrating with NetScaler Application Delivery Controller (ADC), which also provides various GSLB capabilities, such as disaster recovery and load balancing. The DNS redirection technique is used to achieve GSLB in CloudStack.

In order to support this functionality, region level services and service provider are introduced. A new service 'GSLB' is introduced as a region level service. The GSLB service provider is introduced that will provider the GSLB service. Currently, NetScaler is the supported GSLB provider in CloudStack. GSLB functionality works in an Active-Active data center environment.

About Global Server Load Balancing

Global Server Load Balancing (GSLB) is an extension of load balancing functionality, which is highly efficient in avoiding downtime. Based on the nature of deployment, GSLB represents a set of technologies that is used for various purposes, such as load sharing, disaster recovery, performance, and legal obligations. With GSLB, workloads can be distributed across multiple data centers situated at geographically separated locations. GSLB can also provide an alternate location for accessing a resource in the event of a failure, or to provide a means of shifting traffic easily to simplify maintenance, or both.

Components of GSLB

A typical GSLB environment is comprised of the following components:

- **GSLB Site**: In CloudStack terminology, GSLB sites are represented by zones that are mapped to data centers, each of which has various network appliances. Each GSLB site is managed by a NetScaler appliance that is local to that site. Each of these appliances treats its own site as the local site and all other sites, managed by other appliances, as remote sites. It is the central entity in a GSLB deployment, and is represented by a name and an IP address.

- **GSLB Services**: A GSLB service is typically represented by a load balancing or content switching virtual server. In a GSLB environment, you can have a local as well as remote GSLB services. A local GSLB service represents a local load balancing or content switching virtual server. A remote GSLB service is the one configured at one of the other sites in the GSLB setup. At each site in the GSLB setup, you can create one local GSLB service and any number of remote GSLB services.

- **GSLB Virtual Servers**: A GSLB virtual server refers to one or more GSLB services and balances traffic between traffic across the VMs in multiple zones by using the CloudStack functionality. It evaluates the configured GSLB methods or algorithms to select a GSLB service to which to send the client requests. One or more virtual servers from different zones are bound to the GSLB virtual server. GSLB virtual server does not have a public IP associated with it, instead it will have a FQDN DNS name.

- **Load Balancing or Content Switching Virtual Servers**: According to Citrix NetScaler terminology, a load balancing or content switching virtual server represents one or many servers on the local network. Clients send their requests to the load balancing or content switching virtual server's virtual IP (VIP) address, and the virtual server balances the load across the local servers. After a GSLB virtual server selects a GSLB service representing either a local or a remote load balancing or content switching virtual server, the client sends the request to that virtual server's VIP address.

- **DNS VIPs**: DNS virtual IP represents a load balancing DNS virtual server on the GSLB service provider. The DNS requests for domains for which the GSLB service provider is authoritative can be sent to a DNS VIP.

- **Authoritative DNS**: ADNS (Authoritative Domain Name Server) is a service that provides actual answer to DNS queries, such as web site IP address. In a GSLB environment, an ADNS service responds only to DNS requests for domains for which the GSLB service provider is authoritative. When an ADNS service is configured, the service provider owns that IP address and advertises it. When you create an ADNS service, the NetScaler responds to DNS queries on the configured ADNS service IP and port.

How Does GSLB Works in CloudStack?

Global server load balancing is used to manage the traffic flow to a web site hosted on two separate zones that ideally are in different geographic locations. The following is an illustration of how GLSB functionality is provided in CloudStack: An organization, xyztelco, has set up a public cloud that spans two zones, Zone-1 and Zone-2, across geographically separated data centers that are managed by CloudStack. Tenant-A of the cloud launches a highly available solution by using xyztelco cloud. For that purpose, they launch two instances each in both the zones: VM1 and VM2 in Zone-1 and VM5 and VM6 in Zone-2. Tenant-A acquires a public IP, IP-1 in Zone-1, and configures a load balancer rule to load balance the traffic between VM1 and VM2 instances. CloudStack orchestrates setting up a virtual server on the LB service provider in Zone-1. Virtual server 1 that is set up on the LB service provider in Zone-1 represents a publicly accessible virtual server that client reaches at IP-1. The client traffic to virtual server 1 at IP-1 will be load balanced across VM1 and VM2 instances.

Tenant-A acquires another public IP, IP-2 in Zone-2 and sets up a load balancer rule to load balance the traffic between VM5 and VM6 instances. Similarly in Zone-2, CloudStack orchestrates setting up a virtual server on the LB service provider. Virtual server 2 that is setup on the LB service provider in Zone-2 represents a publicly accessible virtual server that client reaches at IP-2. The client traffic that reaches virtual server 2 at IP-2 is load balanced across VM5 and VM6 instances. At this point Tenant-A has the service enabled in both the zones, but has no means to set up a disaster recovery plan if one of the zone fails. Additionally, there is no way for Tenant-A to load balance the traffic intelligently to one of the zones based on load, proximity and so on. The cloud administrator of xyztelco provisions a GSLB service provider to both the zones. A GSLB provider is typically an ADC that has the ability to act as an ADNS (Authoritative Domain Name Server) and has the mechanism to monitor health of virtual servers both at local and remote sites. The cloud admin enables GSLB as a service to the tenants that use zones 1 and 2.

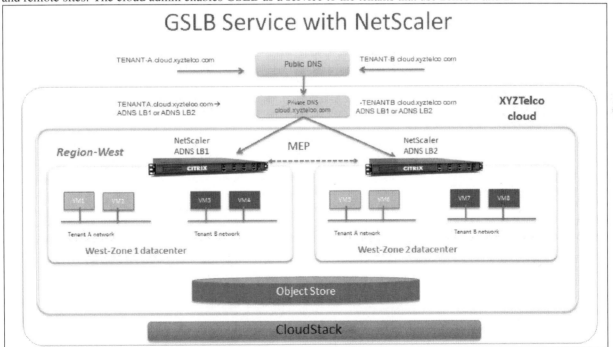

Tenant-A wishes to leverage the GSLB service provided by the xyztelco cloud. Tenant-A configures a GSLB rule to load balance traffic across virtual server 1 at Zone-1 and virtual server 2 at Zone-2. The domain name is provided as A.xyztelco.com. CloudStack orchestrates setting up GSLB virtual server 1 on the GSLB service provider at Zone-1. CloudStack binds virtual server 1 of Zone-1 and virtual server 2 of Zone-2 to GLSB virtual server 1. GSLB virtual server 1 is configured to start monitoring the health of virtual server 1 and 2 in Zone-1. CloudStack will also orchestrate setting up GSLB virtual server 2 on GSLB service provider at Zone-2. CloudStack will bind virtual server 1 of Zone-1 and virtual server 2 of Zone-2 to GLSB virtual server 2. GSLB virtual server 2 is configured to start monitoring the health of virtual server 1 and 2. CloudStack will bind the domain A.xyztelco.com to both the GSLB virtual server 1 and 2. At this point, Tenant-A service will be globally reachable at A.xyztelco.com. The private DNS server for the domain xyztelcom.com is configured by the admin out-of-band to resolve the domain A.xyztelco.com to the GSLB providers at both the zones, which are configured as ADNS for the domain A.xyztelco.com. A client when sends a DNS request to resolve A.xyztelcom.com, will eventually get DNS delegation to the address of GSLB providers at zone 1 and 2. A client DNS request will be received by the GSLB provider. The GSLB provider, depending on the domain for which it needs to resolve, will pick up the GSLB virtual server associated with the domain. Depending on the health of the virtual servers being load balanced, DNS request for the domain will be resolved to the public IP associated with the selected virtual server.

Configuring GSLB

To configure a GSLB deployment, you must first configure a standard load balancing setup for each zone. This enables you to balance load across the different servers in each zone in the region. Then on the NetScaler side, configure both NetScaler appliances that you plan to add to each zone as authoritative DNS (ADNS) servers. Next, create a GSLB site for each zone, configure GSLB virtual servers for each site, create GLSB services, and bind the GSLB services to the GSLB virtual servers. Finally, bind the domain to the GSLB virtual servers. The GSLB configurations on the two appliances at the two different zones are identical, although each sites load-balancing configuration is specific to that site.

Perform the following as a cloud administrator. As per the example given above, the administrator of xyztelco is the one who sets up GSLB:

1. In the cloud.dns.name global parameter, specify the DNS name of your tenant's cloud that make use of the GSLB service.

2. On the NetScaler side, configure GSLB as given in Configuring Global Server Load Balancing (GSLB):

   (a) Configuring a standard load balancing setup.

   (b) Configure Authoritative DNS, as explained in Configuring an Authoritative DNS Service.

   (c) Configure a GSLB site with site name formed from the domain name details.

   Configure a GSLB site with the site name formed from the domain name.

   As per the example given above, the site names are A.xyztelco.com and B.xyztelco.com.

   For more information, see Configuring a Basic GSLB Site.

   (d) Configure a GSLB virtual server.

   For more information, see Configuring a GSLB Virtual Server.

   (e) Configure a GSLB service for each virtual server.

   For more information, see Configuring a GSLB Service.

   (f) Bind the GSLB services to the GSLB virtual server.

   For more information, see Binding GSLB Services to a GSLB Virtual Server.

   (g) Bind domain name to GSLB virtual server. Domain name is obtained from the domain details.

   For more information, see Binding a Domain to a GSLB Virtual Server.

3. In each zone that are participating in GSLB, add GSLB-enabled NetScaler device.

   For more information, see *Enabling GSLB in NetScaler*.

As a domain administrator/ user perform the following:

1. Add a GSLB rule on both the sites.

   See "*Adding a GSLB Rule*".

2. Assign load balancer rules.

   See "*Assigning Load Balancing Rules to GSLB*".

Prerequisites and Guidelines

- The GSLB functionality is supported both Basic and Advanced zones.

- GSLB is added as a new network service.

- GSLB service provider can be added to a physical network in a zone.

- The admin is allowed to enable or disable GSLB functionality at region level.

- The admin is allowed to configure a zone as GSLB capable or enabled.

  A zone shall be considered as GSLB capable only if a GSLB service provider is provisioned in the zone.

- When users have VMs deployed in multiple availability zones which are GSLB enabled, they can use the GSLB functionality to load balance traffic across the VMs in multiple zones.

- The users can use GSLB to load balance across the VMs across zones in a region only if the admin has enabled GSLB in that region.

- The users can load balance traffic across the availability zones in the same region or different regions.

- The admin can configure DNS name for the entire cloud.

- The users can specify an unique name across the cloud for a globally load balanced service. The provided name is used as the domain name under the DNS name associated with the cloud.

  The user-provided name along with the admin-provided DNS name is used to produce a globally resolvable FQDN for the globally load balanced service of the user. For example, if the admin has configured xyztelco.com as the DNS name for the cloud, and user specifies 'foo' for the GSLB virtual service, then the FQDN name of the GSLB virtual service is foo.xyztelco.com.

- While setting up GSLB, users can select a load balancing method, such as round robin, for using across the zones that are part of GSLB.

- The user shall be able to set weight to zone-level virtual server. Weight shall be considered by the load balancing method for distributing the traffic.

- The GSLB functionality shall support session persistence, where series of client requests for particular domain name is sent to a virtual server on the same zone.

  Statistics is collected from each GSLB virtual server.

Enabling GSLB in NetScaler

In each zone, add GSLB-enabled NetScaler device for load balancing.

1. Log in as administrator to the CloudStack UI.

2. In the left navigation bar, click Infrastructure.

3. In Zones, click View More.

4. Choose the zone you want to work with.

5. Click the Physical Network tab, then click the name of the physical network.

6. In the Network Service Providers node of the diagram, click Configure.

   You might have to scroll down to see this.

7. Click NetScaler.

8. Click Add NetScaler device and provide the following:

   For NetScaler:

   - **IP Address**: The IP address of the SDX.

   - **Username/Password**: The authentication credentials to access the device. CloudStack uses these credentials to access the device.

   - **Type**: The type of device that is being added. It could be F5 Big Ip Load Balancer, NetScaler VPX, NetScaler MPX, or NetScaler SDX. For a comparison of the NetScaler types, see the CloudStack Administration Guide.

   - **Public interface**: Interface of device that is configured to be part of the public network.

   - **Private interface**: Interface of device that is configured to be part of the private network.

   - **GSLB service**: Select this option.

   - **GSLB service Public IP**: The public IP address of the NAT translator for a GSLB service that is on a private network.

   - **GSLB service Private IP**: The private IP of the GSLB service.

   - **Number of Retries**. Number of times to attempt a command on the device before considering the operation failed. Default is 2.

   - **Capacity**: The number of networks the device can handle.

   - **Dedicated**: When marked as dedicated, this device will be dedicated to a single account. When Dedicated is checked, the value in the Capacity field has no significance implicitly, its value is 1.

9. Click OK.

Adding a GSLB Rule

1. Log in to the CloudStack UI as a domain administrator or user.

2. In the left navigation pane, click Region.

3. Select the region for which you want to create a GSLB rule.

4. In the Details tab, click View GSLB.

5. Click Add GSLB.

   The Add GSLB page is displayed as follows:

6. Specify the following:

   - **Name**: Name for the GSLB rule.

   - **Description**: (Optional) A short description of the GSLB rule that can be displayed to users.

   - **GSLB Domain Name**: A preferred domain name for the service.

   - **Algorithm**: (Optional) The algorithm to use to load balance the traffic across the zones. The options are Round Robin, Least Connection, and Proximity.

   - **Service Type**: The transport protocol to use for GSLB. The options are TCP and UDP.

   - **Domain**: (Optional) The domain for which you want to create the GSLB rule.

   - **Account**: (Optional) The account on which you want to apply the GSLB rule.

7. Click OK to confirm.

Assigning Load Balancing Rules to GSLB

1. Log in to the CloudStack UI as a domain administrator or user.

2. In the left navigation pane, click Region.

3. Select the region for which you want to create a GSLB rule.

4. In the Details tab, click View GSLB.

5. Select the desired GSLB.

6. Click view assigned load balancing.

7. Click assign more load balancing.

8. Select the load balancing rule you have created for the zone.

9. Click OK to confirm.

Known Limitation

Currently, CloudStack does not support orchestration of services across the zones. The notion of services and service providers in region are to be introduced.

12.1.18 Guest IP Ranges

The IP ranges for guest network traffic are set on a per-account basis by the user. This allows the users to configure their network in a fashion that will enable VPN linking between their guest network and their clients.

In shared networks in Basic zone and Security Group-enabled Advanced networks, you will have the flexibility to add multiple guest IP ranges from different subnets. You can add or remove one IP range at a time. For more information, see *"About Multiple IP Ranges"*.

12.1.19 Acquiring a New IP Address

1. Log in to the CloudStack UI as an administrator or end user.

2. In the left navigation, choose Network.

3. Click the name of the network where you want to work with.

4. Click View IP Addresses.

5. Click Acquire New IP.

   The Acquire New IP window is displayed.

6. Specify whether you want cross-zone IP or not.

   If you want Portable IP click Yes in the confirmation dialog. If you want a normal Public IP click No.

   For more information on Portable IP, see *"Portable IPs"*.

   Within a few moments, the new IP address should appear with the state Allocated. You can now use the IP address in port forwarding or static NAT rules.

12.1.20 Releasing an IP Address

When the last rule for an IP address is removed, you can release that IP address. The IP address still belongs to the VPC; however, it can be picked up for any guest network again.

1. Log in to the CloudStack UI as an administrator or end user.

2. In the left navigation, choose Network.

3. Click the name of the network where you want to work with.

4. Click View IP Addresses.

5. Click the IP address you want to release.

6. Click the Release IP button.

12.1.21 Static NAT

A static NAT rule maps a public IP address to the private IP address of a VM in order to allow Internet traffic into the VM. The public IP address always remains the same, which is why it is called static NAT. This section tells how to enable or disable static NAT for a particular IP address.

Enabling or Disabling Static NAT

If port forwarding rules are already in effect for an IP address, you cannot enable static NAT to that IP.

If a guest VM is part of more than one network, static NAT rules will function only if they are defined on the default network.

1. Log in to the CloudStack UI as an administrator or end user.

2. In the left navigation, choose Network.

3. Click the name of the network where you want to work with.

4. Click View IP Addresses.

5. Click the IP address you want to work with.

6. Click the Static NAT button.

   The button toggles between Enable and Disable, depending on whether static NAT is currently enabled for the IP address.

7. If you are enabling static NAT, a dialog appears where you can choose the destination VM and click Apply.

12.1.22 IP Forwarding and Firewalling

By default, all incoming traffic to the public IP address is rejected. All outgoing traffic from the guests is also blocked by default.

To allow outgoing traffic, follow the procedure in *Egress Firewall Rules in an Advanced Zone*.

To allow incoming traffic, users may set up firewall rules and/or port forwarding rules. For example, you can use a firewall rule to open a range of ports on the public IP address, such as 33 through 44. Then use port forwarding rules to direct traffic from individual ports within that range to specific ports on user VMs. For example, one port forwarding rule could route incoming traffic on the public IP's port 33 to port 100 on one user VM's private IP.

Firewall Rules

By default, all incoming traffic to the public IP address is rejected by the firewall. To allow external traffic, you can open firewall ports by specifying firewall rules. You can optionally specify one or more CIDRs to filter the source IPs. This is useful when you want to allow only incoming requests from certain IP addresses.

You cannot use firewall rules to open ports for an elastic IP address. When elastic IP is used, outside access is instead controlled through the use of security groups. See *"Adding a Security Group"*.

In an advanced zone, you can also create egress firewall rules by using the virtual router. For more information, see *"Egress Firewall Rules in an Advanced Zone"*.

Firewall rules can be created using the Firewall tab in the Management Server UI. This tab is not displayed by default when CloudStack is installed. To display the Firewall tab, the CloudStack administrator must set the global configuration parameter firewall.rule.ui.enabled to "true."

To create a firewall rule:

1. Log in to the CloudStack UI as an administrator or end user.

2. In the left navigation, choose Network.

3. Click the name of the network where you want to work with.

4. Click View IP Addresses.

5. Click the IP address you want to work with.

6. Click the Configuration tab and fill in the following values.

   - **Source CIDR**: (Optional) To accept only traffic from IP addresses within a particular address block, enter a CIDR or a comma-separated list of CIDRs. Example: 192.168.0.0/22. Leave empty to allow all CIDRs.

   - **Protocol**: The communication protocol in use on the opened port(s).

   - **Start Port and End Port**: The port(s) you want to open on the firewall. If you are opening a single port, use the same number in both fields

   - **ICMP Type and ICMP Code**: Used only if Protocol is set to ICMP. Provide the type and code required by the ICMP protocol to fill out the ICMP header. Refer to ICMP documentation for more details if you are not sure what to enter

7. Click Add.

Egress Firewall Rules in an Advanced Zone

The egress traffic originates from a private network to a public network, such as the Internet. By default, the egress traffic is blocked in default network offerings, so no outgoing traffic is allowed from a guest network to the Internet. However, you can control the egress traffic in an Advanced zone by creating egress firewall rules. When an egress firewall rule is applied, the traffic specific to the rule is allowed and the remaining traffic is blocked. When all the firewall rules are removed the default policy, Block, is applied.

Prerequisites and Guidelines

Consider the following scenarios to apply egress firewall rules:

- Egress firewall rules are supported on Juniper SRX and virtual router.

- The egress firewall rules are not supported on shared networks.

- Allow the egress traffic from specified source CIDR. The Source CIDR is part of guest network CIDR.

- Allow the egress traffic with protocol TCP,UDP,ICMP, or ALL.

- Allow the egress traffic with protocol and destination port range. The port range is specified for TCP, UDP or for ICMP type and code.

- The default policy is Allow for the new network offerings, whereas on upgrade existing network offerings with firewall service providers will have the default egress policy Deny.

Configuring an Egress Firewall Rule

1. Log in to the CloudStack UI as an administrator or end user.

2. In the left navigation, choose Network.

3. In Select view, choose Guest networks, then click the Guest network you want.

4. To add an egress rule, click the Egress rules tab and fill out the following fields to specify what type of traffic is allowed to be sent out of VM instances in this guest network:

- **CIDR**: (Add by CIDR only) To send traffic only to the IP addresses within a particular address block, enter a CIDR or a comma-separated list of CIDRs. The CIDR is the base IP address of the destination. For example, 192.168.0.0/22. To allow all CIDRs, set to 0.0.0.0/0.

- **Protocol**: The networking protocol that VMs uses to send outgoing traffic. The TCP and UDP protocols are typically used for data exchange and end-user communications. The ICMP protocol is typically used to send error messages or network monitoring data.

- **Start Port, End Port**: (TCP, UDP only) A range of listening ports that are the destination for the outgoing traffic. If you are opening a single port, use the same number in both fields.

- **ICMP Type, ICMP Code**: (ICMP only) The type of message and error code that are sent.

5. Click Add.

Configuring the Default Egress Policy

The default egress policy for Isolated guest network is configured by using Network offering. Use the create network offering option to determine whether the default policy should be block or allow all the traffic to the public network from a guest network. Use this network offering to create the network. If no policy is specified, by default all the traffic is allowed from the guest network that you create by using this network offering.

You have two options: Allow and Deny.

Allow   If you select Allow for a network offering, by default egress traffic is allowed. However, when an egress rule is configured for a guest network, rules are applied to block the specified traffic and rest are allowed. If no egress rules are configured for the network, egress traffic is accepted.

Deny   If you select Deny for a network offering, by default egress traffic for the guest network is blocked. However, when an egress rules is configured for a guest network, rules are applied to allow the specified traffic. While implementing a guest network, CloudStack adds the firewall egress rule specific to the default egress policy for the guest network.

This feature is supported only on virtual router and Juniper SRX.

1. Create a network offering with your desirable default egress policy:

    (a) Log in with admin privileges to the CloudStack UI.

    (b) In the left navigation bar, click Service Offerings.

    (c) In Select Offering, choose Network Offering.

    (d) Click Add Network Offering.

    (e) In the dialog, make necessary choices, including firewall provider.

(f) In the Default egress policy field, specify the behaviour.

(g) Click OK.

2. Create an isolated network by using this network offering.

   Based on your selection, the network will have the egress public traffic blocked or allowed.

Port Forwarding

A port forward service is a set of port forwarding rules that define a policy. A port forward service is then applied to one or more guest VMs. The guest VM then has its inbound network access managed according to the policy defined by the port forwarding service. You can optionally specify one or more CIDRs to filter the source IPs. This is useful when you want to allow only incoming requests from certain IP addresses to be forwarded.

A guest VM can be in any number of port forward services. Port forward services can be defined but have no members. If a guest VM is part of more than one network, port forwarding rules will function only if they are defined on the default network

You cannot use port forwarding to open ports for an elastic IP address. When elastic IP is used, outside access is instead controlled through the use of security groups. See Security Groups.

To set up port forwarding:

1. Log in to the CloudStack UI as an administrator or end user.

2. If you have not already done so, add a public IP address range to a zone in CloudStack. See Adding a Zone and Pod in the Installation Guide.

3. Add one or more VM instances to CloudStack.

4. In the left navigation bar, click Network.

5. Click the name of the guest network where the VMs are running.

6. Choose an existing IP address or acquire a new IP address. See *"Acquiring a New IP Address"*. Click the name of the IP address in the list.

7. Click the Configuration tab.

8. In the Port Forwarding node of the diagram, click View All.

9. Fill in the following:

   - **Public Port**: The port to which public traffic will be addressed on the IP address you acquired in the previous step.

   - **Private Port**: The port on which the instance is listening for forwarded public traffic.

   - **Protocol**: The communication protocol in use between the two ports

10. Click Add.

12.1.23 IP Load Balancing

The user may choose to associate the same public IP for multiple guests. CloudStack implements a TCP-level load balancer with the following policies.

- Round-robin

- Least connection

- Source IP

This is similar to port forwarding but the destination may be multiple IP addresses.

12.1.24 DNS and DHCP

The Virtual Router provides DNS and DHCP services to the guests. It proxies DNS requests to the DNS server configured on the Availability Zone.

12.1.25 Remote Access VPN

CloudStack account owners can create virtual private networks (VPN) to access their virtual machines. If the guest network is instantiated from a network offering that offers the Remote Access VPN service, the virtual router (based on the System VM) is used to provide the service. CloudStack provides a L2TP-over-IPsec-based remote access VPN service to guest virtual networks. Since each network gets its own virtual router, VPNs are not shared across the networks. VPN clients native to Windows, Mac OS X and iOS can be used to connect to the guest networks. The account owner can create and manage users for their VPN. CloudStack does not use its account database for this purpose but uses a separate table. The VPN user database is shared across all the VPNs created by the account owner. All VPN users get access to all VPNs created by the account owner.

Note: Make sure that not all traffic goes through the VPN. That is, the route installed by the VPN should be only for the guest network and not for all traffic.

- **Road Warrior / Remote Access**. Users want to be able to connect securely from a home or office to a private network in the cloud. Typically, the IP address of the connecting client is dynamic and cannot be preconfigured on the VPN server.

- **Site to Site**. In this scenario, two private subnets are connected over the public Internet with a secure VPN tunnel. The cloud user's subnet (for example, an office network) is connected through a gateway to the network in the cloud. The address of the user's gateway must be preconfigured on the VPN server in the cloud. Note that although L2TP-over-IPsec can be used to set up Site-to-Site VPNs, this is not the primary intent of this feature. For more information, see *"Setting Up a Site-to-Site VPN Connection"*.

Configuring Remote Access VPN

To set up VPN for the cloud:

1. Log in to the CloudStack UI as an administrator or end user.

2. In the left navigation, click Global Settings.

3. Set the following global configuration parameters.

   - remote.access.vpn.client.ip.range - The range of IP addresses to be allocated to remote access VPN clients. The first IP in the range is used by the VPN server.

   - remote.access.vpn.psk.length - Length of the IPSec key.

   - remote.access.vpn.user.limit - Maximum number of VPN users per account.

To enable VPN for a particular network:

1. Log in as a user or administrator to the CloudStack UI.

2. In the left navigation, click Network.

3. Click the name of the network you want to work with.

4. Click View IP Addresses.

5. Click one of the displayed IP address names.

6. Click the Enable VPN button.

The IPsec key is displayed in a popup window.

Configuring Remote Access VPN in VPC

On enabling Remote Access VPN on a VPC, any VPN client present outside the VPC can access VMs present in the VPC by using the Remote VPN connection. The VPN client can be present anywhere except inside the VPC on which the user enabled the Remote Access VPN service.

To enable VPN for a VPC:

1. Log in as a user or administrator to the CloudStack UI.

2. In the left navigation, click Network.

3. In the Select view, select VPC.

   All the VPCs that you have created for the account is listed in the page.

4. Click the Configure button of the VPC.

   For each tier, the following options are displayed:

   - Internal LB
   - Public LB IP
   - Static NAT
   - Virtual Machines
   - CIDR

   The following router information is displayed:

   - Private Gateways
   - Public IP Addresses
   - Site-to-Site VPNs
   - Network ACL Lists

5. In the Router node, select Public IP Addresses.

   The IP Addresses page is displayed.

6. Click Source NAT IP address.

7. Click the Enable VPN button.

   Click OK to confirm. The IPsec key is displayed in a pop-up window.

Now, you need to add the VPN users.

1. Click the Source NAT IP.

2. Select the VPN tab.

3. Add the username and the corresponding password of the user you wanted to add.

4. Click Add.

5. Repeat the same steps to add the VPN users.

Setting Up a Site-to-Site VPN Connection

A Site-to-Site VPN connection helps you establish a secure connection from an enterprise datacenter to the cloud infrastructure. This allows users to access the guest VMs by establishing a VPN connection to the virtual router of the account from a device in the datacenter of the enterprise. You can also establish a secure connection between two VPC setups or high availability zones in your environment. Having this facility eliminates the need to establish VPN connections to individual VMs.

The difference from Remote VPN is that Site-to-site VPNs connects entire networks to each other, for example, connecting a branch office network to a company headquarters network. In a site-to-site VPN, hosts do not have VPN client software; they send and receive normal TCP/IP traffic through a VPN gateway.

The supported endpoints on the remote datacenters are:

- Cisco ISR with IOS 12.4 or later
- Juniper J-Series routers with JunOS 9.5 or later
- CloudStack virtual routers

Note: In addition to the specific Cisco and Juniper devices listed above, the expectation is that any Cisco or Juniper device running on the supported operating systems are able to establish VPN connections.

To set up a Site-to-Site VPN connection, perform the following:

1. Create a Virtual Private Cloud (VPC).

   See "*Configuring a Virtual Private Cloud*".

2. Create a VPN Customer Gateway.

3. Create a VPN gateway for the VPC that you created.

4. Create VPN connection from the VPC VPN gateway to the customer VPN gateway.

Creating and Updating a VPN Customer Gateway

Note: A VPN customer gateway can be connected to only one VPN gateway at a time.

To add a VPN Customer Gateway:

1. Log in to the CloudStack UI as an administrator or end user.

2. In the left navigation, choose Network.

3. In the Select view, select VPN Customer Gateway.

4. Click Add VPN Customer Gateway.

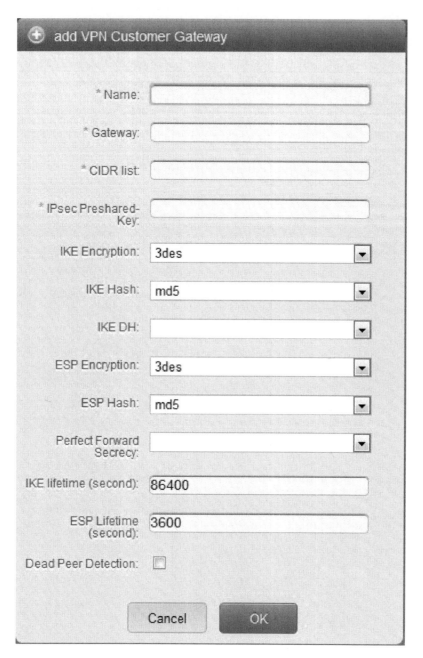

Provide the following information:

- **Name**: A unique name for the VPN customer gateway you create.

- **Gateway**: The IP address for the remote gateway.

- **CIDR list**: The guest CIDR list of the remote subnets. Enter a CIDR or a comma-separated list of CIDRs. Ensure that a guest CIDR list is not overlapped with the VPC's CIDR, or another guest CIDR. The CIDR must be RFC1918-compliant.

- **IPsec Preshared Key**: Preshared keying is a method where the endpoints of the VPN share a secret key. This key value is used to authenticate the customer gateway and the VPC VPN gateway to each other.

Note: The IKE peers (VPN end points) authenticate each other by computing and sending a keyed hash of data that includes the Preshared key. If the receiving peer is able to create the same hash independently by using its Preshared key, it knows that both peers must share the same secret, thus authenticating the

---

customer gateway.

- **IKE Encryption**: The Internet Key Exchange (IKE) policy for phase-1. The supported encryption algorithms are AES128, AES192, AES256, and 3DES. Authentication is accomplished through the Preshared Keys.

Note: The phase-1 is the first phase in the IKE process. In this initial negotiation phase, the two VPN endpoints agree on the methods to be used to provide security for the underlying IP traffic. The phase-1 authenticates the two VPN gateways to each other, by confirming that the remote gateway has a matching Preshared Key.

- **IKE Hash**: The IKE hash for phase-1. The supported hash algorithms are SHA1 and MD5.
- **IKE DH**: A public-key cryptography protocol which allows two parties to establish a shared secret over an insecure communications channel. The 1536-bit Diffie-Hellman group is used within IKE to establish session keys. The supported options are None, Group-5 (1536-bit) and Group-2 (1024-bit).
- **ESP Encryption**: Encapsulating Security Payload (ESP) algorithm within phase-2. The supported encryption algorithms are AES128, AES192, AES256, and 3DES.

Note: The phase-2 is the second phase in the IKE process. The purpose of IKE phase-2 is to negotiate IPSec security associations (SA) to set up the IPSec tunnel. In phase-2, new keying material is extracted from the Diffie-Hellman key exchange in phase-1, to provide session keys to use in protecting the VPN data flow.

- **ESP Hash**: Encapsulating Security Payload (ESP) hash for phase-2. Supported hash algorithms are SHA1 and MD5.
- **Perfect Forward Secrecy**: Perfect Forward Secrecy (or PFS) is the property that ensures that a session key derived from a set of long-term public and private keys will not be compromised. This property enforces a new Diffie-Hellman key exchange. It provides the keying material that has greater key material life and thereby greater resistance to cryptographic attacks. The available options are None, Group-5 (1536-bit) and Group-2 (1024-bit). The security of the key exchanges increase as the DH groups grow larger, as does the time of the exchanges.

Note: When PFS is turned on, for every negotiation of a new phase-2 SA the two gateways must generate a new set of phase-1 keys. This adds an extra layer of protection that PFS adds, which ensures if the phase-2 SA's have expired, the keys used for new phase-2 SA's have not been generated from the current phase-1 keying material.

- **IKE Lifetime (seconds)**: The phase-1 lifetime of the security association in seconds. Default is 86400 seconds (1 day). Whenever the time expires, a new phase-1 exchange is performed.
- **ESP Lifetime (seconds)**: The phase-2 lifetime of the security association in seconds. Default is 3600 seconds (1 hour). Whenever the value is exceeded, a re-key is initiated to provide a new IPsec encryption and authentication session keys.
- **Dead Peer Detection**: A method to detect an unavailable Internet Key Exchange (IKE) peer. Select this option if you want the virtual router to query the liveliness of its IKE peer at regular intervals. It's recommended to have the same configuration of DPD on both side of VPN connection.

5. Click OK.

Updating and Removing a VPN Customer Gateway You can update a customer gateway either with no VPN connection, or related VPN connection is in error state.

1. Log in to the CloudStack UI as an administrator or end user.

2. In the left navigation, choose Network.

3. In the Select view, select VPN Customer Gateway.

4. Select the VPN customer gateway you want to work with.

5. To modify the required parameters, click the Edit VPN Customer Gateway button

6. To remove the VPN customer gateway, click the Delete VPN Customer Gateway button

7. Click OK.

Creating a VPN gateway for the VPC

1. Log in to the CloudStack UI as an administrator or end user.

2. In the left navigation, choose Network.

3. In the Select view, select VPC.

   All the VPCs that you have created for the account is listed in the page.

4. Click the Configure button of the VPC to which you want to deploy the VMs.

   The VPC page is displayed where all the tiers you created are listed in a diagram.

   For each tier, the following options are displayed:

   - Internal LB

   - Public LB IP

   - Static NAT

   - Virtual Machines

   - CIDR

   The following router information is displayed:

   - Private Gateways

   - Public IP Addresses

   - Site-to-Site VPNs

   - Network ACL Lists

5. Select Site-to-Site VPN.

   If you are creating the VPN gateway for the first time, selecting Site-to-Site VPN prompts you to create a VPN gateway.

6. In the confirmation dialog, click Yes to confirm.

   Within a few moments, the VPN gateway is created. You will be prompted to view the details of the VPN gateway you have created. Click Yes to confirm.

   The following details are displayed in the VPN Gateway page:

   - IP Address

   - Account

- Domain

Creating a VPN Connection

Note: CloudStack supports creating up to 8 VPN connections.

1. Log in to the CloudStack UI as an administrator or end user.

2. In the left navigation, choose Network.

3. In the Select view, select VPC.

   All the VPCs that you create for the account are listed in the page.

4. Click the Configure button of the VPC to which you want to deploy the VMs.

   The VPC page is displayed where all the tiers you created are listed in a diagram.

5. Click the Settings icon.

   For each tier, the following options are displayed:

   - Internal LB
   - Public LB IP
   - Static NAT
   - Virtual Machines
   - CIDR

   The following router information is displayed:

   - Private Gateways
   - Public IP Addresses
   - Site-to-Site VPNs
   - Network ACL Lists

6. Select Site-to-Site VPN.

   The Site-to-Site VPN page is displayed.

7. From the Select View drop-down, ensure that VPN Connection is selected.

8. Click Create VPN Connection.

   The Create VPN Connection dialog is displayed:

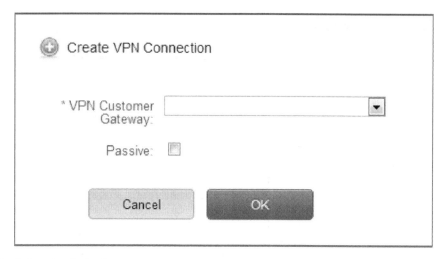

9. Select the desired customer gateway.

10. Select Passive if you want to establish a connection between two VPC virtual routers.

    If you want to establish a connection between two VPC virtual routers, select Passive only on one of the VPC virtual routers, which waits for the other VPC virtual router to initiate the connection. Do not select Passive on the VPC virtual router that initiates the connection.

11. Click OK to confirm.

    Within a few moments, the VPN Connection is displayed.

    The following information on the VPN connection is displayed:

    - IP Address

    - Gateway

    - State

    - IPSec Preshared Key

    - IKE Policy

    - ESP Policy

Site-to-Site VPN Connection Between VPC Networks

CloudStack provides you with the ability to establish a site-to-site VPN connection between CloudStack virtual routers. To achieve that, add a passive mode Site-to-Site VPN. With this functionality, users can deploy applications in multiple Availability Zones or VPCs, which can communicate with each other by using a secure Site-to-Site VPN Tunnel.

This feature is supported on all the hypervisors.

1. Create two VPCs. For example, VPC A and VPC B.

   For more information, see *"Configuring a Virtual Private Cloud"*.

2. Create VPN gateways on both the VPCs you created.

   For more information, see *"Creating a VPN gateway for the VPC"*.

3. Create VPN customer gateway for both the VPCs.

   For more information, see *"Creating and Updating a VPN Customer Gateway"*.

4. Enable a VPN connection on VPC A in passive mode.

   For more information, see *"Creating a VPN Connection"*.

   Ensure that the customer gateway is pointed to VPC B. The VPN connection is shown in the Disconnected state.

5. Enable a VPN connection on VPC B.

   Ensure that the customer gateway is pointed to VPC A. Because virtual router of VPC A, in this case, is in passive mode and is waiting for the virtual router of VPC B to initiate the connection, VPC B virtual router should not be in passive mode.

   The VPN connection is shown in the Disconnected state.

   Creating VPN connection on both the VPCs initiates a VPN connection. Wait for few seconds. The default is 30 seconds for both the VPN connections to show the Connected state.

Restarting and Removing a VPN Connection

1. Log in to the CloudStack UI as an administrator or end user.

2. In the left navigation, choose Network.

3. In the Select view, select VPC.

   All the VPCs that you have created for the account is listed in the page.

4. Click the Configure button of the VPC to which you want to deploy the VMs.

   The VPC page is displayed where all the tiers you created are listed in a diagram.

5. Click the Settings icon.

   For each tier, the following options are displayed:

   - Internal LB
   - Public LB IP
   - Static NAT
   - Virtual Machines
   - CIDR

   The following router information is displayed:

   - Private Gateways
   - Public IP Addresses
   - Site-to-Site VPNs
   - Network ACL Lists

6. Select Site-to-Site VPN.

   The Site-to-Site VPN page is displayed.

7. From the Select View drop-down, ensure that VPN Connection is selected.

   All the VPN connections you created are displayed.

8. Select the VPN connection you want to work with.

   The Details tab is displayed.

9. To remove a VPN connection, click the Delete VPN connection button

To restart a VPN connection, click the Reset VPN connection button present in the Details tab.

12.1.26 About Inter-VLAN Routing (nTier Apps)

Inter-VLAN Routing (nTier Apps) is the capability to route network traffic between VLANs. This feature enables you to build Virtual Private Clouds (VPC), an isolated segment of your cloud, that can hold multi-tier applications. These tiers are deployed on different VLANs that can communicate with each other. You provision VLANs to the tiers your create, and VMs can be deployed on different tiers. The VLANs are connected to a virtual router, which facilitates communication between the VMs. In effect, you can segment VMs by means of VLANs into different networks that can host multi-tier applications, such as Web, Application, or Database. Such segmentation by means of VLANs logically separate application VMs for higher security and lower broadcasts, while remaining physically connected to the same device.

This feature is supported on XenServer, KVM, and VMware hypervisors.

The major advantages are:

- The administrator can deploy a set of VLANs and allow users to deploy VMs on these VLANs. A guest VLAN is randomly alloted to an account from a pre-specified set of guest VLANs. All the VMs of a certain tier of an account reside on the guest VLAN allotted to that account.

Note: A VLAN allocated for an account cannot be shared between multiple accounts.

- The administrator can allow users create their own VPC and deploy the application. In this scenario, the VMs that belong to the account are deployed on the VLANs allotted to that account.

- Both administrators and users can create multiple VPCs. The guest network NIC is plugged to the VPC virtual router when the first VM is deployed in a tier.

- The administrator can create the following gateways to send to or receive traffic from the VMs:

    - **VPN Gateway**: For more information, see *"Creating a VPN gateway for the VPC"*.

    - **Public Gateway**: The public gateway for a VPC is added to the virtual router when the virtual router is created for VPC. The public gateway is not exposed to the end users. You are not allowed to list it, nor allowed to create any static routes.

    - **Private Gateway**: For more information, see *"Adding a Private Gateway to a VPC"*.

- Both administrators and users can create various possible destinations-gateway combinations. However, only one gateway of each type can be used in a deployment.

    For example:

    - **VLANs and Public Gateway**: For example, an application is deployed in the cloud, and the Web application VMs communicate with the Internet.

    - **VLANs, VPN Gateway, and Public Gateway**: For example, an application is deployed in the cloud; the Web application VMs communicate with the Internet; and the database VMs communicate with the on-premise devices.

- The administrator can define Network Access Control List (ACL) on the virtual router to filter the traffic among the VLANs or between the Internet and a VLAN. You can define ACL based on CIDR, port range, protocol, type code (if ICMP protocol is selected) and Ingress/Egress type.

The following figure shows the possible deployment scenarios of a Inter-VLAN setup:

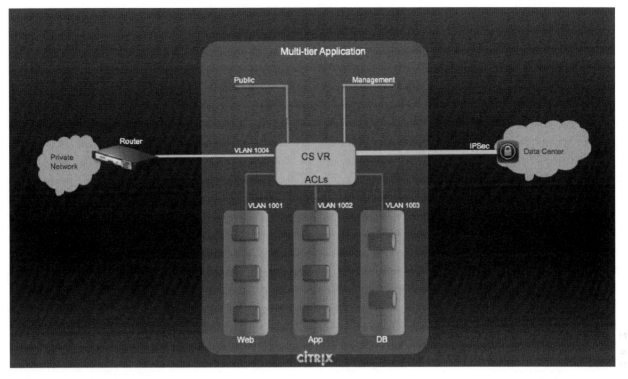

To set up a multi-tier Inter-VLAN deployment, see *"Configuring a Virtual Private Cloud"*.

12.1.27 Configuring a Virtual Private Cloud

About Virtual Private Clouds

CloudStack Virtual Private Cloud is a private, isolated part of CloudStack. A VPC can have its own virtual network topology that resembles a traditional physical network. You can launch VMs in the virtual network that can have private addresses in the range of your choice, for example: 10.0.0.0/16. You can define network tiers within your VPC network range, which in turn enables you to group similar kinds of instances based on IP address range.

For example, if a VPC has the private range 10.0.0.0/16, its guest networks can have the network ranges 10.0.1.0/24, 10.0.2.0/24, 10.0.3.0/24, and so on.

Major Components of a VPC

A VPC is comprised of the following network components:

- **VPC**: A VPC acts as a container for multiple isolated networks that can communicate with each other via its virtual router.

- **Network Tiers**: Each tier acts as an isolated network with its own VLANs and CIDR list, where you can place groups of resources, such as VMs. The tiers are segmented by means of VLANs. The NIC of each tier acts as its gateway.

- **Virtual Router**: A virtual router is automatically created and started when you create a VPC. The virtual router connect the tiers and direct traffic among the public gateway, the VPN gateways, and the NAT instances. For each tier, a corresponding NIC and IP exist in the virtual router. The virtual router provides DNS and DHCP services through its IP.

- **Public Gateway**: The traffic to and from the Internet routed to the VPC through the public gateway. In a VPC, the public gateway is not exposed to the end user; therefore, static routes are not support for the public gateway.

- **Private Gateway**: All the traffic to and from a private network routed to the VPC through the private gateway. For more information, see *"Adding a Private Gateway to a VPC"*.

- **VPN Gateway**: The VPC side of a VPN connection.

- **Site-to-Site VPN Connection**: A hardware-based VPN connection between your VPC and your datacenter, home network, or co-location facility. For more information, see *"Setting Up a Site-to-Site VPN Connection"*.

- **Customer Gateway**: The customer side of a VPN Connection. For more information, see *"Creating and Updating a VPN Customer Gateway"*.

- **NAT Instance**: An instance that provides Port Address Translation for instances to access the Internet via the public gateway. For more information, see *"Enabling or Disabling Static NAT on a VPC"*.

- **Network ACL**: Network ACL is a group of Network ACL items. Network ACL items are nothing but numbered rules that are evaluated in order, starting with the lowest numbered rule. These rules determine whether traffic is allowed in or out of any tier associated with the network ACL. For more information, see *"Configuring Network Access Control List"*.

Network Architecture in a VPC

In a VPC, the following four basic options of network architectures are present:
- VPC with a public gateway only
- VPC with public and private gateways
- VPC with public and private gateways and site-to-site VPN access
- VPC with a private gateway only and site-to-site VPN access

Connectivity Options for a VPC

You can connect your VPC to:
- The Internet through the public gateway.
- The corporate datacenter by using a site-to-site VPN connection through the VPN gateway.
- Both the Internet and your corporate datacenter by using both the public gateway and a VPN gateway.

VPC Network Considerations

Consider the following before you create a VPC:
- A VPC, by default, is created in the enabled state.
- A VPC can be created in Advance zone only, and can't belong to more than one zone at a time.
- The default number of VPCs an account can create is 20. However, you can change it by using the max.account.vpcs global parameter, which controls the maximum number of VPCs an account is allowed to create.
- The default number of tiers an account can create within a VPC is 3. You can configure this number by using the vpc.max.networks parameter.

- Each tier should have an unique CIDR in the VPC. Ensure that the tier's CIDR should be within the VPC CIDR range.

- A tier belongs to only one VPC.

- All network tiers inside the VPC should belong to the same account.

- When a VPC is created, by default, a SourceNAT IP is allocated to it. The Source NAT IP is released only when the VPC is removed.

- A public IP can be used for only one purpose at a time. If the IP is a sourceNAT, it cannot be used for StaticNAT or port forwarding.

- The instances can only have a private IP address that you provision. To communicate with the Internet, enable NAT to an instance that you launch in your VPC.

- Only new networks can be added to a VPC. The maximum number of networks per VPC is limited by the value you specify in the vpc.max.networks parameter. The default value is three.

- The load balancing service can be supported by only one tier inside the VPC.

- If an IP address is assigned to a tier:

    - That IP can't be used by more than one tier at a time in the VPC. For example, if you have tiers A and B, and a public IP1, you can create a port forwarding rule by using the IP either for A or B, but not for both.

    - That IP can't be used for StaticNAT, load balancing, or port forwarding rules for another guest network inside the VPC.

- Remote access VPN is not supported in VPC networks.

Adding a Virtual Private Cloud

When creating the VPC, you simply provide the zone and a set of IP addresses for the VPC network address space. You specify this set of addresses in the form of a Classless Inter-Domain Routing (CIDR) block.

1. Log in to the CloudStack UI as an administrator or end user.

2. In the left navigation, choose Network.

3. In the Select view, select VPC.

4. Click Add VPC. The Add VPC page is displayed as follows:

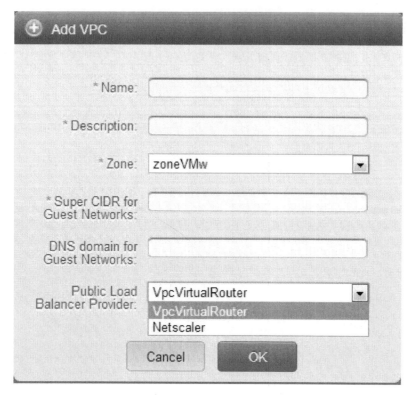

Provide the following information:

- **Name**: A short name for the VPC that you are creating.

- **Description**: A brief description of the VPC.

- **Zone**: Choose the zone where you want the VPC to be available.

- **Super CIDR for Guest Networks**: Defines the CIDR range for all the tiers (guest networks) within a VPC. When you create a tier, ensure that its CIDR is within the Super CIDR value you enter. The CIDR must be RFC1918 compliant.

- **DNS domain for Guest Networks**: If you want to assign a special domain name, specify the DNS suffix. This parameter is applied to all the tiers within the VPC. That implies, all the tiers you create in the VPC belong to the same DNS domain. If the parameter is not specified, a DNS domain name is generated automatically.

- **Public Load Balancer Provider**: You have two options: VPC Virtual Router and Netscaler.

5. Click OK.

Adding Tiers

Tiers are distinct locations within a VPC that act as isolated networks, which do not have access to other tiers by default. Tiers are set up on different VLANs that can communicate with each other by using a virtual router. Tiers provide inexpensive, low latency network connectivity to other tiers within the VPC.

1. Log in to the CloudStack UI as an administrator or end user.

2. In the left navigation, choose Network.

3. In the Select view, select VPC.

   All the VPC that you have created for the account is listed in the page.

Note: The end users can see their own VPCs, while root and domain admin can see any VPC they are authorized to see.

4. Click the Configure button of the VPC for which you want to set up tiers.

5. Click Create network.

   The Add new tier dialog is displayed, as follows:

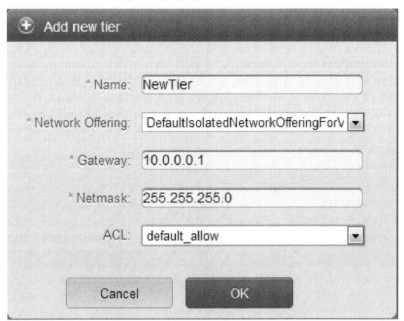

   If you have already created tiers, the VPC diagram is displayed. Click Create Tier to add a new tier.

6. Specify the following:

   All the fields are mandatory.

   • **Name**: A unique name for the tier you create.

   • **Network Offering**: The following default network offerings are listed: Internal LB, DefaultIsolatedNetworkOfferingForVpcNetworksNoLB, DefaultIsolatedNetworkOfferingForVpcNetworks

     In a VPC, only one tier can be created by using LB-enabled network offering.

   • **Gateway**: The gateway for the tier you create. Ensure that the gateway is within the Super CIDR range that you specified while creating the VPC, and is not overlapped with the CIDR of any existing tier within the VPC.

   • **VLAN**: The VLAN ID for the tier that the root admin creates.

     This option is only visible if the network offering you selected is VLAN-enabled.

     For more information, see "Assigning VLANs to Isolated Networks".

   • **Netmask**: The netmask for the tier you create.

     For example, if the VPC CIDR is 10.0.0.0/16 and the network tier CIDR is 10.0.1.0/24, the gateway of the tier is 10.0.1.1, and the netmask of the tier is 255.255.255.0.

7. Click OK.

8. Continue with configuring access control list for the tier.

Configuring Network Access Control List

Define Network Access Control List (ACL) on the VPC virtual router to control incoming (ingress) and outgoing (egress) traffic between the VPC tiers, and the tiers and Internet. By default, all incoming traffic to the guest networks is blocked and all outgoing traffic from guest networks is allowed, once you add an ACL rule for outgoing traffic, then only outgoing traffic specified in this ACL rule is allowed, the rest is blocked. To open the ports, you must create a new network ACL. The network ACLs can be created for the tiers only if the NetworkACL service is supported.

About Network ACL Lists

In CloudStack terminology, Network ACL is a group of Network ACL items. Network ACL items are nothing but numbered rules that are evaluated in order, starting with the lowest numbered rule. These rules determine whether traffic is allowed in or out of any tier associated with the network ACL. You need to add the Network ACL items to the Network ACL, then associate the Network ACL with a tier. Network ACL is associated with a VPC and can be assigned to multiple VPC tiers within a VPC. A Tier is associated with a Network ACL at all the times. Each tier can be associated with only one ACL.

The default Network ACL is used when no ACL is associated. Default behavior is all the incoming traffic is blocked and outgoing traffic is allowed from the tiers. Default network ACL cannot be removed or modified. Contents of the default Network ACL is:

Rule	Protocol	Traffic type	Action	CIDR
1	All	Ingress	Deny	0.0.0.0/0
2	All	Egress	Deny	0.0.0.0/0

Creating ACL Lists

1. Log in to the CloudStack UI as an administrator or end user.

2. In the left navigation, choose Network.

3. In the Select view, select VPC.

   All the VPCs that you have created for the account is listed in the page.

4. Click the Configure button of the VPC.

   For each tier, the following options are displayed:

   - Internal LB
   - Public LB IP
   - Static NAT
   - Virtual Machines
   - CIDR

   The following router information is displayed:

   - Private Gateways
   - Public IP Addresses
   - Site-to-Site VPNs
   - Network ACL Lists

5. Select Network ACL Lists.

   The following default rules are displayed in the Network ACLs page: default_allow, default_deny.

6. Click Add ACL Lists, and specify the following:

- **ACL List Name**: A name for the ACL list.

- **Description**: A short description of the ACL list that can be displayed to users.

Creating an ACL Rule

1. Log in to the CloudStack UI as an administrator or end user.

2. In the left navigation, choose Network.

3. In the Select view, select VPC.

   All the VPCs that you have created for the account is listed in the page.

4. Click the Configure button of the VPC.

5. Select Network ACL Lists.

   In addition to the custom ACL lists you have created, the following default rules are displayed in the Network ACLs page: default_allow, default_deny.

6. Select the desired ACL list.

7. Select the ACL List Rules tab.

   To add an ACL rule, fill in the following fields to specify what kind of network traffic is allowed in the VPC.

   - **Rule Number**: The order in which the rules are evaluated.

   - **CIDR**: The CIDR acts as the Source CIDR for the Ingress rules, and Destination CIDR for the Egress rules. To accept traffic only from or to the IP addresses within a particular address block, enter a CIDR or a comma-separated list of CIDRs. The CIDR is the base IP address of the incoming traffic. For example, 192.168.0.0/22. To allow all CIDRs, set to 0.0.0.0/0.

   - **Action**: What action to be taken. Allow traffic or block.

   - **Protocol**: The networking protocol that sources use to send traffic to the tier. The TCP and UDP protocols are typically used for data exchange and end-user communications. The ICMP protocol is typically used to send error messages or network monitoring data. All supports all the traffic. Other option is Protocol Number.

   - **Start Port**, **End Port** (TCP, UDP only): A range of listening ports that are the destination for the incoming traffic. If you are opening a single port, use the same number in both fields.

   - **Protocol Number**: The protocol number associated with IPv4 or IPv6. For more information, see Protocol Numbers.

   - **ICMP Type**, **ICMP Code** (ICMP only): The type of message and error code that will be sent.

   - **Traffic Type**: The type of traffic: Incoming or outgoing.

8. Click Add. The ACL rule is added.

   You can edit the tags assigned to the ACL rules and delete the ACL rules you have created. Click the appropriate button in the Details tab.

Creating a Tier with Custom ACL List

1. Create a VPC.

2. Create a custom ACL list.

---

3. Add ACL rules to the ACL list.

4. Create a tier in the VPC.

   Select the desired ACL list while creating a tier.

5. Click OK.

Assigning a Custom ACL List to a Tier

1. Create a VPC.

2. Create a tier in the VPC.

3. Associate the tier with the default ACL rule.

4. Create a custom ACL list.

5. Add ACL rules to the ACL list.

6. Select the tier for which you want to assign the custom ACL.

7. Click the Replace ACL List icon.

   The Replace ACL List dialog is displayed.

8. Select the desired ACL list.

9. Click OK.

Adding a Private Gateway to a VPC

A private gateway can be added by the root admin only. The VPC private network has 1:1 relationship with the NIC of the physical network. You can configure multiple private gateways to a single VPC. No gateways with duplicated VLAN and IP are allowed in the same data center.

1. Log in to the CloudStack UI as an administrator or end user.

2. In the left navigation, choose Network.

3. In the Select view, select VPC.

   All the VPCs that you have created for the account is listed in the page.

4. Click the Configure button of the VPC to which you want to configure load balancing rules.

   The VPC page is displayed where all the tiers you created are listed in a diagram.

5. Click the Settings icon.

   The following options are displayed.

   • Internal LB

   • Public LB IP

   • Static NAT

   • Virtual Machines

   • CIDR

   The following router information is displayed:

   • Private Gateways

- Public IP Addresses
- Site-to-Site VPNs
- Network ACL Lists

6. Select Private Gateways.

   The Gateways page is displayed.

7. Click Add new gateway:

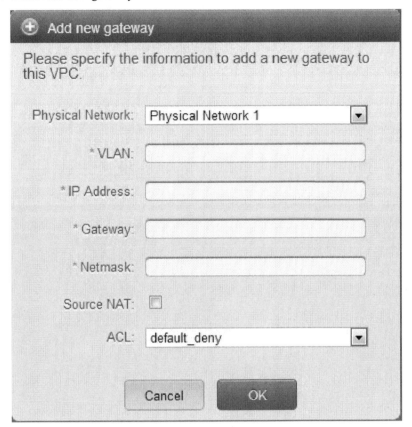

8. Specify the following:

   - **Physical Network**: The physical network you have created in the zone.
   - **IP Address**: The IP address associated with the VPC gateway.
   - **Gateway**: The gateway through which the traffic is routed to and from the VPC.
   - **Netmask**: The netmask associated with the VPC gateway.
   - **VLAN**: The VLAN associated with the VPC gateway.
   - **Source NAT**: Select this option to enable the source NAT service on the VPC private gateway.

     See "*Source NAT on Private Gateway*".
   - **ACL**: Controls both ingress and egress traffic on a VPC private gateway. By default, all the traffic is blocked.

     See "*ACL on Private Gateway*".

   The new gateway appears in the list. You can repeat these steps to add more gateway for this VPC.

Source NAT on Private Gateway

You might want to deploy multiple VPCs with the same super CIDR and guest tier CIDR. Therefore, multiple guest VMs from different VPCs can have the same IPs to reach a enterprise data center through the private gateway. In such cases, a NAT service need to be configured on the private gateway to avoid IP conflicts. If Source NAT is enabled, the guest VMs in VPC reaches the enterprise network via private gateway IP address by using the NAT service.

The Source NAT service on a private gateway can be enabled while adding the private gateway. On deletion of a private gateway, source NAT rules specific to the private gateway are deleted.

To enable source NAT on existing private gateways, delete them and create afresh with source NAT.

ACL on Private Gateway

The traffic on the VPC private gateway is controlled by creating both ingress and egress network ACL rules. The ACLs contains both allow and deny rules. As per the rule, all the ingress traffic to the private gateway interface and all the egress traffic out from the private gateway interface are blocked.

You can change this default behaviour while creating a private gateway. Alternatively, you can do the following:

1. In a VPC, identify the Private Gateway you want to work with.

2. In the Private Gateway page, do either of the following:

    • Use the Quickview. See 3.

    • Use the Details tab. See 4 through .

3. In the Quickview of the selected Private Gateway, click Replace ACL, select the ACL rule, then click OK

4. Click the IP address of the Private Gateway you want to work with.

5. In the Detail tab, click the Replace ACL button.

   The Replace ACL dialog is displayed.

6. select the ACL rule, then click OK.

   Wait for few seconds. You can see that the new ACL rule is displayed in the Details page.

Creating a Static Route

CloudStack enables you to specify routing for the VPN connection you create. You can enter one or CIDR addresses to indicate which traffic is to be routed back to the gateway.

1. In a VPC, identify the Private Gateway you want to work with.

2. In the Private Gateway page, click the IP address of the Private Gateway you want to work with.

3. Select the Static Routes tab.

4. Specify the CIDR of destination network.

5. Click Add.

   Wait for few seconds until the new route is created.

Blacklisting Routes

CloudStack enables you to block a list of routes so that they are not assigned to any of the VPC private gateways. Specify the list of routes that you want to blacklist in the `blacklisted.routes` global parameter. Note that the parameter update affects only new static route creations. If you block an existing static route, it remains intact and continue functioning. You cannot add a static route if the route is blacklisted for the zone.

Deploying VMs to the Tier

1. Log in to the CloudStack UI as an administrator or end user.

2. In the left navigation, choose Network.

3. In the Select view, select VPC.

   All the VPCs that you have created for the account is listed in the page.

4. Click the Configure button of the VPC to which you want to deploy the VMs.

   The VPC page is displayed where all the tiers you have created are listed.

5. Click Virtual Machines tab of the tier to which you want to add a VM.

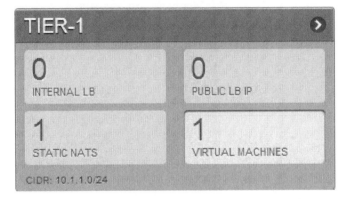

   The Add Instance page is displayed.

   Follow the on-screen instruction to add an instance. For information on adding an instance, see the Installation Guide.

Deploying VMs to VPC Tier and Shared Networks

CloudStack allows you deploy VMs on a VPC tier and one or more shared networks. With this feature, VMs deployed in a multi-tier application can receive monitoring services via a shared network provided by a service provider.

1. Log in to the CloudStack UI as an administrator.

2. In the left navigation, choose Instances.

3. Click Add Instance.

4. Select a zone.

5. Select a template or ISO, then follow the steps in the wizard.

6. Ensure that the hardware you have allows starting the selected service offering.

7. Under Networks, select the desired networks for the VM you are launching.

   You can deploy a VM to a VPC tier and multiple shared networks.

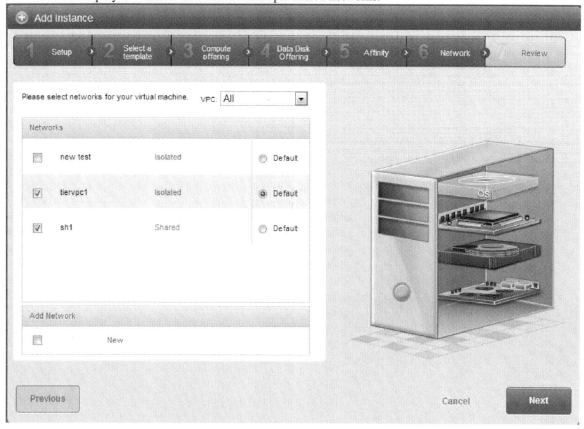

8. Click Next, review the configuration and click Launch.

   Your VM will be deployed to the selected VPC tier and shared network.

Acquiring a New IP Address for a VPC

When you acquire an IP address, all IP addresses are allocated to VPC, not to the guest networks within the VPC. The IPs are associated to the guest network only when the first port-forwarding, load balancing, or Static NAT rule is created for the IP or the network. IP can't be associated to more than one network at a time.

1. Log in to the CloudStack UI as an administrator or end user.

2. In the left navigation, choose Network.

3. In the Select view, select VPC.

   All the VPCs that you have created for the account is listed in the page.

4. Click the Configure button of the VPC to which you want to deploy the VMs.

   The VPC page is displayed where all the tiers you created are listed in a diagram.

   The following options are displayed.

   - Internal LB
   - Public LB IP
   - Static NAT

- Virtual Machines
- CIDR

The following router information is displayed:

- Private Gateways
- Public IP Addresses
- Site-to-Site VPNs
- Network ACL Lists

5. Select IP Addresses.

The Public IP Addresses page is displayed.

6. Click Acquire New IP, and click Yes in the confirmation dialog.

You are prompted for confirmation because, typically, IP addresses are a limited resource. Within a few moments, the new IP address should appear with the state Allocated. You can now use the IP address in port forwarding, load balancing, and static NAT rules.

Releasing an IP Address Alloted to a VPC

The IP address is a limited resource. If you no longer need a particular IP, you can disassociate it from its VPC and return it to the pool of available addresses. An IP address can be released from its tier, only when all the networking (port forwarding, load balancing, or StaticNAT) rules are removed for this IP address. The released IP address will still belongs to the same VPC.

1. Log in to the CloudStack UI as an administrator or end user.

2. In the left navigation, choose Network.

3. In the Select view, select VPC.

All the VPCs that you have created for the account is listed in the page.

4. Click the Configure button of the VPC whose IP you want to release.

The VPC page is displayed where all the tiers you created are listed in a diagram.

The following options are displayed.

- Internal LB
- Public LB IP
- Static NAT
- Virtual Machines
- CIDR

The following router information is displayed:

- Private Gateways
- Public IP Addresses
- Site-to-Site VPNs
- Network ACL Lists

5. Select Public IP Addresses.

The IP Addresses page is displayed.

6. Click the IP you want to release.

7. In the Details tab, click the Release IP button

Enabling or Disabling Static NAT on a VPC

A static NAT rule maps a public IP address to the private IP address of a VM in a VPC to allow Internet traffic to it. This section tells how to enable or disable static NAT for a particular IP address in a VPC.

If port forwarding rules are already in effect for an IP address, you cannot enable static NAT to that IP.

If a guest VM is part of more than one network, static NAT rules will function only if they are defined on the default network.

1. Log in to the CloudStack UI as an administrator or end user.

2. In the left navigation, choose Network.

3. In the Select view, select VPC.

   All the VPCs that you have created for the account is listed in the page.

4. Click the Configure button of the VPC to which you want to deploy the VMs.

   The VPC page is displayed where all the tiers you created are listed in a diagram.

   For each tier, the following options are displayed.

   - Internal LB

   - Public LB IP

   - Static NAT

   - Virtual Machines

   - CIDR

   The following router information is displayed:

   - Private Gateways

   - Public IP Addresses

   - Site-to-Site VPNs

   - Network ACL Lists

5. In the Router node, select Public IP Addresses.

   The IP Addresses page is displayed.

6. Click the IP you want to work with.

7. In the Details tab,click the Static NAT button. The button toggles between Enable and Disable, depending on whether static NAT is currently enabled for the IP address.

8. If you are enabling static NAT, a dialog appears as follows:

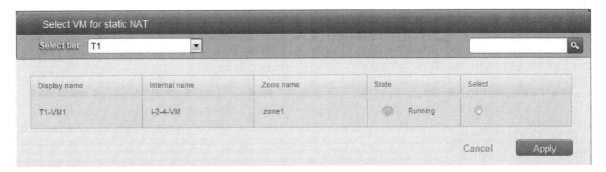

9. Select the tier and the destination VM, then click Apply.

Adding Load Balancing Rules on a VPC

In a VPC, you can configure two types of load balancing: external LB and internal LB. External LB is nothing but a LB rule created to redirect the traffic received at a public IP of the VPC virtual router. The traffic is load balanced within a tier based on your configuration. Citrix NetScaler and VPC virtual router are supported for external LB. When you use internal LB service, traffic received at a tier is load balanced across different VMs within that tier. For example, traffic reached at Web tier is redirected to another VM in that tier. External load balancing devices are not supported for internal LB. The service is provided by a internal LB VM configured on the target tier.

Load Balancing Within a Tier (External LB)

A CloudStack user or administrator may create load balancing rules that balance traffic received at a public IP to one or more VMs that belong to a network tier that provides load balancing service in a VPC. A user creates a rule, specifies an algorithm, and assigns the rule to a set of VMs within a tier.

Enabling NetScaler as the LB Provider on a VPC Tier

1. Add and enable Netscaler VPX in dedicated mode.

   Netscaler can be used in a VPC environment only if it is in dedicated mode.

2. Create a network offering, as given in *"Creating a Network Offering for External LB"*.

3. Create a VPC with Netscaler as the Public LB provider.

   For more information, see *"Adding a Virtual Private Cloud"*.

4. For the VPC, acquire an IP.

5. Create an external load balancing rule and apply, as given in *Creating an External LB Rule*.

Creating a Network Offering for External LB   To have external LB support on VPC, create a network offering as follows:

1. Log in to the CloudStack UI as a user or admin.

2. From the Select Offering drop-down, choose Network Offering.

3. Click Add Network Offering.

4. In the dialog, make the following choices:

   - **Name**: Any desired name for the network offering.

   - **Description**: A short description of the offering that can be displayed to users.

- **Network Rate**: Allowed data transfer rate in MB per second.

- **Traffic Type**: The type of network traffic that will be carried on the network.

- **Guest Type**: Choose whether the guest network is isolated or shared.

- **Persistent**: Indicate whether the guest network is persistent or not. The network that you can provision without having to deploy a VM on it is termed persistent network.

- **VPC**: This option indicate whether the guest network is Virtual Private Cloud-enabled. A Virtual Private Cloud (VPC) is a private, isolated part of CloudStack. A VPC can have its own virtual network topology that resembles a traditional physical network. For more information on VPCs, see *"About Virtual Private Clouds"*.

- **Specify VLAN**: (Isolated guest networks only) Indicate whether a VLAN should be specified when this offering is used.

- **Supported Services**: Select Load Balancer. Use Netscaler or VpcVirtualRouter.

- **Load Balancer Type**: Select Public LB from the drop-down.

- **LB Isolation**: Select Dedicated if Netscaler is used as the external LB provider.

- **System Offering**: Choose the system service offering that you want virtual routers to use in this network.

- **Conserve mode**: Indicate whether to use conserve mode. In this mode, network resources are allocated only when the first virtual machine starts in the network.

5. Click OK and the network offering is created.

Creating an External LB Rule

1. Log in to the CloudStack UI as an administrator or end user.

2. In the left navigation, choose Network.

3. In the Select view, select VPC.

   All the VPCs that you have created for the account is listed in the page.

4. Click the Configure button of the VPC, for which you want to configure load balancing rules.

   The VPC page is displayed where all the tiers you created listed in a diagram.

   For each tier, the following options are displayed:

   - Internal LB
   - Public LB IP
   - Static NAT
   - Virtual Machines
   - CIDR

   The following router information is displayed:

   - Private Gateways
   - Public IP Addresses
   - Site-to-Site VPNs
   - Network ACL Lists

5. In the Router node, select Public IP Addresses.

   The IP Addresses page is displayed.

6. Click the IP address for which you want to create the rule, then click the Configuration tab.

7. In the Load Balancing node of the diagram, click View All.

8. Select the tier to which you want to apply the rule.

9. Specify the following:

   - **Name**: A name for the load balancer rule.

   - **Public Port**: The port that receives the incoming traffic to be balanced.

   - **Private Port**: The port that the VMs will use to receive the traffic.

   - **Algorithm**. Choose the load balancing algorithm you want CloudStack to use. CloudStack supports the following well-known algorithms:

     - Round-robin

     - Least connections

     - Source

   - **Stickiness**. (Optional) Click Configure and choose the algorithm for the stickiness policy. See Sticky Session Policies for Load Balancer Rules.

   - **Add VMs**: Click Add VMs, then select two or more VMs that will divide the load of incoming traffic, and click Apply.

The new load balancing rule appears in the list. You can repeat these steps to add more load balancing rules for this IP address.

Load Balancing Across Tiers

CloudStack supports sharing workload across different tiers within your VPC. Assume that multiple tiers are set up in your environment, such as Web tier and Application tier. Traffic to each tier is balanced on the VPC virtual router on the public side, as explained in *"Adding Load Balancing Rules on a VPC"*. If you want the traffic coming from the Web tier to the Application tier to be balanced, use the internal load balancing feature offered by CloudStack.

How Does Internal LB Work in VPC? In this figure, a public LB rule is created for the public IP 72.52.125.10 with public port 80 and private port 81. The LB rule, created on the VPC virtual router, is applied on the traffic coming from the Internet to the VMs on the Web tier. On the Application tier two internal load balancing rules are created. An internal LB rule for the guest IP 10.10.10.4 with load balancer port 23 and instance port 25 is configured on the VM, InternalLBVM1. Another internal LB rule for the guest IP 10.10.10.4 with load balancer port 45 and instance port 46 is configured on the VM, InternalLBVM1. Another internal LB rule for the guest IP 10.10.10.6, with load balancer port 23 and instance port 25 is configured on the VM, InternalLBVM2.

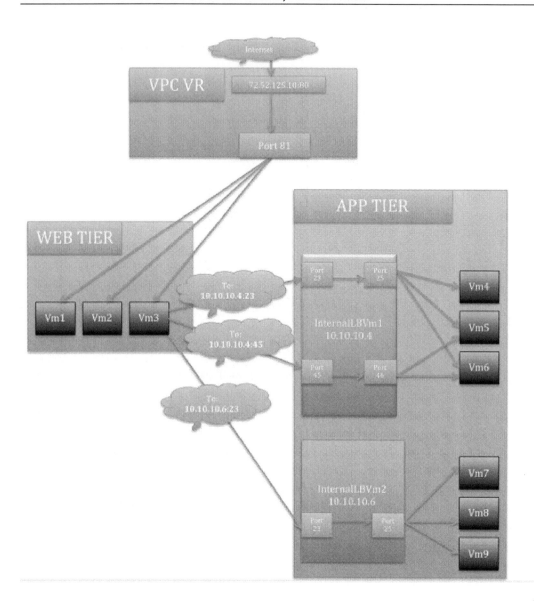

Guidelines

- Internal LB and Public LB are mutually exclusive on a tier. If the tier has LB on the public side, then it can't have the Internal LB.

- Internal LB is supported just on VPC networks in CloudStack 4.2 release.

- Only Internal LB VM can act as the Internal LB provider in CloudStack 4.2 release.

- Network upgrade is not supported from the network offering with Internal LB to the network offering with Public LB.

- Multiple tiers can have internal LB support in a VPC.

- Only one tier can have Public LB support in a VPC.

Enabling Internal LB on a VPC Tier

1. Create a network offering, as given in *Creating a Network Offering for Internal LB*.

2. Create an internal load balancing rule and apply, as given in *Creating an Internal LB Rule*.

Creating a Network Offering for Internal LB   To have internal LB support on VPC, either use the default offering, DefaultIsolatedNetworkOfferingForVpcNetworksWithInternalLB, or create a network offering as follows:

1. Log in to the CloudStack UI as a user or admin.

2. From the Select Offering drop-down, choose Network Offering.

3. Click Add Network Offering.

4. In the dialog, make the following choices:

    - **Name**: Any desired name for the network offering.

    - **Description**: A short description of the offering that can be displayed to users.

    - **Network Rate**: Allowed data transfer rate in MB per second.

    - **Traffic Type**: The type of network traffic that will be carried on the network.

    - **Guest Type**: Choose whether the guest network is isolated or shared.

    - **Persistent**: Indicate whether the guest network is persistent or not. The network that you can provision without having to deploy a VM on it is termed persistent network.

    - **VPC**: This option indicate whether the guest network is Virtual Private Cloud-enabled. A Virtual Private Cloud (VPC) is a private, isolated part of CloudStack. A VPC can have its own virtual network topology that resembles a traditional physical network. For more information on VPCs, see *"About Virtual Private Clouds"*.

    - **Specify VLAN**: (Isolated guest networks only) Indicate whether a VLAN should be specified when this offering is used.

    - **Supported Services**: Select Load Balancer. Select `InternalLbVM` from the provider list.

    - **Load Balancer Type**: Select Internal LB from the drop-down.

    - **System Offering**: Choose the system service offering that you want virtual routers to use in this network.

    - **Conserve mode**: Indicate whether to use conserve mode. In this mode, network resources are allocated only when the first virtual machine starts in the network.

5. Click OK and the network offering is created.

Creating an Internal LB Rule   When you create the Internal LB rule and applies to a VM, an Internal LB VM, which is responsible for load balancing, is created.

You can view the created Internal LB VM in the Instances page if you navigate to **Infrastructure > Zones** > <zone_name> > <physical_network_name> > **Network Service Providers > Internal LB VM**. You can manage the Internal LB VMs as and when required from the location.

1. Log in to the CloudStack UI as an administrator or end user.

2. In the left navigation, choose Network.

3. In the Select view, select VPC.

    All the VPCs that you have created for the account is listed in the page.

4. Locate the VPC for which you want to configure internal LB, then click Configure.

    The VPC page is displayed where all the tiers you created listed in a diagram.

5. Locate the Tier for which you want to configure an internal LB rule, click Internal LB.

    In the Internal LB page, click Add Internal LB.

6. In the dialog, specify the following:

- **Name**: A name for the load balancer rule.

- **Description**: A short description of the rule that can be displayed to users.

- **Source IP Address**: (Optional) The source IP from which traffic originates. The IP is acquired from the CIDR of that particular tier on which you want to create the Internal LB rule. If not specified, the IP address is automatically allocated from the network CIDR.

  For every Source IP, a new Internal LB VM is created for load balancing.

- **Source Port**: The port associated with the source IP. Traffic on this port is load balanced.

- **Instance Port**: The port of the internal LB VM.

- **Algorithm**. Choose the load balancing algorithm you want CloudStack to use. CloudStack supports the following well-known algorithms:

  - Round-robin

  - Least connections

  - Source

Adding a Port Forwarding Rule on a VPC

1. Log in to the CloudStack UI as an administrator or end user.

2. In the left navigation, choose Network.

3. In the Select view, select VPC.

   All the VPCs that you have created for the account is listed in the page.

4. Click the Configure button of the VPC to which you want to deploy the VMs.

   The VPC page is displayed where all the tiers you created are listed in a diagram.

   For each tier, the following options are displayed:

   - Internal LB

   - Public LB IP

   - Static NAT

   - Virtual Machines

   - CIDR

   The following router information is displayed:

   - Private Gateways

   - Public IP Addresses

   - Site-to-Site VPNs

   - Network ACL Lists

5. In the Router node, select Public IP Addresses.

   The IP Addresses page is displayed.

6. Click the IP address for which you want to create the rule, then click the Configuration tab.

7. In the Port Forwarding node of the diagram, click View All.

8. Select the tier to which you want to apply the rule.

9. Specify the following:

   - **Public Port**: The port to which public traffic will be addressed on the IP address you acquired in the previous step.

   - **Private Port**: The port on which the instance is listening for forwarded public traffic.

   - **Protocol**: The communication protocol in use between the two ports.

     - TCP

     - UDP

   - **Add VM**: Click Add VM. Select the name of the instance to which this rule applies, and click Apply.

   You can test the rule by opening an SSH session to the instance.

Removing Tiers

You can remove a tier from a VPC. A removed tier cannot be revoked. When a tier is removed, only the resources of the tier are expunged. All the network rules (port forwarding, load balancing and staticNAT) and the IP addresses associated to the tier are removed. The IP address still be belonging to the same VPC.

1. Log in to the CloudStack UI as an administrator or end user.

2. In the left navigation, choose Network.

3. In the Select view, select VPC.

   All the VPC that you have created for the account is listed in the page.

4. Click the Configure button of the VPC for which you want to set up tiers.

   The Configure VPC page is displayed. Locate the tier you want to work with.

5. Select the tier you want to remove.

6. In the Network Details tab, click the Delete Network button.

   Click Yes to confirm. Wait for some time for the tier to be removed.

Editing, Restarting, and Removing a Virtual Private Cloud

Note: Ensure that all the tiers are removed before you remove a VPC.

1. Log in to the CloudStack UI as an administrator or end user.

2. In the left navigation, choose Network.

3. In the Select view, select VPC.

   All the VPCs that you have created for the account is listed in the page.

4. Select the VPC you want to work with.

5. In the Details tab, click the Remove VPC button

   You can remove the VPC by also using the remove button in the Quick View.

   You can edit the name and description of a VPC. To do that, select the VPC, then click the Edit button.

To restart a VPC, select the VPC, then click the Restart button.

12.1.28 Persistent Networks

The network that you can provision without having to deploy any VMs on it is called a persistent network. A persistent network can be part of a VPC or a non-VPC environment.

When you create other types of network, a network is only a database entry until the first VM is created on that network. When the first VM is created, a VLAN ID is assigned and the network is provisioned. Also, when the last VM is destroyed, the VLAN ID is released and the network is no longer available. With the addition of persistent network, you will have the ability to create a network in CloudStack in which physical devices can be deployed without having to run any VMs. Additionally, you can deploy physical devices on that network.

One of the advantages of having a persistent network is that you can create a VPC with a tier consisting of only physical devices. For example, you might create a VPC for a three-tier application, deploy VMs for Web and Application tier, and use physical machines for the Database tier. Another use case is that if you are providing services by using physical hardware, you can define the network as persistent and therefore even if all its VMs are destroyed the services will not be discontinued.

Persistent Network Considerations

- Persistent network is designed for isolated networks.
- All default network offerings are non-persistent.
- A network offering cannot be editable because changing it affects the behavior of the existing networks that were created using this network offering.
- When you create a guest network, the network offering that you select defines the network persistence. This in turn depends on whether persistent network is enabled in the selected network offering.
- An existing network can be made persistent by changing its network offering to an offering that has the Persistent option enabled. While setting this property, even if the network has no running VMs, the network is provisioned.
- An existing network can be made non-persistent by changing its network offering to an offering that has the Persistent option disabled. If the network has no running VMs, during the next network garbage collection run the network is shut down.
- When the last VM on a network is destroyed, the network garbage collector checks if the network offering associated with the network is persistent, and shuts down the network only if it is non-persistent.

Creating a Persistent Guest Network

To create a persistent network, perform the following:

1. Create a network offering with the Persistent option enabled.

   See "Creating a New Network Offering".

2. Select Network from the left navigation pane.
3. Select the guest network that you want to offer this network service to.
4. Click the Edit button.
5. From the Network Offering drop-down, select the persistent network offering you have just created.
6. Click OK.

12.1.29 Setup a Palo Alto Networks Firewall

Functionality Provided

This implementation enables the orchestration of a Palo Alto Networks Firewall from within CloudStack UI and API.

The following features are supported:

- List/Add/Delete Palo Alto Networks service provider
- List/Add/Delete Palo Alto Networks network service offering
- List/Add/Delete Palo Alto Networks network using the above service offering
- Add an instance to a Palo Alto Networks network
- Source NAT management on network create and delete
- List/Add/Delete Ingress Firewall rule
- List/Add/Delete Egress Firewall rule (both 'Allow' and 'Deny' default rules supported)
- List/Add/Delete Port Forwarding rule
- List/Add/Delete Static NAT rule
- Apply a Threat Profile to all firewall rules (more details in the Additional Features section)
- Apply a Log Forwarding profile to all firewall rules (more details in the Additional Features section)

Initial Palo Alto Networks Firewall Configuration

Anatomy of the Palo Alto Networks Firewall

- In **'Network > Interfaces'** there is a list of physical interfaces as well as aggregated physical interfaces which are used for managing traffic in and out of the Palo Alto Networks Firewall device.
- In **'Network > Zones'** there is a list of the different configuration zones. This implementation will use two zones; a public (defaults to 'untrust') and private (defaults to 'trust') zone.
- In **'Network > Virtual Routers'** there is a list of VRs which handle traffic routing for the Palo Alto Firewall. We only use a single Virtual Router on the firewall and it is used to handle all the routing to the next network hop.
- In **'Objects > Security Profile Groups'** there is a list of profiles which can be applied to firewall rules. These profiles are used to better understand the types of traffic that is flowing through your network. Configured when you add the firewall provider to CloudStack.
- In **'Objects > Log Forwarding'** there is a list of profiles which can be applied to firewall rules. These profiles are used to better track the logs generated by the firewall. Configured when you add the firewall provider to CloudStack.
- In **'Policies > Security'** there is a list of firewall rules that are currently configured. You will not need to modify this section because it will be completely automated by CloudStack, but you can review the firewall rules which have been created here.
- In **'Policies > NAT'** there is a list of the different NAT rules. You will not need to modify this section because it will be completely automated by CloudStack, but you can review the different NAT rules that have been created here. Source NAT, Static NAT and Destination NAT (Port Forwarding) rules will show up in this list.

Configure the Public / Private Zones on the firewall

No manual configuration is required to setup these zones because CloudStack will configure them automatically when you add the Palo Alto Networks firewall device to CloudStack as a service provider. This implementation depends on two zones, one for the public side and one for the private side of the firewall.

- The public zone (defaults to 'untrust') will contain all of the public interfaces and public IPs.
- The private zone (defaults to 'trust') will contain all of the private interfaces and guest network gateways.

The NAT and firewall rules will be configured between these zones.

Configure the Public / Private Interfaces on the firewall

This implementation supports standard physical interfaces as well as grouped physical interfaces called aggregated interfaces. Both standard interfaces and aggregated interfaces are treated the same, so they can be used interchangeably. For this document, we will assume that we are using 'ethernet1/1' as the public interface and 'ethernet1/2' as the private interface. If aggregated interfaces where used, you would use something like 'ae1' and 'ae2' as the interfaces.

This implementation requires that the 'Interface Type' be set to 'Layer3' for both the public and private interfaces. If you want to be able to use the 'Untagged' VLAN tag for public traffic in CloudStack, you will need to enable support for it in the public 'ethernet1/1' interface (details below).

Steps to configure the Public Interface:

1. Log into Palo Alto Networks Firewall
2. Navigate to 'Network > Interfaces'
3. Click on 'ethernet1/1' (for aggregated ethernet, it will probably be called 'ae1')
4. Select 'Layer3' from the 'Interface Type' list
5. Click 'Advanced'
6. Check the 'Untagged Subinterface' check-box
7. Click 'OK'

Steps to configure the Private Interface:

1. Click on 'ethernet1/2' (for aggregated ethernet, it will probably be called 'ae2')
2. Select 'Layer3' from the 'Interface Type' list
3. Click 'OK'

Configure a Virtual Router on the firewall

The Virtual Router on the Palo Alto Networks Firewall is not to be confused with the Virtual Routers that CloudStack provisions. For this implementation, the Virtual Router on the Palo Alto Networks Firewall will ONLY handle the upstream routing from the Firewall to the next hop.

Steps to configure the Virtual Router:

1. Log into Palo Alto Networks Firewall
2. Navigate to 'Network > Virtual Routers'
3. Select the 'default' Virtual Router or Add a new Virtual Router if there are none in the list
   - If you added a new Virtual Router, you will need to give it a 'Name'

4. Navigate to 'Static Routes > IPv4'

5. 'Add' a new static route

   - **Name**: next_hop (you can name it anything you want)

   - **Destination**: 0.0.0.0/0 (send all traffic to this route)

   - **Interface**: ethernet1/1 (or whatever you set your public interface as)

   - **Next Hop**: (specify the gateway IP for the next hop in your network)

   - Click 'OK'

6. Click 'OK'

Configure the default Public Subinterface

The current implementation of the Palo Alto Networks firewall integration uses CIDRs in the form of 'w.x.y.z/32' for the public IP addresses that CloudStack provisions. Because no broadcast or gateway IPs are in this single IP range, there is no way for the firewall to route the traffic for these IPs. To route the traffic for these IPs, we create a single subinterface on the public interface with an IP and a CIDR which encapsulates the CloudStack public IP range. This IP will need to be inside the subnet defined by the CloudStack public range netmask, but outside the CloudStack public IP range. The CIDR should reflect the same subnet defined by the CloudStack public range netmask. The name of the subinterface is determined by the VLAN configured for the public range in CloudStack.

To clarify this concept, we will use the following example.

Example CloudStack Public Range Configuration:

- **Gateway**: 172.30.0.1

- **Netmask**: 255.255.255.0

- **IP Range**: 172.30.0.100 - 172.30.0.199

- **VLAN**: Untagged

Configure the Public Subinterface:

1. Log into Palo Alto Networks Firewall

2. Navigate to 'Network > Interfaces'

3. Select the 'ethernet1/1' line (not clicking on the name)

4. Click 'Add Subinterface' at the bottom of the window

5. Enter 'Interface Name': 'ethernet1/1' . '9999'

   - 9999 is used if the CloudStack public range VLAN is 'Untagged'

   - If the CloudStack public range VLAN is tagged (eg: 333), then the name will reflect that tag

6. The 'Tag' is the VLAN tag that the traffic is sent to the next hop with, so set it accordingly. If you are passing 'Untagged' traffic from CloudStack to your next hop, leave it blank. If you want to pass tagged traffic from CloudStack, specify the tag.

7. Select 'default' from the 'Config > Virtual Router' drop-down (assuming that is what your virtual router is called)

8. Click the 'IPv4' tab

9. Select 'Static' from the 'Type' radio options

10. Click 'Add' in the 'IP' section

11. Enter '172.30.0.254/24' in the new line

   • The IP can be any IP outside the CloudStack public IP range, but inside the CloudStack public range netmask (it can NOT be the gateway IP)

   • The subnet defined by the CIDR should match the CloudStack public range netmask

12. Click 'OK'

Commit configuration on the Palo Alto Networks Firewall

In order for all the changes we just made to take effect, we need to commit the changes.

1. Click the 'Commit' link in the top right corner of the window

2. Click 'OK' in the commit window overlay

3. Click 'Close' to the resulting commit status window after the commit finishes

Setup the Palo Alto Networks Firewall in CloudStack

Add the Palo Alto Networks Firewall as a Service Provider

1. Navigate to 'Infrastructure > Zones > ZONE_NAME > Physical Network > NETWORK_NAME (guest) > Configure; Network Service Providers'

2. Click on 'Palo Alto' in the list

3. Click 'View Devices'

4. Click 'Add Palo Alto Device'

5. Enter your configuration in the overlay. This example will reflect the details previously used in this guide.

   • **IP Address**: (the IP of the Palo Alto Networks Firewall)

   • **Username**: (the admin username for the firewall)

   • **Password**: (the admin password for the firewall)

   • **Type**: Palo Alto Firewall

   • **Public Interface**: ethernet1/1 (use what you setup earlier as the public interface if it is different from my examples)

   • **Private Interface**: ethernet1/2 (use what you setup earlier as the private interface if it is different from my examples)

   • **Number of Retries**: 2 (the default is fine)

   • **Timeout**: 300 (the default is fine)

   • **Public Network**: untrust (this is the public zone on the firewall and did not need to be configured)

   • **Private Network**: trust (this is the private zone on the firewall and did not need to be configured)

   • **Virtual Router**: default (this is the name of the Virtual Router we setup on the firewall)

   • **Palo Alto Threat Profile**: (not required. name of the 'Security Profile Groups' to apply. more details in the 'Additional Features' section)

   • **Palo Alto Log Profile**: (not required. name of the 'Log Forwarding' profile to apply. more details in the 'Additional Features' section)

- **Capacity**: (not required)
- **Dedicated**: (not required)

6. Click 'OK'

7. Click on 'Palo Alto' in the breadcrumbs to go back one screen.

8. Click on 'Enable Provider'

Add a Network Service Offering to use the new Provider

There are 6 'Supported Services' that need to be configured in the network service offering for this functionality. They are DHCP, DNS, Firewall, Source NAT, Static NAT and Port Forwarding. For the other settings, there are probably additional configurations which will work, but I will just document a common case.

1. Navigate to 'Service Offerings'

2. In the drop-down at the top, select 'Network Offerings'

3. Click 'Add Network Offering'

   - **Name**: (name it whatever you want)
   - **Description**: (again, can be whatever you want)
   - **Guest Type**: Isolated
   - **Supported Services**:
     - **DHCP**: Provided by 'VirtualRouter'
     - **DNS**: Provided by 'VirtualRouter'
     - **Firewall**: Provided by 'PaloAlto'
     - **Source NAT**: Provided by 'PaloAlto'
     - **Static NAT**: Provided by 'PaloAlto'
     - **Port Forwarding**: Provided by 'PaloAlto'
   - **System Offering for Router**: System Offering For Software Router
   - **Supported Source NAT Type**: Per account (this is the only supported option)
   - **Default egress policy**: (both 'Allow' and 'Deny' are supported)

4. Click 'OK'

5. Click on the newly created service offering

6. Click 'Enable network offering'

When adding networks in CloudStack, select this network offering to use the Palo Alto Networks firewall.

Additional Features

In addition to the standard functionality exposed by CloudStack, we have added a couple additional features to this implementation. We did not add any new screens to CloudStack, but we have added a couple fields to the 'Add Palo Alto Service Provider' screen which will add functionality globally for the device.

Palo Alto Networks Threat Profile

This feature allows you to specify a 'Security Profile Group' to be applied to all of the firewall rules which are created on the Palo Alto Networks firewall device.

To create a 'Security Profile Group' on the Palo Alto Networks firewall, do the following:

1. Log into the Palo Alto Networks firewall
2. Navigate to 'Objects > Security Profile Groups'
3. Click 'Add' at the bottom of the page to add a new group
4. Give the group a Name and specify the profiles you would like to include in the group
5. Click 'OK'
6. Click the 'Commit' link in the top right of the screen and follow the on screen instructions

Once you have created a profile, you can reference it by Name in the 'Palo Alto Threat Profile' field in the 'Add the Palo Alto Networks Firewall as a Service Provider' step.

Palo Alto Networks Log Forwarding Profile

This feature allows you to specify a 'Log Forwarding' profile to better manage where the firewall logs are sent to. This is helpful for keeping track of issues that can arise on the firewall.

To create a 'Log Forwarding' profile on the Palo Alto Networks Firewall, do the following:

1. Log into the Palo Alto Networks firewall
2. Navigate to 'Objects > Log Forwarding'
3. Click 'Add' at the bottom of the page to add a new profile
4. Give the profile a Name and specify the details you want for the traffic and threat settings
5. Click 'OK'
6. Click the 'Commit' link in the top right of the screen and follow the on screen instructions

Once you have created a profile, you can reference it by Name in the 'Palo Alto Log Profile' field in the 'Add the Palo Alto Networks Firewall as a Service Provider' step.

Limitations

- The implementation currently only supports a single public IP range in CloudStack
- Usage tracking is not yet implemented

12.2 Using Remote Access VPN

Clients

Per Operating System instructions

- *Mac OSX*
- *Microsoft Windows 8*

Remote Access VPN connection to VPC or Guest Network to access Instances and applications. This section consider you have enable Remonte acccess VPN, refer to: *Remote Access VPN*.

When connected to a VPC via VPN, the client have access to all Tiers.

Following information is required to confiture VPN client:

- `Public IP`: source NAT with VPN enabled.
- `IPsec pre-shared key`: Provide at the VPN activation.
- `Username` VPN account username.
- `Password` VPN account password.

12.2.1 Mac OSX

Mac OSX provide native IPsec VPN client.

1. Into System Preferences -> Network
2. Click "+" button and add a VPN:
   - Interface: VPN
   - VPN Type: L2TP over IPSec
   - Service Name: (ex: test-vpc1)

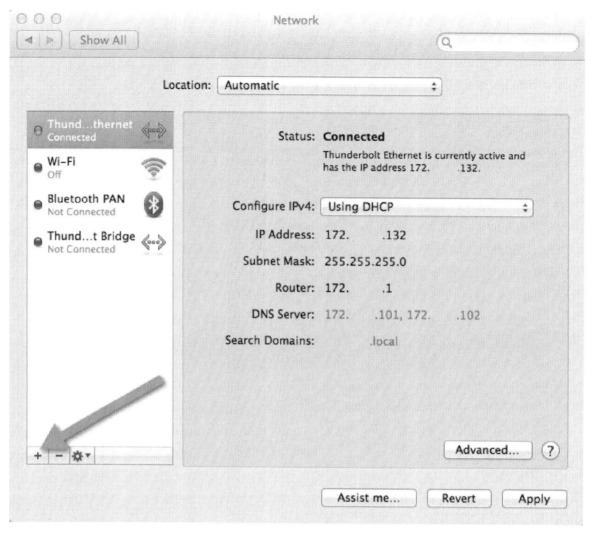

3. Configure L2TP over IPsec

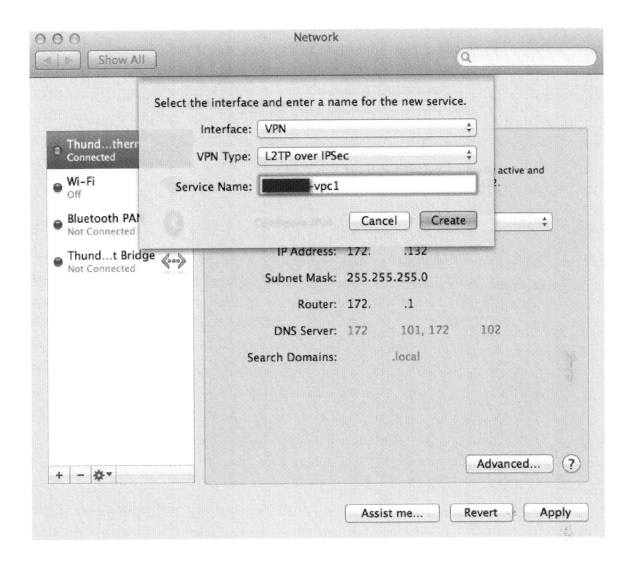

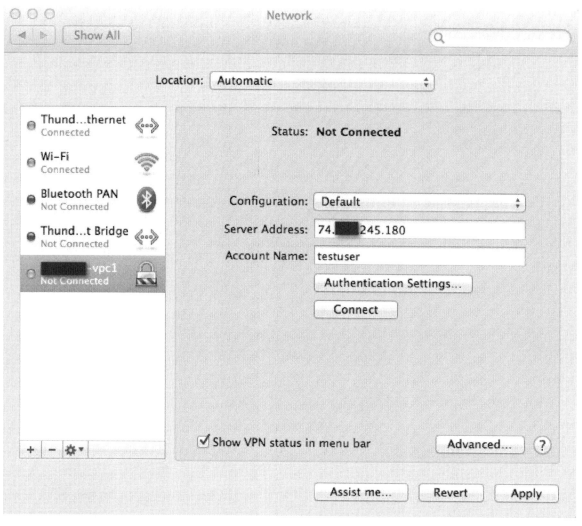

4. Inside Authentication Settings...

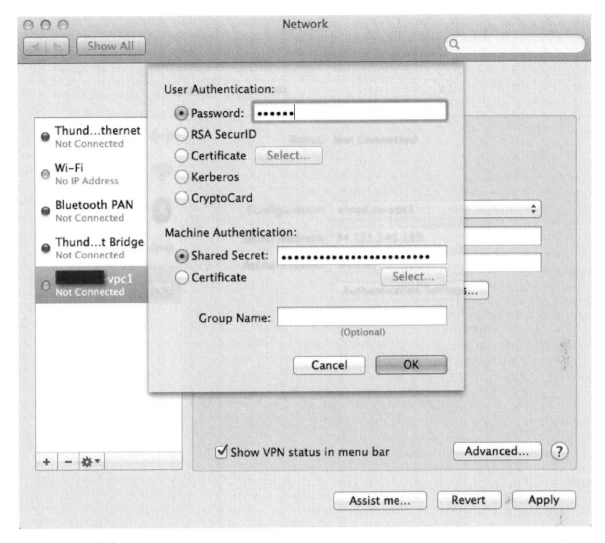

5. Connect into VPN

   (a) Click Apply to apply Network configuration changes.

   (b) Click Connect to initiate VPN connection.

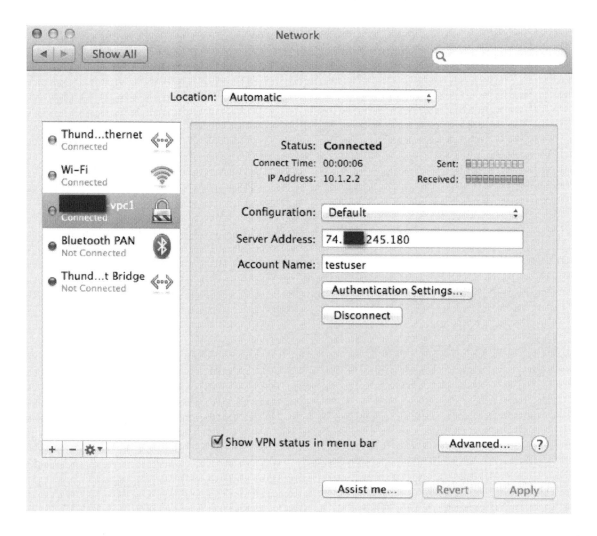

12.2.2 Microsoft Windows 8

Following instruction have been perform using Windows 8.1 using Native VPN client.

1. Create network VPN connection

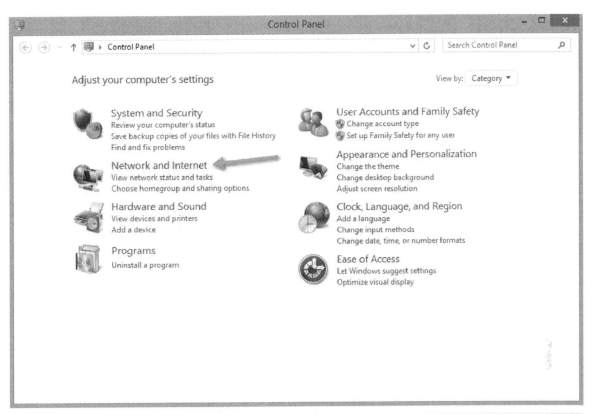

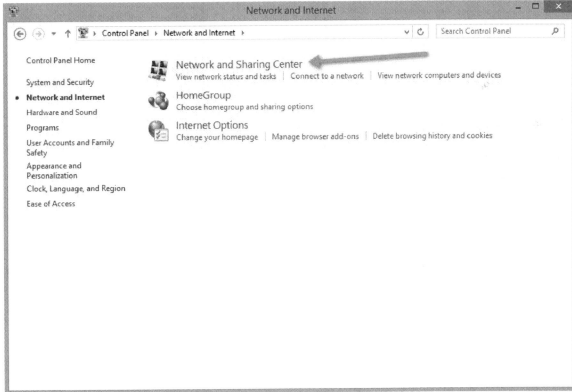

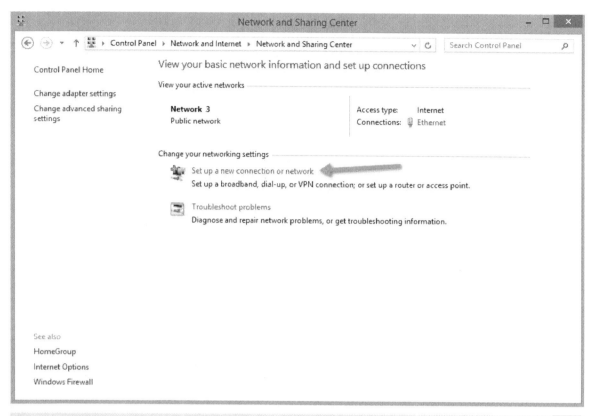

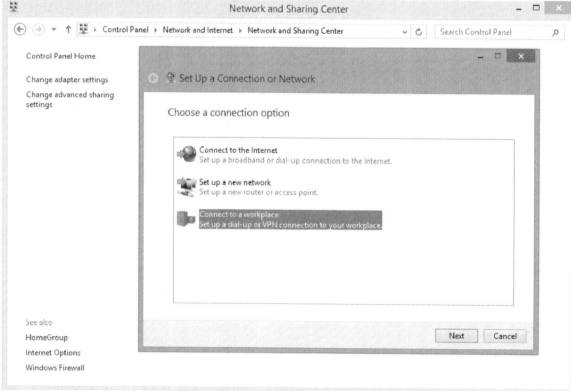

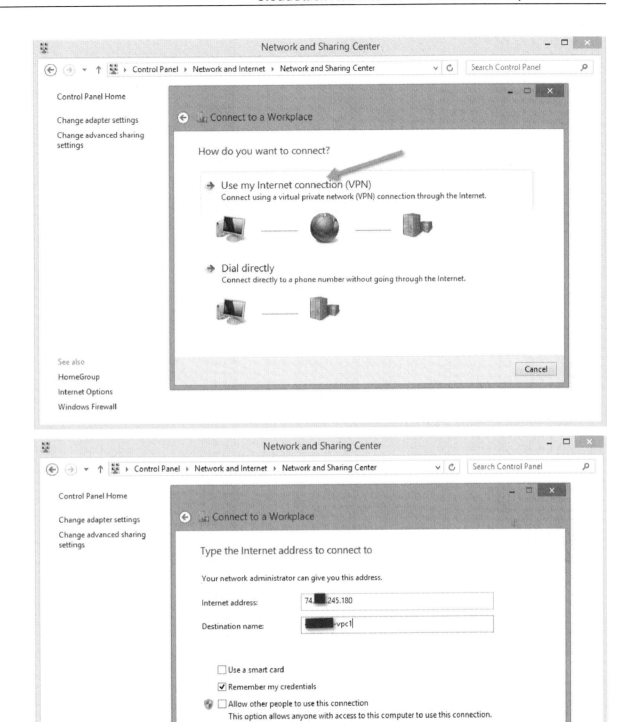

2. Configure VPN settings

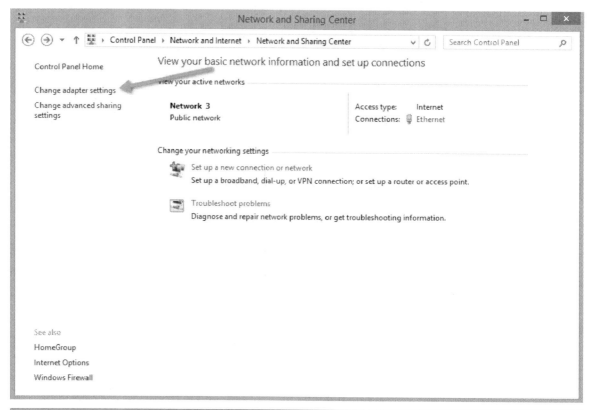

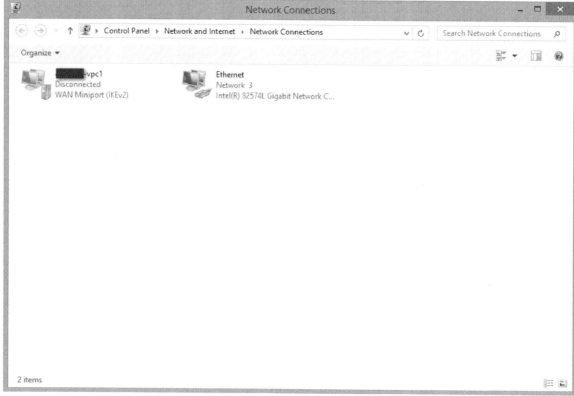

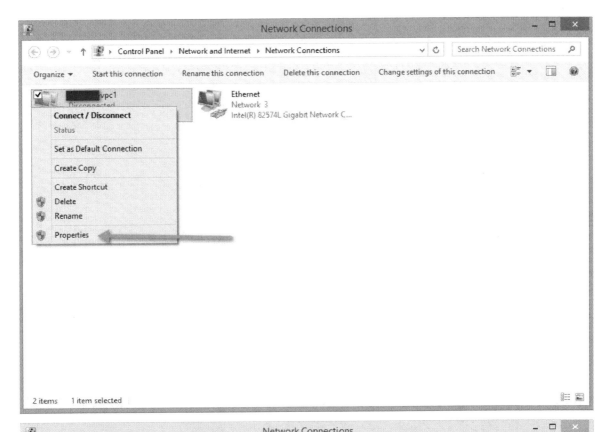

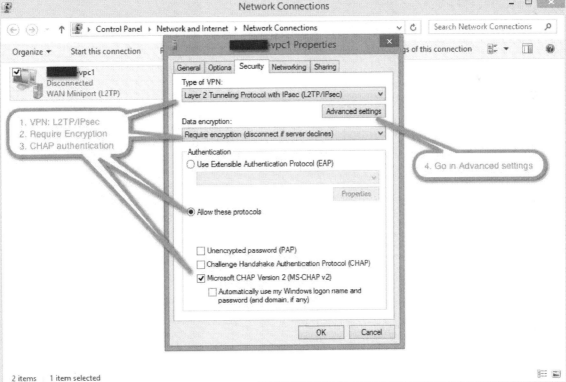

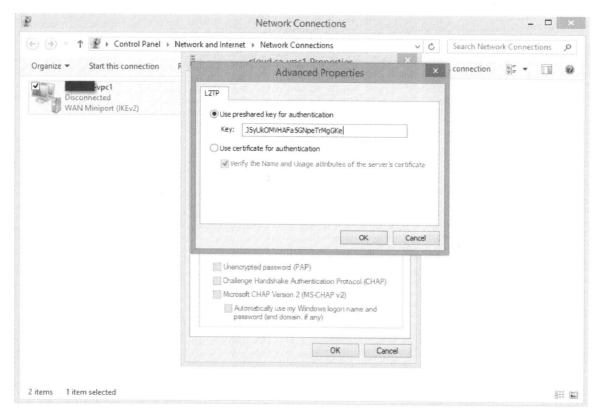

3. Initiate VPN connection

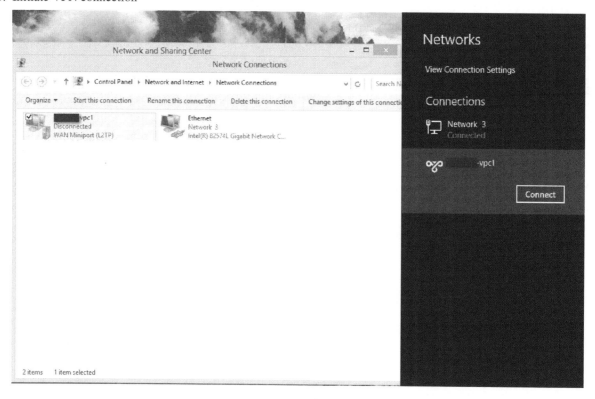

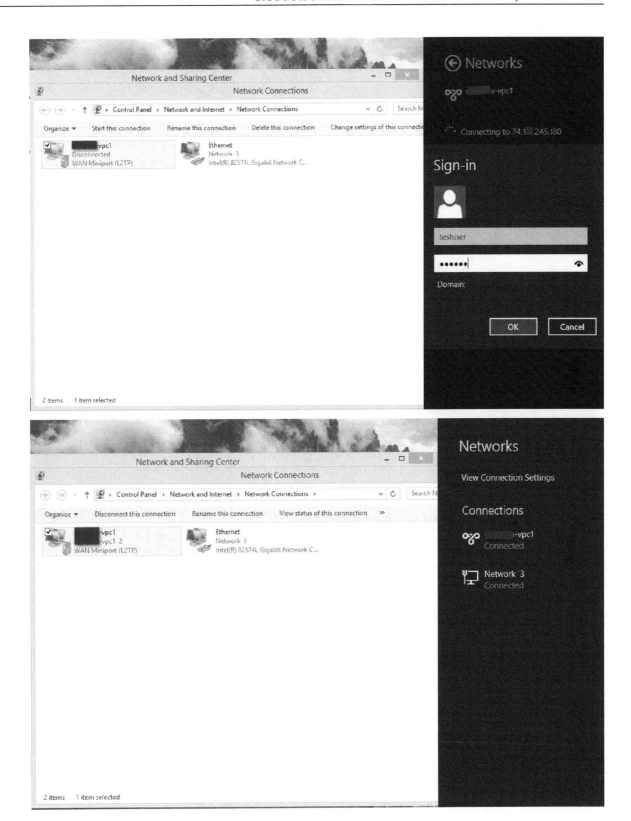

Managing the Cloud

13.1 Managing the Cloud

13.1.1 Using Tags to Organize Resources in the Cloud

A tag is a key-value pair that stores metadata about a resource in the cloud. Tags are useful for categorizing resources. For example, you can tag a user VM with a value that indicates the user's city of residence. In this case, the key would be "city" and the value might be "Toronto" or "Tokyo." You can then request CloudStack to find all resources that have a given tag; for example, VMs for users in a given city.

You can tag a user virtual machine, volume, snapshot, guest network, template, ISO, firewall rule, port forwarding rule, public IP address, security group, load balancer rule, project, VPC, network ACL, or static route. You can not tag a remote access VPN.

You can work with tags through the UI or through the API commands createTags, deleteTags, and listTags. You can define multiple tags for each resource. There is no limit on the number of tags you can define. Each tag can be up to 255 characters long. Users can define tags on the resources they own, and administrators can define tags on any resources in the cloud.

An optional input parameter, "tags," exists on many of the list* API commands. The following example shows how to use this new parameter to find all the volumes having tag region=canada OR tag city=Toronto:

```
command=listVolumes
   &listAll=true
   &tags[0].key=region
   &tags[0].value=canada
   &tags[1].key=city
   &tags[1].value=Toronto
```

The following API commands have the "tags" input parameter:

- listVirtualMachines
- listVolumes
- listSnapshots
- listNetworks
- listTemplates
- listIsos
- listFirewallRules
- listPortForwardingRules

- listPublicIpAddresses
- listSecurityGroups
- listLoadBalancerRules
- listProjects
- listVPCs
- listNetworkACLs
- listStaticRoutes

13.1.2 Reporting CPU Sockets

PRODUCT manages different types of hosts that contains one or more physical CPU sockets. CPU socket is considered as a unit of measure used for licensing and billing cloud infrastructure. PRODUCT provides both UI and API support to collect the CPU socket statistics for billing purpose. The Infrastructure tab has a new tab for CPU sockets. You can view the statistics for CPU sockets managed by PRODUCT, which in turn reflects the size of the cloud. The CPU Socket page will give you the number of hosts and sockets used for each host type.

1. Log in to the PRODUCT UI.

2. In the left navigation bar, click Infrastructure.

3. On CPU Sockets, click View all.

   The CPU Socket page is displayed. The page shows the number of hosts and CPU sockets based on hypervisor types.

13.1.3 Changing the Database Configuration

The CloudStack Management Server stores database configuration information (e.g., hostname, port, credentials) in the file /etc/cloudstack/management/db.properties. To effect a change, edit this file on each Management Server, then restart the Management Server.

13.1.4 Changing the Database Password

You may need to change the password for the MySQL account used by CloudStack. If so, you'll need to change the password in MySQL, and then add the encrypted password to /etc/cloudstack/management/db.properties.

1. Before changing the password, you'll need to stop CloudStack's management server and the usage engine if you've deployed that component.

```
# service cloudstack-management stop
# service cloudstack-usage stop
```

2. Next, you'll update the password for the CloudStack user on the MySQL server.

```
# mysql -u root -p
```

At the MySQL shell, you'll change the password and flush privileges:

```
update mysql.user set password=PASSWORD("newpassword123") where User='cloud';
flush privileges;
quit;
```

3. The next step is to encrypt the password and copy the encrypted password to CloudStack's database configuration (`/etc/cloudstack/management/db.properties`).

```
# java -classpath /usr/share/cloudstack-common/lib/jasypt-1.9.0.jar \ org.jasypt.i
```

13.1.5 File encryption type

Note that this is for the file encryption type. If you're using the web encryption type then you'll use password="management_server_secret_key"

1. Now, you'll update `/etc/cloudstack/management/db.properties` with the new ciphertext. Open `/etc/cloudstack/management/db.properties` in a text editor, and update these parameters:

```
db.cloud.password=ENC(encrypted_password_from_above)
db.usage.password=ENC(encrypted_password_from_above)
```

2. After copying the new password over, you can now start CloudStack (and the usage engine, if necessary).

```
# service cloudstack-management start
# service cloud-usage start
```

13.1.6 Administrator Alerts

The system provides alerts and events to help with the management of the cloud. Alerts are notices to an administrator, generally delivered by e-mail, notifying the administrator that an error has occurred in the cloud. Alert behavior is configurable.

Events track all of the user and administrator actions in the cloud. For example, every guest VM start creates an associated event. Events are stored in the Management Server's database.

Emails will be sent to administrators under the following circumstances:

- The Management Server cluster runs low on CPU, memory, or storage resources
- The Management Server loses heartbeat from a Host for more than 3 minutes
- The Host cluster runs low on CPU, memory, or storage resources

Sending Alerts to External SNMP and Syslog Managers

In addition to showing administrator alerts on the Dashboard in the CloudStack UI and sending them in email, CloudStack can also send the same alerts to external SNMP or Syslog management software. This is useful if you prefer to use an SNMP or Syslog manager to monitor your cloud.

The alerts which can be sent are:

The following is the list of alert type numbers. The current alerts can be found by calling listAlerts.

```
MEMORY = 0 // Available Memory below configured threshold
```

```
CPU = 1 // Unallocated CPU below configured threshold
```

```
STORAGE =2 // Available Storage below configured threshold
```

```
STORAGE_ALLOCATED = 3 // Remaining unallocated Storage is below configured threshold
```

```
PUBLIC_IP = 4 // Number of unallocated virtual network public IPs is below configured th
```

```
PRIVATE_IP = 5 // Number of unallocated private IPs is below configured threshold
```

```
SECONDARY_STORAGE = 6 //  Available Secondary Storage in availability zone is below conf
```

```
HOST = 7 // Host related alerts like host disconnected
```

```
USERVM = 8 // User VM stopped unexpectedly
```

```
DOMAIN_ROUTER = 9 // Domain Router VM stopped unexpectedly
```

```
CONSOLE_PROXY = 10 // Console Proxy VM stopped unexpectedly
```

```
ROUTING = 11 // Lost connection to default route (to the gateway)
```

```
STORAGE_MISC = 12 // Storage issue in system VMs
```

```
USAGE_SERVER = 13 // No usage server process running
```

```
MANAGMENT_NODE = 14 // Management network CIDR is not configured originally
```

```
DOMAIN_ROUTER_MIGRATE = 15 // Domain Router VM Migration was unsuccessful
```

```
CONSOLE_PROXY_MIGRATE = 16 // Console Proxy VM Migration was unsuccessful
```

```
USERVM_MIGRATE = 17 // User VM Migration was unsuccessful
```

```
VLAN = 18 // Number of unallocated VLANs is below configured threshold in availability z
```

```
SSVM = 19 // SSVM stopped unexpectedly
```

```
USAGE_SERVER_RESULT = 20 // Usage job failed
```

```
STORAGE_DELETE = 21 // Failed to delete storage pool
```

```
UPDATE_RESOURCE_COUNT = 22 // Failed to update the resource count
```

```
USAGE_SANITY_RESULT = 23 // Usage Sanity Check failed
```

```
DIRECT_ATTACHED_PUBLIC_IP = 24 // Number of unallocated shared network IPs is low in ava
```

```
LOCAL_STORAGE = 25 // Remaining unallocated Local Storage is below configured threshold
```

```
RESOURCE_LIMIT_EXCEEDED = 26 //Generated when the resource limit exceeds the limit. Curr
```

You can also display the most up to date list by calling the API command `listAlerts`.

SNMP Alert Details

The supported protocol is SNMP version 2.

Each SNMP trap contains the following information: message, podId, dataCenterId, clusterId, and generationTime.

Syslog Alert Details

CloudStack generates a syslog message for every alert. Each syslog message incudes the fields alertType, message, podId, dataCenterId, and clusterId, in the following format. If any field does not have a valid value, it will not be included.

```
Date severity_level Management_Server_IP_Address/Name  alertType:: value dataCenterId::
```

For example:

```
Mar  4 10:13:47    WARN    localhost    alertType:: managementNode message:: Management
```

Configuring SNMP and Syslog Managers

To configure one or more SNMP managers or Syslog managers to receive alerts from CloudStack:

1. For an SNMP manager, install the CloudStack MIB file on your SNMP manager system. This maps the SNMP OIDs to trap types that can be more easily read by users. The file must be publicly available. For more information on how to install this file, consult the documentation provided with the SNMP manager.

2. Edit the file /etc/cloudstack/management/log4j-cloud.xml.

```
# vi /etc/cloudstack/management/log4j-cloud.xml
```

3. Add an entry using the syntax shown below. Follow the appropriate example depending on whether you are adding an SNMP manager or a Syslog manager. To specify multiple external managers, separate the IP addresses and other configuration values with commas (,).

Note: The recommended maximum number of SNMP or Syslog managers is 20 for each.

The following example shows how to configure two SNMP managers at IP addresses 10.1.1.1 and 10.1.1.2. Substitute your own IP addresses, ports, and communities. Do not change the other values (name, threshold, class, and layout values).

```
<appender name="SNMP" class="org.apache.cloudstack.alert.snmp.SnmpTrapAppender">
  <param name="Threshold" value="WARN"/>  <!-- Do not edit. The alert feature assum
  <param name="SnmpManagerIpAddresses" value="10.1.1.1,10.1.1.2"/>
  <param name="SnmpManagerPorts" value="162,162"/>
  <param name="SnmpManagerCommunities" value="public,public"/>
  <layout class="org.apache.cloudstack.alert.snmp.SnmpEnhancedPatternLayout"> <!--
    <param name="PairDelimeter" value="//"/>
    <param name="KeyValueDelimeter" value="::"/>
  </layout>
</appender>
```

The following example shows how to configure two Syslog managers at IP addresses 10.1.1.1 and 10.1.1.2. Substitute your own IP addresses. You can set Facility to any syslog-defined value, such as LOCAL0 - LOCAL7. Do not change the other values.

```
<appender name="ALERTSYSLOG">
  <param name="Threshold" value="WARN"/>
  <param name="SyslogHosts" value="10.1.1.1,10.1.1.2"/>
  <param name="Facility" value="LOCAL6"/>
  <layout>
    <param name="ConversionPattern" value=""/>
  </layout>
</appender>
```

4. If your cloud has multiple Management Server nodes, repeat these steps to edit log4j-cloud.xml on every instance.

5. If you have made these changes while the Management Server is running, wait a few minutes for the change to take effect.

Troubleshooting: If no alerts appear at the configured SNMP or Syslog manager after a reasonable amount of time, it is likely that there is an error in the syntax of the <appender> entry in log4j-cloud.xml. Check to be sure that the format and settings are correct.

Deleting an SNMP or Syslog Manager

To remove an external SNMP manager or Syslog manager so that it no longer receives alerts from CloudStack, remove the corresponding entry from the file /etc/cloudstack/management/log4j-cloud.xml.

13.1.7 Customizing the Network Domain Name

The root administrator can optionally assign a custom DNS suffix at the level of a network, account, domain, zone, or entire CloudStack installation, and a domain administrator can do so within their own domain. To specify a custom domain name and put it into effect, follow these steps.

1. Set the DNS suffix at the desired scope

   - At the network level, the DNS suffix can be assigned through the UI when creating a new network, as described in "Adding an Additional Guest Network" or with the updateNetwork command in the CloudStack API.

   - At the account, domain, or zone level, the DNS suffix can be assigned with the appropriate CloudStack API commands: createAccount, editAccount, createDomain, editDomain, createZone, or editZone.

   - At the global level, use the configuration parameter guest.domain.suffix. You can also use the CloudStack API command updateConfiguration. After modifying this global configuration, restart the Management Server to put the new setting into effect.

2. To make the new DNS suffix take effect for an existing network, call the CloudStack API command updateNetwork. This step is not necessary when the DNS suffix was specified while creating a new network.

The source of the network domain that is used depends on the following rules.

- For all networks, if a network domain is specified as part of a network's own configuration, that value is used.

- For an account-specific network, the network domain specified for the account is used. If none is specified, the system looks for a value in the domain, zone, and global configuration, in that order.

- For a domain-specific network, the network domain specified for the domain is used. If none is specified, the system looks for a value in the zone and global configuration, in that order.

- For a zone-specific network, the network domain specified for the zone is used. If none is specified, the system looks for a value in the global configuration.

13.1.8 Stopping and Restarting the Management Server

The root administrator will need to stop and restart the Management Server from time to time.

For example, after changing a global configuration parameter, a restart is required. If you have multiple Management Server nodes, restart all of them to put the new parameter value into effect consistently throughout the cloud..

To stop the Management Server, issue the following command at the operating system prompt on the Management Server node:

```
# service cloudstack-management stop
```

To start the Management Server:

```
# service cloudstack-management start
```

## CHAPTER 14

System Reliability and Availability

14.1 System Reliability and High Availability

14.1.1 HA for Management Server

The CloudStack Management Server should be deployed in a multi-node configuration such that it is not susceptible to individual server failures. The Management Server itself (as distinct from the MySQL database) is stateless and may be placed behind a load balancer.

Normal operation of Hosts is not impacted by an outage of all Management Serves. All guest VMs will continue to work.

When the Management Server is down, no new VMs can be created, and the end user and admin UI, API, dynamic load distribution, and HA will cease to work.

14.1.2 Management Server Load Balancing

CloudStack can use a load balancer to provide a virtual IP for multiple Management Servers. The administrator is responsible for creating the load balancer rules for the Management Servers. The application requires persistence or stickiness across multiple sessions. The following chart lists the ports that should be load balanced and whether or not persistence is required.

Even if persistence is not required, enabling it is permitted.

Source Port	Destination Port	Protocol	Persistence Required?
80 or 443	8080 (or 20400 with AJP)	HTTP (or AJP)	Yes
8250	8250	TCP	Yes
8096	8096	HTTP	No

In addition to above settings, the administrator is responsible for setting the 'host' global config value from the management server IP to load balancer virtual IP address. If the 'host' value is not set to the VIP for Port 8250 and one of your management servers crashes, the UI is still available but the system VMs will not be able to contact the management server.

14.1.3 HA-Enabled Virtual Machines

The user can specify a virtual machine as HA-enabled. By default, all virtual router VMs and Elastic Load Balancing VMs are automatically configured as HA-enabled. When an HA-enabled VM crashes, CloudStack detects the crash and restarts the VM automatically within the same Availability Zone. HA is never performed across different Availability Zones. CloudStack has a conservative policy towards restarting VMs and ensures that there will never be two instances of the same VM running at the same time. The Management Server attempts to start the VM on another Host in the same cluster.

HA features work with iSCSI or NFS primary storage. HA with local storage is not supported.

14.1.4 HA for Hosts

The user can specify a virtual machine as HA-enabled. By default, all virtual router VMs and Elastic Load Balancing VMs are automatically configured as HA-enabled. When an HA-enabled VM crashes, CloudStack detects the crash and restarts the VM automatically within the same Availability Zone. HA is never performed across different Availability Zones. CloudStack has a conservative policy towards restarting VMs and ensures that there will never be two instances of the same VM running at the same time. The Management Server attempts to start the VM on another Host in the same cluster.

HA features work with iSCSI or NFS primary storage. HA with local storage is not supported.

Dedicated HA Hosts

One or more hosts can be designated for use only by HA-enabled VMs that are restarting due to a host failure. Setting up a pool of such dedicated HA hosts as the recovery destination for all HA-enabled VMs is useful to:

- Make it easier to determine which VMs have been restarted as part of the CloudStack high-availability function. If a VM is running on a dedicated HA host, then it must be an HA-enabled VM whose original host failed. (With one exception: It is possible for an administrator to manually migrate any VM to a dedicated HA host.).

- Keep HA-enabled VMs from restarting on hosts which may be reserved for other purposes.

The dedicated HA option is set through a special host tag when the host is created. To allow the administrator to dedicate hosts to only HA-enabled VMs, set the global configuration variable ha.tag to the desired tag (for example, "ha_host"), and restart the Management Server. Enter the value in the Host Tags field when adding the host(s) that you want to dedicate to HA-enabled VMs.

Note: If you set ha.tag, be sure to actually use that tag on at least one host in your cloud. If the tag specified in ha.tag is not set for any host in the cloud, the HA-enabled VMs will fail to restart after a crash.

14.1.5 Primary Storage Outage and Data Loss

When a primary storage outage occurs the hypervisor immediately stops all VMs stored on that storage device. Guests that are marked for HA will be restarted as soon as practical when the primary storage comes back on line. With NFS, the hypervisor may allow the virtual machines to continue running depending on the nature of the issue. For example, an NFS hang will cause the guest VMs to be suspended until storage connectivity is restored.Primary storage is not designed to be backed up. Individual volumes in primary storage can be backed up using snapshots.

14.1.6 Secondary Storage Outage and Data Loss

For a Zone that has only one secondary storage server, a secondary storage outage will have feature level impact to the system but will not impact running guest VMs. It may become impossible to create a VM with the selected template for a user. A user may also not be able to save snapshots or examine/restore saved snapshots. These features will automatically be available when the secondary storage comes back online.

Secondary storage data loss will impact recently added user data including templates, snapshots, and ISO images. Secondary storage should be backed up periodically. Multiple secondary storage servers can be provisioned within each zone to increase the scalability of the system.

14.1.7 Database High Availability

To help ensure high availability of the databases that store the internal data for CloudStack, you can set up database replication. This covers both the main CloudStack database and the Usage database. Replication is achieved using the MySQL connector parameters and two-way replication. Tested with MySQL 5.1 and 5.5.

How to Set Up Database Replication

Database replication in CloudStack is provided using the MySQL replication capabilities. The steps to set up replication can be found in the MySQL documentation (links are provided below). It is suggested that you set up two-way replication, which involves two database nodes. In this case, for example, you might have node1 and node2.

You can also set up chain replication, which involves more than two nodes. In this case, you would first set up two-way replication with node1 and node2. Next, set up one-way replication from node2 to node3. Then set up one-way replication from node3 to node4, and so on for all the additional nodes.

References:

- http://dev.mysql.com/doc/refman/5.0/en/replication-howto.html

- https://wikis.oracle.com/display/CommSuite/MySQL+High+Availability+and+Replication+Information+For+C

Configuring Database High Availability

To control the database high availability behavior, use the following configuration settings in the file /etc/cloudstack/management/db.properties.

Required Settings

Be sure you have set the following in db.properties:

- db.ha.enabled: set to true if you want to use the replication feature.

  Example: db.ha.enabled=true

- db.cloud.slaves: set to a comma-delimited set of slave hosts for the cloud database. This is the list of nodes set up with replication. The master node is not in the list, since it is already mentioned elsewhere in the properties file.

  Example: db.cloud.slaves=node2,node3,node4

- db.usage.slaves: set to a comma-delimited set of slave hosts for the usage database. This is the list of nodes set up with replication. The master node is not in the list, since it is already mentioned elsewhere in the properties file.

  Example: db.usage.slaves=node2,node3,node4

Optional Settings

The following settings must be present in db.properties, but you are not required to change the default values unless you wish to do so for tuning purposes:

- db.cloud.secondsBeforeRetryMaster: The number of seconds the MySQL connector should wait before trying again to connect to the master after the master went down. Default is 1 hour. The retry might happen sooner if db.cloud.queriesBeforeRetryMaster is reached first.

  Example: db.cloud.secondsBeforeRetryMaster=3600

- db.cloud.queriesBeforeRetryMaster: The minimum number of queries to be sent to the database before trying again to connect to the master after the master went down. Default is 5000. The retry might happen sooner if db.cloud.secondsBeforeRetryMaster is reached first.

Example: `db.cloud.queriesBeforeRetryMaster=5000`

- `db.cloud.initialTimeout`: Initial time the MySQL connector should wait before trying again to connect to the master. Default is 3600.

    Example: `db.cloud.initialTimeout=3600`

Limitations on Database High Availability

The following limitations exist in the current implementation of this feature.

- Slave hosts can not be monitored through CloudStack. You will need to have a separate means of monitoring.

- Events from the database side are not integrated with the CloudStack Management Server events system.

- You must periodically perform manual clean-up of bin log files generated by replication on database nodes. If you do not clean up the log files, the disk can become full.

## CHAPTER 15

Tuning

15.1 Tuning

This section provides tips on how to improve the performance of your cloud.

15.1.1 Performance Monitoring

Host and guest performance monitoring is available to end users and administrators. This allows the user to monitor their utilization of resources and determine when it is appropriate to choose a more powerful service offering or larger disk.

15.1.2 Increase Management Server Maximum Memory

If the Management Server is subject to high demand, the default maximum JVM memory allocation can be insufficient. To increase the memory:

1. Edit the Tomcat configuration file:

```
/etc/cloudstack/management/tomcat6.conf
```

2. Change the command-line parameter -XmxNNNm to a higher value of N.

   For example, if the current value is -Xmx128m, change it to -Xmx1024m or higher.

3. To put the new setting into effect, restart the Management Server.

```
# service cloudstack-management restart
```

For more information about memory issues, see "FAQ: Memory" at Tomcat Wiki.

15.1.3 Set Database Buffer Pool Size

It is important to provide enough memory space for the MySQL database to cache data and indexes:

1. Edit the MySQL configuration file:

```
/etc/my.cnf
```

2. Insert the following line in the [mysqld] section, below the datadir line. Use a value that is appropriate for your situation. We recommend setting the buffer pool at 40% of RAM if MySQL is on the same server as the management server or 70% of RAM if MySQL has a dedicated server. The following example assumes a dedicated server with 1024M of RAM.

```
innodb_buffer_pool_size=700M
```

3. Restart the MySQL service.

```
# service mysqld restart
```

For more information about the buffer pool, see "The InnoDB Buffer Pool" at MySQL Reference Manual.

15.1.4 Set and Monitor Total VM Limits per Host

The CloudStack administrator should monitor the total number of VM instances in each cluster, and disable allocation to the cluster if the total is approaching the maximum that the hypervisor can handle. Be sure to leave a safety margin to allow for the possibility of one or more hosts failing, which would increase the VM load on the other hosts as the VMs are automatically redeployed. Consult the documentation for your chosen hypervisor to find the maximum permitted number of VMs per host, then use CloudStack global configuration settings to set this as the default limit. Monitor the VM activity in each cluster at all times. Keep the total number of VMs below a safe level that allows for the occasional host failure. For example, if there are N hosts in the cluster, and you want to allow for one host in the cluster to be down at any given time, the total number of VM instances you can permit in the cluster is at most (N-1) * (per-host-limit). Once a cluster reaches this number of VMs, use the CloudStack UI to disable allocation of more VMs to the cluster.

15.1.5 Configure XenServer dom0 Memory

Configure the XenServer dom0 settings to allocate more memory to dom0. This can enable XenServer to handle larger numbers of virtual machines. We recommend 2940 MB of RAM for XenServer dom0. For instructions on how to do this, see Citrix Knowledgebase Article.The article refers to XenServer 5.6, but the same information applies to XenServer 6

## CHAPTER 16

Events and Troubleshooting

16.1 Event Notification

An event is essentially a significant or meaningful change in the state of both virtual and physical resources associated with a cloud environment. Events are used by monitoring systems, usage and billing systems, or any other event-driven workflow systems to discern a pattern and make the right business decision. In CloudStack an event could be a state change of virtual or physical resources, an action performed by an user (action events), or policy based events (alerts).

16.1.1 Event Logs

There are two types of events logged in the CloudStack Event Log. Standard events log the success or failure of an event and can be used to identify jobs or processes that have failed. There are also long running job events. Events for asynchronous jobs log when a job is scheduled, when it starts, and when it completes. Other long running synchronous jobs log when a job starts, and when it completes. Long running synchronous and asynchronous event logs can be used to gain more information on the status of a pending job or can be used to identify a job that is hanging or has not started. The following sections provide more information on these events..

16.1.2 Notification

Event notification framework provides a means for the Management Server components to publish and subscribe to CloudStack events. Event notification is achieved by implementing the concept of event bus abstraction in the Management Server.

A new event for state change, resource state change, is introduced as part of Event notification framework. Every resource, such as user VM, volume, NIC, network, public IP, snapshot, and template, is associated with a state machine and generates events as part of the state change. That implies that a change in the state of a resource results in a state change event, and the event is published in the corresponding state machine on the event bus. All the CloudStack events (alerts, action events, usage events) and the additional category of resource state change events, are published on to the events bus.

Implementations

An event bus is introduced in the Management Server that allows the CloudStack components and extension plug-ins to subscribe to the events by using the Advanced Message Queuing Protocol (AMQP) client. In CloudStack, a default implementation of event bus is provided as a plug-in that uses the RabbitMQ AMQP client. The AMQP client pushes the published events to a compatible AMQP server. Therefore all the CloudStack events are published to an exchange in the AMQP server.

Additionally, both an in-memory implementation and an Apache Kafka implementation are also available.

Use Cases

The following are some of the use cases:

- Usage or Billing Engines: A third-party cloud usage solution can implement a plug-in that can connects to CloudStack to subscribe to CloudStack events and generate usage data. The usage data is consumed by their usage software.

- AMQP plug-in can place all the events on the a message queue, then a AMQP message broker can provide topic-based notification to the subscribers.

- Publish and Subscribe notification service can be implemented as a pluggable service in CloudStack that can provide rich set of APIs for event notification, such as topics-based subscription and notification. Additionally, the pluggable service can deal with multi-tenancy, authentication, and authorization issues.

AMQP Configuration

As a CloudStack administrator, perform the following one-time configuration to enable event notification framework. At run time no changes can control the behaviour.

1. Create the folder `/etc/cloudstack/management/META-INF/cloudstack/core`

2. Inside that folder, open `spring-event-bus-context.xml`.

3. Define a bean named `eventNotificationBus` as follows:

    - name : Specify a name for the bean.

    - server : The name or the IP address of the RabbitMQ AMQP server.

    - port : The port on which RabbitMQ server is running.

    - username : The username associated with the account to access the RabbitMQ server.

    - password : The password associated with the username of the account to access the RabbitMQ server.

    - exchange : The exchange name on the RabbitMQ server where CloudStack events are published.

    A sample bean is given below:

```
<beans xmlns="http://www.springframework.org/schema/beans"
xmlns:xsi="http://www.w3.org/2001/XMLSchema-instance"
xmlns:context="http://www.springframework.org/schema/context"
xmlns:aop="http://www.springframework.org/schema/aop"
xsi:schemaLocation="http://www.springframework.org/schema/beans
http://www.springframework.org/schema/beans/spring-beans-3.0.xsd
http://www.springframework.org/schema/aop http://www.springframework.org/schema
http://www.springframework.org/schema/context
http://www.springframework.org/schema/context/spring-context-3.0.xsd">
    <bean id="eventNotificationBus" class="org.apache.cloudstack.mom.rabbitmq.Ra
        <property name="name" value="eventNotificationBus"/>
        <property name="server" value="127.0.0.1"/>
        <property name="port" value="5672"/>
        <property name="username" value="guest"/>
        <property name="password" value="guest"/>
        <property name="exchange" value="cloudstack-events"/>
    </bean>
</beans>
```

The eventNotificationBus bean represents the org.apache.cloudstack.mom.rabbitmq. class.

If you want to use encrypted values for the username and password, you have to include a bean to pass those as variables from a credentials file.

A sample is given below

```
<beans xmlns="http://www.springframework.org/schema/beans"
       xmlns:xsi="http://www.w3.org/2001/XMLSchema-instance"
       xmlns:context="http://www.springframework.org/schema/context"
       xmlns:aop="http://www.springframework.org/schema/aop"
       xsi:schemaLocation="http://www.springframework.org/schema/beans
        http://www.springframework.org/schema/beans/spring-beans-3.0.xsd
        http://www.springframework.org/schema/aop http://www.springframework.or
        http://www.springframework.org/schema/context
        http://www.springframework.org/schema/context/spring-context-3.0.xsd"
 >

    <bean id="eventNotificationBus" class="org.apache.cloudstack.mom.rabbitmq.Ra
        <property name="name" value="eventNotificationBus"/>
        <property name="server" value="127.0.0.1"/>
        <property name="port" value="5672"/>
        <property name="username" value="${username}"/>
        <property name="password" value="${password}"/>
        <property name="exchange" value="cloudstack-events"/>
    </bean>

    <bean id="environmentVariablesConfiguration" class="org.jasypt.encryption.pb
        <property name="algorithm" value="PBEWithMD5AndDES" />
        <property name="passwordEnvName" value="APP_ENCRYPTION_PASSWORD" />
    </bean>

    <bean id="configurationEncryptor" class="org.jasypt.encryption.pbe.StandardP
        <property name="config" ref="environmentVariablesConfiguration" />
    </bean>

    <bean id="propertyConfigurer" class="org.jasypt.spring3.properties.Encryptab
        <constructor-arg ref="configurationEncryptor" />
        <property name="location" value="classpath:/cred.properties" />
    </bean>
</beans>
```

Create a new file in the same folder called cred.properties and the specify the values for username and password as jascrypt encrypted strings

Sample, with guest as values for both fields:

```
username=nh2XrM7jWHMG4VQK18iiBQ==
password=nh2XrM7jWHMG4VQK18iiBQ==
```

4. Restart the Management Server.

Kafka Configuration

As a CloudStack administrator, perform the following one-time configuration to enable event notification framework. At run time no changes can control the behaviour.

1. Create an appropriate configuration file in `/etc/cloudstack/management/kafka.producer.prope`
which contains valid kafka configuration properties as documented in
http://kafka.apache.org/documentation.html#newproducerconfigs The properties may contain an additional `topic` property which if not provided will default to `cloudstack`. While `key.serializer` and `value.serializer` are usually required for a producer to correctly start, they may be omitted and will
default to `org.apache.kafka.common.serialization.StringSerializer`.

2. Create the folder `/etc/cloudstack/management/META-INF/cloudstack/core`

3. Inside that folder, open `spring-event-bus-context.xml`.

4. Define a bean named `eventNotificationBus` with a single `name` attribute, A sample bean is given below:

```
<beans xmlns="http://www.springframework.org/schema/beans"
       xmlns:xsi="http://www.w3.org/2001/XMLSchema-instance"
       xmlns:context="http://www.springframework.org/schema/context"
       xmlns:aop="http://www.springframework.org/schema/aop"
       xsi:schemaLocation="http://www.springframework.org/schema/beans
                     http://www.springframework.org/schema/beans/spring-beans
                     http://www.springframework.org/schema/aop http://www.spr
                     http://www.springframework.org/schema/context
                     http://www.springframework.org/schema/context/spring-con
    <bean id="eventNotificationBus" class="org.apache.cloudstack.mom.kafka.KafkaEven
      <property name="name" value="eventNotificationBus"/>
    </bean>
</beans>
```

5. Restart the Management Server.

16.1.3 Standard Events

The events log records three types of standard events.

- INFO. This event is generated when an operation has been successfully performed.
- WARN. This event is generated in the following circumstances.
    - When a network is disconnected while monitoring a template download.
    - When a template download is abandoned.
    - When an issue on the storage server causes the volumes to fail over to the mirror storage server.
- ERROR. This event is generated when an operation has not been successfully performed

16.1.4 Long Running Job Events

The events log records three types of standard events.

- INFO. This event is generated when an operation has been successfully performed.
- WARN. This event is generated in the following circumstances.
    - When a network is disconnected while monitoring a template download.
    - When a template download is abandoned.
    - When an issue on the storage server causes the volumes to fail over to the mirror storage server.
- ERROR. This event is generated when an operation has not been successfully performed

16.1.5 Event Log Queries

Database logs can be queried from the user interface. The list of events captured by the system includes:

- Virtual machine creation, deletion, and on-going management operations
- Virtual router creation, deletion, and on-going management operations
- Template creation and deletion
- Network/load balancer rules creation and deletion
- Storage volume creation and deletion
- User login and logout

16.1.6 Deleting and Archiving Events and Alerts

CloudStack provides you the ability to delete or archive the existing alerts and events that you no longer want to implement. You can regularly delete or archive any alerts or events that you cannot, or do not want to resolve from the database.

You can delete or archive individual alerts or events either directly by using the Quickview or by using the Details page. If you want to delete multiple alerts or events at the same time, you can use the respective context menu. You can delete alerts or events by category for a time period. For example, you can select categories such as **USER.LOGOUT**, **VM.DESTROY**, **VM.AG.UPDATE**, **CONFIGURATION.VALUE.EDI**, and so on. You can also view the number of events or alerts archived or deleted.

In order to support the delete or archive alerts, the following global parameters have been added:

- **alert.purge.delay**: The alerts older than specified number of days are purged. Set the value to 0 to never purge alerts automatically.
- **alert.purge.interval**: The interval in seconds to wait before running the alert purge thread. The default is 86400 seconds (one day).

Note: Archived alerts or events cannot be viewed in the UI or by using the API. They are maintained in the database for auditing or compliance purposes.

Permissions

Consider the following:

- The root admin can delete or archive one or multiple alerts or events.
- The domain admin or end user can delete or archive one or multiple events.

Procedure

1. Log in as administrator to the CloudStack UI.
2. In the left navigation, click Events.
3. Perform either of the following:
   - To archive events, click Archive Events, and specify event type and date.
   - To archive events, click Delete Events, and specify event type and date.
4. Click OK.

16.2 TroubleShooting

16.2.1 Working with Server Logs

The CloudStack Management Server logs all web site, middle tier, and database activities for diagnostics purposes in */var/log/cloudstack/management/*. The CloudStack logs a variety of error messages. We recommend this command to find the problematic output in the Management Server log:.

Note: When copying and pasting a command, be sure the command has pasted as a single line before executing. Some document viewers may introduce unwanted line breaks in copied text.

```
grep -i -E 'exception|unable|fail|invalid|leak|warn|error' /var/log/cloudstack/managemen
```

The CloudStack processes requests with a Job ID. If you find an error in the logs and you are interested in debugging the issue you can grep for this job ID in the management server log. For example, suppose that you find the following ERROR message:

```
2010-10-04 13:49:32,595 ERROR [cloud.vm.UserVmManagerImpl] (Job-Executor-11:job-1076) Un
```

Note that the job ID is 1076. You can track back the events relating to job 1076 with the following grep:

```
grep "job-1076)" management-server.log
```

The CloudStack Agent Server logs its activities in */var/log/cloudstack/agent/*.

16.2.2 Data Loss on Exported Primary Storage

Symptom

Loss of existing data on primary storage which has been exposed as a Linux NFS server export on an iSCSI volume.

Cause

It is possible that a client from outside the intended pool has mounted the storage. When this occurs, the LVM is wiped and all data in the volume is lost

Solution

When setting up LUN exports, restrict the range of IP addresses that are allowed access by specifying a subnet mask. For example:

```
echo "/export 192.168.1.0/24(rw,async,no_root_squash,no_subtree_check)" > /etc/exports
```

Adjust the above command to suit your deployment needs.

More Information

See the export procedure in the "Secondary Storage" section of the CloudStack Installation Guide

16.2.3 Recovering a Lost Virtual Router

Symptom

A virtual router is running, but the host is disconnected. A virtual router no longer functions as expected.

Cause

The Virtual router is lost or down.

Solution

If you are sure that a virtual router is down forever, or no longer functions as expected, destroy it. You must create one afresh while keeping the backup router up and running (it is assumed this is in a redundant router setup):

- Force stop the router. Use the stopRouter API with forced=true parameter to do so.
- Before you continue with destroying this router, ensure that the backup router is running. Otherwise the network connection will be lost.
- Destroy the router by using the destroyRouter API.

Recreate the missing router by using the restartNetwork API with cleanup=false parameter. For more information about redundant router setup, see Creating a New Network Offering.

For more information about the API syntax, see the API Reference at http://cloudstack.apache.org/docs/api/.

16.2.4 Maintenance mode not working on vCenter

Symptom

Host was placed in maintenance mode, but still appears live in vCenter.

Cause

The CloudStack administrator UI was used to place the host in scheduled maintenance mode. This mode is separate from vCenter's maintenance mode.

Solution

Use vCenter to place the host in maintenance mode.

16.2.5 Unable to deploy VMs from uploaded vSphere template

Symptom

When attempting to create a VM, the VM will not deploy.

Cause

If the template was created by uploading an OVA file that was created using vSphere Client, it is possible the OVA contained an ISO image. If it does, the deployment of VMs from the template will fail.

Solution

Remove the ISO and re-upload the template.

16.2.6 Unable to power on virtual machine on VMware

Symptom

Virtual machine does not power on. You might see errors like:

- Unable to open Swap File
- Unable to access a file since it is locked
- Unable to access Virtual machine configuration

Cause

A known issue on VMware machines. ESX hosts lock certain critical virtual machine files and file systems to prevent concurrent changes. Sometimes the files are not unlocked when the virtual machine is powered off. When a virtual machine attempts to power on, it can not access these critical files, and the virtual machine is unable to power on.

Solution

See the following:

VMware Knowledge Base Article

16.2.7 Load balancer rules fail after changing network offering

Symptom

After changing the network offering on a network, load balancer rules stop working.

Cause

Load balancing rules were created while using a network service offering that includes an external load balancer device such as NetScaler, and later the network service offering changed to one that uses the CloudStack virtual router.

Solution

Create a firewall rule on the virtual router for each of your existing load balancing rules so that they continue to function.

16.2.8 Troubleshooting Internet Traffic

Below are a few troubleshooting steps to check whats going wrong with your network...

Trouble Shooting Steps

1. The switches have to be configured correctly to pass VLAN traffic. You can verify if VLAN traffic is working by bringing up a tagged interface on the hosts and pinging between them as below...

   On *host1 (kvm1)*

   ```
   kvm1 ~$ vconfig add eth0 64
   kvm1 ~$ ifconfig eth0.64 1.2.3.4 netmask 255.255.255.0 up
   kvm1 ~$ ping 1.2.3.5
   ```

   On *host2 (kvm2)*

   ```
   kvm2 ~$ vconfig add eth0 64
   kvm2 ~$ ifconfig eth0.64 1.2.3.5 netmask 255.255.255.0 up
   kvm2 ~$ ping 1.2.3.4
   ```

   If the pings dont work, run *tcpdump(8)* all over the place to check who is gobbling up the packets. Ultimately, if the switches are not configured correctly, CloudStack networking wont work so fix the physical networking issues before you proceed to the next steps

2. Ensure Traffic Labels are set for the Zone.

   Traffic labels need to be set for all hypervisors including XenServer, KVM and VMware types. You can configure traffic labels when you creating a new zone from the *Add Zone Wizard*.

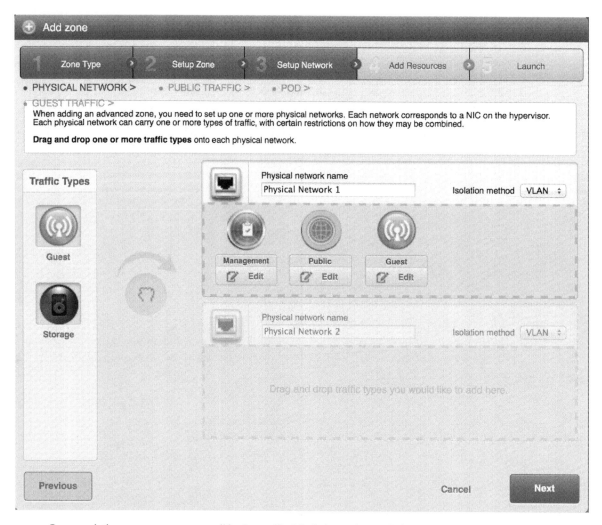

On an existing zone, you can modify the traffic labels by going to *Infrastructure, Zones, Physical Network* tab.

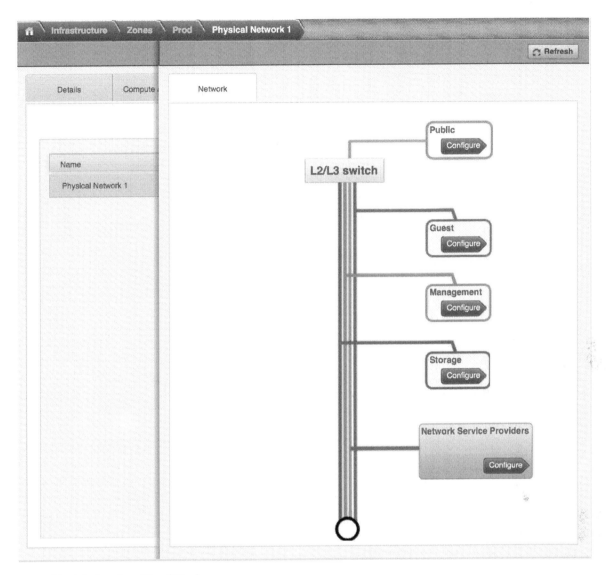

List labels using *CloudMonkey*

```
acs-manager ~$ cloudmonkey list traffictypes physicalnetworkid=41cb7ff6-8eb2-4630-b
count = 4
traffictype:
id = cd0915fe-a660-4a82-9df7-34aebf90003e
kvmnetworklabel = cloudbr0
physicalnetworkid = 41cb7ff6-8eb2-4630-b577-1da25e0e1145
traffictype = Guest
xennetworklabel = MGMT
========================================================
id = f5524b8f-6605-41e4-a982-81a356b2a196
kvmnetworklabel = cloudbr0
physicalnetworkid = 41cb7ff6-8eb2-4630-b577-1da25e0e1145
traffictype = Management
xennetworklabel = MGMT
========================================================
id = 266bad0e-7b68-4242-b3ad-f59739346cfd
kvmnetworklabel = cloudbr0
physicalnetworkid = 41cb7ff6-8eb2-4630-b577-1da25e0e1145
traffictype = Public
```

```
xennetworklabel = MGMT
============================================================
id = a2baad4f-7ce7-45a8-9caf-a0b9240adf04
kvmnetworklabel = cloudbr0
physicalnetworkid = 41cb7ff6-8eb2-4630-b577-1da25e0e1145
traffictype = Storage
xennetworklabel = MGMT
============================================================
```

3. KVM traffic labels require to be named as *"cloudbr0", "cloudbr2", "cloudbrN"* etc and the corresponding bridge must exist on the KVM hosts. If you create labels/bridges with any other names, CloudStack (atleast earlier versions did) seems to ignore them. CloudStack does not create the physical bridges on the KVM hosts, you need to create them **before** before adding the host to Cloudstack.

```
kvm1 ~$ ifconfig cloudbr0
cloudbr0   Link encap:Ethernet   HWaddr 00:0C:29:EF:7D:78
    inet addr:192.168.44.22  Bcast:192.168.44.255  Mask:255.255.255.0
    inet6 addr: fe80::20c:29ff:feef:7d78/64 Scope:Link
    UP BROADCAST RUNNING MULTICAST  MTU:1500  Metric:1
    RX packets:92435 errors:0 dropped:0 overruns:0 frame:0
    TX packets:50596 errors:0 dropped:0 overruns:0 carrier:0
    collisions:0 txqueuelen:0
    RX bytes:94985932 (90.5 MiB)  TX bytes:61635793 (58.7 MiB)
```

4. The Virtual Router, SSVM, CPVM *public* interface would be bridged to a physical interface on the host. In the example below, *cloudbr0* is the public interface and CloudStack has correctly created the virtual interfaces bridge. This virtual interface to physical interface mapping is done automatically by CloudStack using the traffic label settings for the Zone. If you have provided correct settings and still dont have a working working Internet, check the switching layer before you debug any further. You can verify traffic using tcpdump on the virtual, physical and bridge interfaces.

```
kvm-host1 ~$ brctl show
bridge name    bridge id            STP enabled  interfaces
breth0-64      8000.000c29ef7d78    no           eth0.64
                                                 vnet2
cloud0         8000.fe00a9fe0219    no           vnet0
cloudbr0       8000.000c29ef7d78    no           eth0
                                                 vnet1
                                                 vnet3
virbr0         8000.5254008e321a    yes          virbr0-nic
```

```
xenserver1 ~$ brctl show
bridge name  bridge id            STP enabled  interfaces
xapi0        0000.e2b76d0a1149    no           vif1.0
xenbr0       0000.000c299b54dc    no           eth0
                                               xapi1
                                               vif1.1
                                               vif1.2
```

5. Pre-create labels on the XenServer Hosts. Similar to KVM bridge setup, traffic labels must also be pre-created on the XenServer hosts before adding them to CloudStack.

```
xenserver1 ~$ xe network-list
uuid ( RO)                    : aaa-bbb-ccc-ddd
        name-label ( RW): MGMT
    name-description ( RW):
            bridge ( RO): xenbr0
```

6. The Internet would be accessible from both the SSVM and CPVM instances by default. Their public IPs will

also be directly pingable from the Internet. Please note that these test would work only if your switches and traffic labels are configured correctly for your environment. If your SSVM/CPVM cant reach the Internet, its very unlikely that the Virtual Router (VR) can also the reach the Internet suggesting that its either a switching issue or incorrectly assigned traffic labels. Fix the SSVM/CPVM issues before you debug VR issues.

```
root@s-1-VM:~# ping -c 3 google.com
PING google.com (74.125.236.164): 56 data bytes
64 bytes from 74.125.236.164: icmp_seq=0 ttl=55 time=26.932 ms
64 bytes from 74.125.236.164: icmp_seq=1 ttl=55 time=29.156 ms
64 bytes from 74.125.236.164: icmp_seq=2 ttl=55 time=25.000 ms
--- google.com ping statistics ---
3 packets transmitted, 3 packets received, 0% packet loss
round-trip min/avg/max/stddev = 25.000/27.029/29.156/1.698 ms
```

```
root@v-2-VM:~# ping -c 3 google.com
PING google.com (74.125.236.164): 56 data bytes
64 bytes from 74.125.236.164: icmp_seq=0 ttl=55 time=32.125 ms
64 bytes from 74.125.236.164: icmp_seq=1 ttl=55 time=26.324 ms
64 bytes from 74.125.236.164: icmp_seq=2 ttl=55 time=37.001 ms
--- google.com ping statistics ---
3 packets transmitted, 3 packets received, 0% packet loss
round-trip min/avg/max/stddev = 26.324/31.817/37.001/4.364 ms
```

7. The Virtual Router (VR) should also be able to reach the Internet without having any Egress rules. The Egress rules only control forwarded traffic and not traffic that originates on the VR itself.

```
root@r-4-VM:~# ping -c 3 google.com
PING google.com (74.125.236.164): 56 data bytes
64 bytes from 74.125.236.164: icmp_seq=0 ttl=55 time=28.098 ms
64 bytes from 74.125.236.164: icmp_seq=1 ttl=55 time=34.785 ms
64 bytes from 74.125.236.164: icmp_seq=2 ttl=55 time=69.179 ms
--- google.com ping statistics ---
3 packets transmitted, 3 packets received, 0% packet loss
round-trip min/avg/max/stddev = 28.098/44.021/69.179/17.998 ms
```

8. However, the Virtual Router's (VR) Source NAT Public IP address **WONT** be reachable until appropriate Ingress rules are in place. You can add *Ingress* rules under *Network, Guest Network, IP Address, Firewall* setting page.

9. The VM Instances by default wont be able to access the Internet. Add Egress rules to permit traffic.

10. Some users have reported that flushing IPTables rules (or changing routes) on the SSVM, CPVM or the Virtual Router makes the Internet work. This is not expected behaviour and suggests that your networking settings are incorrect. No IPtables/route changes are required on the SSVM, CPVM or the VR. Go back and double check all your settings.

In a vast majority of the cases, the problem has turned out to be at the switching layer where the L3 switches were configured incorrectly.

This section was contibuted by Shanker Balan and was originally published on Shapeblue's blog

Printed in Great Britain
by Amazon